Data Warehousing
Architecture and Implementation

ISBN 0-13-080902-0

9 780130 809025

ARRIS KERN'S ENTERPRISE COMPUTING INSTITUTE

Data Warehousing
Architecture and Implementation

Humphries, Hawkins, and Dy

Prentice Hall PTR
Upper Saddle River, NJ 07458
http://www.phptr.com

Acquisitions editor: Greg Doench
Cover designer: Talar Agasyan
Cover design director: Jerry Votta
Manufacturing editor: Alexis R. Heydt
Marketing manager: Kaylie Smith
Compositor/Production services: Pine Tree Composition, Inc.

Reprinted with corrections May, 1999

© 1999 by Prentice Hall PTR
Prentice-Hall, Inc.
Upper Saddle River, New Jersey 07458

Printed in the United States of America
10 9 8 7 6 5 4 3 2

ISBN: 0-13-080902-0

Prentice-Hall International (UK) Limited, *London*
Prentice-Hall of Australia Pty. Limited, *Sydney*
Prentice-Hall Canada Inc., *Toronto*
Prentice-Hall Hispanoamericana, S.A., *Mexico*
Prentice-Hall of India Private Limited, *New Delhi*
Prentice-Hall of Japan, Inc., *Tokyo*
Prentice-Hall Asia Pte. Ltd., *Singapore*
Editora Prentice-Hall do Brasil, Ltda., *Rio de Janeiro*

Contents

Chapter 4

The CIO 73

Chapter 5

The Project Manager 103

Part 3
Process   121

Chapter 6

Warehousing Strategy   123

Chapter 7

Warehouse Management and Support Processes   135

Data Warehouse Planning ... 143

Data Warehouse Implementation ... 165

Part 4

Technology   189

Chapter 10

Hardware and Operating Systems   191

Chapter 11

Warehousing Software   195

Chapter 12

Warehouse Schema Design   211

Chapter 13

Warehouse Metadata   229

Chapter 14

Warehousing Applications   239

Part 5

Where to Now?   247

Chapter 15

Warehouse Maintenance and Evolution   249

Chapter 16

Warehousing Trends 261

Preface

This book is intended for Information Technology (IT) professionals who have been hearing about or have been tasked to evaluate, learn or implement data warehousing technologies.

Far from being just a passing fad, data warehousing technology has grown much in scale and reputation in the past few years, as evidenced by the increasing number of products, vendors, organizations, and yes, even books, devoted to the subject. Enterprises that have successfully implemented data warehouses find it strategic and often wonder how they ever managed to survive without it in the past.

As early as 1995, a Gartner Group survey of Fortune 500 IT managers found that 90 percent of all organizations had planned to implement data warehouses by 1998. Virtually all Top-100 US banks will actively use a data warehouse-based profitability application by 1998. Nearly 30 percent of companies that actively pursue this technology have created a permanent or semipermanent unit to plan, create, maintain, promote, and support the data warehouse.

If you are an IT professional who has been tasked with planning, managing, designing, implementing, supporting, or maintaining your organization's data warehouse, then this book is intended for you.

The first section introduces the Enterprise Architecture and Data Warehouse concepts, the basis of the reasons for writing this book.

The second section of this book focuses on three of the key **People** in any data warehousing initiative: the Project Sponsor, the CIO, and the Project Manager. This section is devoted to addressing the primary concerns of these individuals.

The third section presents a **Process** for planning and implementing a data warehouse and provides guidelines that will prove extremely helpful for both first-time and experienced warehouse developers.

The fourth section of this book focuses on the **Technology** aspect of data warehousing. It lends order to the dizzying array of technology components that you may use to build your data warehouse.

The fifth section of this book opens a window to the future of data warehousing.

This book also comes with a CD-ROM that contains two software products. Please refer to the **readme.txt** file on the CD-ROM for any last minute changes and updates.

The enclosed software products are:

- **R/olapXL®**. R/olapXL is a powerful query and reporting tool that allows users to draw data directly into Microsoft Excel spreadsheets from any dimensional data mart or data warehouse that resides on an ODBC-compliant database. Once the data are in Microsoft Excel, you are free to use any of Excel's standard features to analyze, report, or graph the retrieved data.
- **WAREHOUSE DESIGNER®**. Warehouse Designer is a tool that generates DDL statements for creating dimensional data warehouse or data mart tables. Users specify the required data structure through a GUI front-end. The tool generates statements to create primary keys, foreign keys, indexes, constraints, and table structures. It recognizes key dimensional modeling concepts such as fact and dimension tables, core and custom schemas, as well as base and aggregate schemas.

Also enclosed is a License Agreement that you must read and agree to before using any of the software provided on the disk. Manuals for both products are included as appendices in this book. The latest information on these products is available at the website of Intranet Business Systems, Inc. The URL is http://www.intranetsys.com.

Part 1

Introduction

The term *Enterprise Architecture* refers to a collection of technology components and their interrelationships, which are integrated to meet the information requirements of an enterprise. This section introduces the concept of Enterprise IT Architectures with the intention of providing a framework for the various types of technologies used to meet an enterprise's computing needs.

Data warehousing technologies belong to just one of the many components in an IT architecture. This chapter aims to define how data warehousing fits within the overall IT architecture, in the hope that IT professionals will be better positioned to use and integrate data warehousing technologies with the other IT components used by the enterprise.

1

The Enterprise IT Architecture

This chapter begins with a brief look at how changing business requirements have, over time, influenced the evolution of Enterprise Architectures. The Info*Motion* ("Information in Motion") Enterprise Architecture is introduced to provide IT professionals with a framework with which to classify the various technologies currently available.

▶ The Past: Evolution of Enterprise Architectures

The IT architecture of an enterprise at a given time depends on three main factors:

- the business requirements of the enterprise;
- the available technology at that time; and
- the accumulated investments of the enterprise from earlier technology generations.

3

The business requirements of an enterprise are constantly changing, and the changes are coming at an exponential rate. Business requirements have, over the years, evolved from the day-to-day clerical recording of transactions to the automation of business processes. Exception reporting has shifted from tracking and correcting daily transactions that have gone astray to the development of self-adjusting business processes.

Technology has likewise advanced by delivering exponential increases in computing power and communications capabilities. However, for all these advances in computing hardware, a significant lag exists in the realms of software development and architecture definition. Enterprise Architectures thus far have displayed a general inability to gracefully evolve in line with business requirements, without either compromising on prior technology investments or seriously limiting their own ability to evolve further.

In hindsight, the evolution of the typical Enterprise Architecture reflects the continuous, piecemeal efforts of IT professionals to take advantage of the latest technology to improve the support of business operations. Unfortunately, this piecemeal effort has often resulted in a morass of incompatible components.

▶ The Present: The IT Professional's Responsibility

Today, the IT professional continues to have a two-fold responsibility: Meet business requirements through Information Technology and integrate new technology into the existing Enterprise Architecture.

Meet Business Requirements

The IT professional must ensure that the enterprise IT infrastructure properly supports a myriad set of requirements from different business users, each of whom has different and constantly changing needs, as illustrated in Figure 1–1.

Figure 1–1   Different Business Needs

Take Advantage of Technology Advancements

At the same time, the IT professional must also constantly learn new buzzwords, review new methodologies, evaluate new tools, and maintain ties with technology partners. Not all the latest technologies are useful; the IT professional must first sift through the technology jigsaw puzzle (see Figure 1–2) to find the pieces that meet the needs of the en-

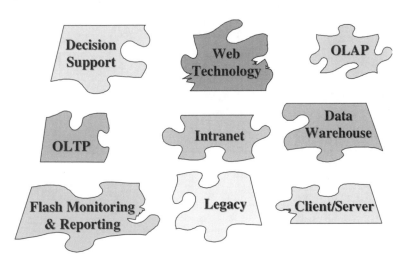

Figure 1–2   The Technology Jigsaw Puzzle

terprise, then integrate the newer pieces with the existing ones to form a coherent whole.

One of the key constraints the IT professional faces today is the current Enterprise IT Architecture itself. At this point, therefore, it is prudent to step back, assess the current state of affairs and identify the distinct but related components of modern Enterprise Architectures.

The two orthogonal perspectives of business and technology are merged to form one unified framework, as shown in Figure 1–3.

▶ Business Perspective

From the business perspective, the requirements of the enterprise fall into categories illustrated in Figure 1–4 and described below.

Operational

Technology supports the smooth execution and continuous improvement of day-to-day operations, the identification and correction of er-

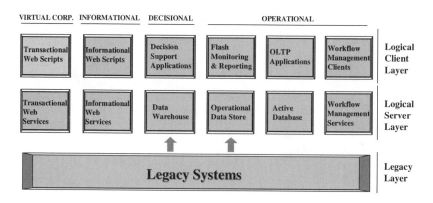

Figure 1–3   The InfoMotion Enterprise Architecture

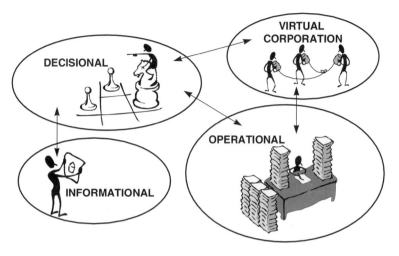

Figure 1–4   The Enterprise Architecture (Business Perspective)

rors through exception reporting and workflow management, and the overall monitoring of operations. Information retrieved about the business from an operational viewpoint is used to either complete or optimize the execution of a business process.

Decisional

Technology supports managerial decision-making and long-term planning. Decision-makers are provided with views of enterprise data from multiple dimensions and in varying levels of detail. Historical patterns in sales and other customer behavior are analyzed. Decisional systems also support decision-making and planning through scenario-based modeling, what-if analysis, trend analysis, and rule discovery.

Informational

Technology makes current, relatively static information widely and readily available to as many people as need access to it. Examples include company policies, product and service information, organizational setup, office location, corporate forms, training materials, company profiles.

Virtual Corporation

Technology enables the creation of strategic links with key suppliers and customers to better meet customer needs. In the past, such links were feasible only for large companies because of economies of scale. Now, the affordability of Internet technology provides any enterprise with this same capability.

▶ Technology Perspective

This section presents each architectural component from a technology standpoint and highlights the business need that each is best suited to support.

Operational Needs

Legacy Systems

The term *legacy system* refers to any information system currently in use that was built using previous technology generations. Most legacy systems are operational in nature, largely because the automation of transaction-oriented business processes had long been the priority of Information Technology projects.

OPERATIONAL
- Legacy Systems
- OLTP Application
- Active Database
- Operational Data Store
- Flash Monitoring and Reporting
- Workflow Management (Groupware)

OLTP Applications

The term *Online Transaction Processing* refers to systems that automate and capture business transactions through the use of computer systems. In addition, these applications traditionally produce reports that allow business users to track the status of transactions. OLTP applications and their related active databases compose the majority of client/server systems today.

Active Databases

Databases store the data produced by Online Transaction Processing applications. These databases were traditionally passive repositories of data manipulated by business applications. It is not unusual to find legacy systems with processing logic and business rules contained entirely in the user interface or randomly interspersed in procedural code.

With the advent of client/server architecture, distributed systems, and advances in database technology, databases began to take on a more active role through database programming (e.g., stored procedures) and event management. IT professionals are now able to bullet-proof the application by placing processing logic in the database itself. This contrasts with the still-popular practice of replicating processing logic (sometimes in an inconsistent manner) across the different parts of a client application or across different client applications that update the same database. Through active databases, applications are more robust and conducive to evolution.

Operational Data Stores

An Operational Data Store or ODS is a collection of integrated databases designed to support the monitoring of operations. Unlike the databases of OLTP applications (that are function oriented), the Operational Data Store contains subject-oriented, volatile, and current enterprise-wide detailed information; it serves as a system of record that provides comprehensive views of data in operational systems.

Data are transformed and integrated into a consistent, unified whole as they are obtained from legacy and other operational systems to provide business users with an integrated and current view of operations (see Figure 1–5). Data in the Operational Data Store are constantly refreshed so that the resulting image reflects the latest state of operations.

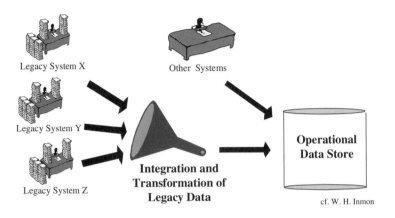

Figure 1–5   Legacy Systems and the Operational Data Store

Flash Monitoring and Reporting

These tools provide business users with a dashboard—meaningful online information on the operational status of the enterprise by making use of the data in the Operational Data Store. The business user obtains a constantly refreshed, enterprise-wide view of operations without creating unwanted interruptions or additional load on transaction processing systems.

Workflow Management and Groupware

Workflow management systems are tools that allow groups to communicate and coordinate their work. Early incarnations of this technology supported group scheduling, e-mail, online discussions, and resource sharing. More advanced implementations of this technology are integrated with OLTP applications to support the execution of business processes.

Decisional Needs

Data Warehouse

The data warehouse concept developed as IT professionals increasingly realized that the structure of data required for transaction reporting was significantly different from the structure required to analyze data.

DECISIONAL
- Data Warehouse
- Decision Support Applications (OLAP)

The data warehouse was originally envisioned as a separate architectural component that converted and integrated masses of raw data from legacy and other operational systems and from external sources. It was designed to contain summarized, historical views of data in production systems. This collection provides business users and decision-makers with a cross-functional, integrated, subject-oriented view of the enterprise.

The introduction of the Operational Data Store has now caused the data warehouse concept to evolve further. The data warehouse now contains summarized, historical views of the data in the Operational Data Store. This is achieved by taking regular "snapshots" of the contents of the Operational Data Store and using these snapshots as the basis for warehouse loads.

In so doing, the enterprise obtains the information required for long-term and historical analysis, decision-making, and planning.

Decision Support Applications

Also known as OLAP (Online Analytical Processing), these applications provide managerial users with meaningful views of past and present enterprise data. User-friendly formats, such as graphs and charts are frequently employed to quickly convey meaningful data relationships.

Decision support processing typically does not involve the update of data; however, some OLAP software allows users to enter data for budgeting, forecasting, and "what-if" analysis.

Informational Needs

Informational Web Services and Scripts

Web browsers provide their users with a universal tool or front-end for accessing information from web servers. They provide users with a new ability to both explore and publish information with relative ease. Unlike other technologies, web technology makes any user an instant publisher by enabling the distribution of knowledge and expertise, with no more effort than it takes to record the information in the first place.

By its very nature, this technology supports a paperless distribution process. Maintenance and update of information is straightforward since the information is stored on the web server.

Virtual Corporation Needs

Transactional Web Services and Scripts

Several factors now make Internet technology and electronic commerce a realistic option for enterprises that wish to use the Internet for business transactions.

- **Cost:** The increasing affordability of Internet access allows businesses to establish cost-effective and strategic links with business partners. This option was originally open only to large enterprises through expensive, dedicated wide-area networks or metropolitan area networks.
- **Security.** Improved security and encryption for sensitive data now provide customers with the confidence to transact over the Internet. At the same time, improvements in security provide the

enterprise with the confidence to link corporate computing environments to the Internet.

- **User-friendliness.** Improved user-friendliness and navigability from web technology make Internet technology and its use within the enterprise increasingly popular.

Figure 1–6 recapitulates the architectural components for the different types of business needs.

The majority of the architectural components support the enterprise at the operational level. However, separate components are now clearly defined for decisional and information purposes, and the virtual corporation becomes possible through Internet technologies.

Other Components

Other architectural components are so pervasive that most enterprises have begun to take their presence for granted. One example is the group of applications collectively known as office productivity tools (such as Microsoft Office or Lotus SmartSuite). Components of this type can and should be used across the various layers of the Enterprise Architecture and, therefore, are not described here as a separate item.

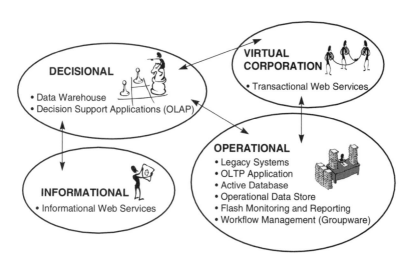

Figure 1–6 Info*Motion* Enterprise Architecture Components (Applicability to Business Needs)

▶ Architecture Migration Scenarios

Given the typical path that most Enterprise Architectures have followed, an enterprise will find itself in need of one or more of the following six migration scenarios. We offer recommendations for fulfilling those needs.

Legacy Integration

The Need

The integration of new and legacy systems is a constant challenge because of the architectural templates upon which legacy systems were built. Legacy systems often attempt to meet all types of information requirements through a single architectural component; consequently, these systems are brittle and resistant to evolution.

Despite attempts to replace them with new applications, many legacy systems remain in use because they continue to meet a set of business requirements: they represent significant investments that the enterprise cannot afford to scrap, or their massive replacement would result in unacceptable levels of disruption to business operations.

The Recommended Approach

The integration of legacy systems with the rest of the architecture is best achieved through the Operational Data Store and/or the data warehouse. Figure 1–7 modifies Figure 1–5 to show the integration of legacy systems.

Legacy programs that produce and maintain summary information are migrated to the data warehouse. Historical data are likewise migrated to the data warehouse. Reporting functionality in legacy systems is moved either to the flash reporting and monitoring tools (for operational concerns), or to decision support applications (for long-term planning and decision-making). Data required for operational monitoring are moved to the Operational Data Store. Table 1–1 summarizes the migration avenues.

The Operational Data Store and the data warehouse present IT professionals with a natural migration path for legacy migration. By migrating legacy systems to these two components, enterprises can gain a

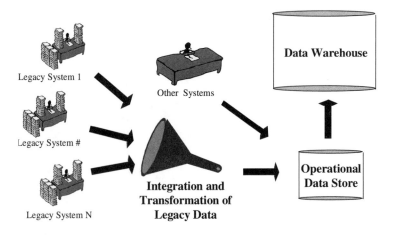

Figure 1–7 Legacy Integration

measure of independence from legacy components that were designed with old, possibly obsolete, technology. Figure 1–8 highlights how this approach fits into the Enterprise Architecture.

Operational Monitoring

The Need

Today's typical legacy systems are not suitable for supporting the operational monitoring needs of an enterprise. Legacy systems are typically structured around functional or organizational areas, in contrast

Table 1–1 Migration of Legacy Functionality to the Appropriate Architectural Component

Functionality in Legacy Systems	Should be Migrated to . . .
Summary Information	Data Warehouse
Historical Data	Data Warehouse
Operational Reporting	Flash Monitoring and Reporting Tools
Data for Operational Monitoring	Operational Data Store
Decisional Reporting	Decision Support Applications

INFO*MOTION*
LEGACY INTEGRATION

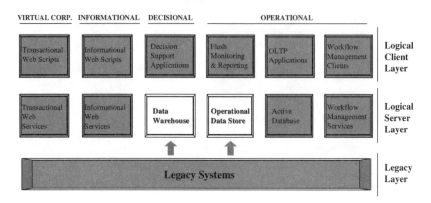

Figure 1–8   Legacy Integration: Architectural View

to the cross-functional view required by operations monitoring. Different and potentially incompatible technology platforms may have been used for different systems. Data may be available in legacy databases but are not extracted in the format required by business users. Or data may be available but may be too raw to be of use for operational decision-making (further summarization, calculation, or conversion is required). And lastly, several systems may contain data about the same item but may examine the data from different viewpoints or at different time frames, therefore requiring reconciliation.

The Recommended Approach

An integrated view of current, operational information is required for the successful monitoring of operations. Extending the functionality of legacy applications to meet this requirement would merely increase the enterprise's dependence on increasingly obsolete technology. Instead, an Operational Data Store, coupled with flash monitoring and reporting tools, as shown in Figure 1–9, meets this requirement without sacrificing architectural integrity.

Like a dashboard on a car, flash monitoring and reporting tools keep business users apprised of the latest cross-functional status of opera-

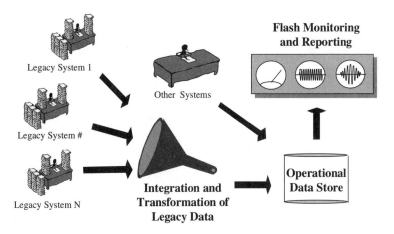

Legacy System 1

Legacy System #

Legacy System N

Other Systems

Integration and
Transformation of
Legacy Data

Operational
Data Store

**Flash Monitoring
and Reporting**

Figure 1–9   Operational Monitoring

tions. These tools obtain data from the Operational Data Store, which is regularly refreshed with the latest information from legacy and other operational systems.

Business users are consequently able to step in and correct problems in operations while they are still small or, better still, prevent problems from occurring altogether. Once alerted of a potential problem, the business user can manually intervene or make use of automated tools (i.e., control panel mechanisms) to fine-tune operational processes. Figure 1–10 highlights how this approach fits into the Enterprise Architecture.

Process Implementation

The Need

In the early 90s, the popularity of business process reengineering (BPR) caused businesses to focus on the implementation of new and redefined business processes.

Raymond Manganelli and Mark Klein, in their book *The Reengineering Handbook* (AMACOM, 1994, ISBN: 0-8144-0236-4) define BPR as "the rapid and radical redesign of *strategic, value-added business processes*—and the systems, policies, and organizational structures

INFO*MOTION*
OPERATIONAL MONITORING

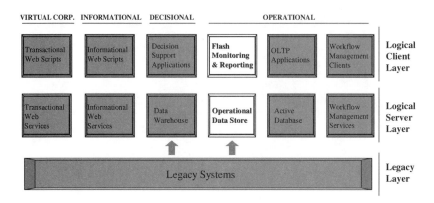

Figure 1–10   Operational Monitoring: Architectural View

that support them—to optimize the work flow and productivity in an organization." Business processes are redesigned to achieve desired results in an optimum manner.

The Recommended Approach

With BPR, the role of Information Technology shifted from simple automation to enabling radically redesigned processes. Client/server technology, such as OLTP applications serviced by active databases, is particularly suited to supporting this type of business need. Technology advances have made it possible to build and modify systems quickly in response to changes in business processes. New policies, procedures, and controls are supported and enforced by the systems.

In addition, workflow management systems can be used to supplement OLTP applications. A workflow management system converts business activities into a goal-directed process that flows through the enterprise in an orderly fashion (see Figure 1–11). The workflow management system alerts users through the automatic generation of notification messages or reminders and routes work so that the desired business result is achieved in an expedited manner.

Figure 1–11   Process Implementation

Figure 1–12 highlights how this approach fits into the Enterprise Architecture.

Decision Support

The Need

It is not possible to anticipate the information requirements of decision-makers for the simple reason that their needs depend on the business situation that they face. Decision-makers need to review enterprise data from different dimensions and at different levels of detail to find the source of a business problem before they can attack it. They likewise need information for detecting business opportunities to exploit.

Decision-makers also need to analyze trends in the performance of the enterprise. Rather than waiting for problems to present themselves, decision-makers need to proactively mobilize the resources of the enterprise in anticipation of a business situation.

Since these information requirements cannot be anticipated, the decision-maker often resorts to reviewing predesigned inquiries or reports in an attempt to find or derive needed information. Alternatively, the IT professional is pressured to produce an ad hoc report from legacy sys-

INFO*MOTION*
PROCESS IMPLEMENTATION

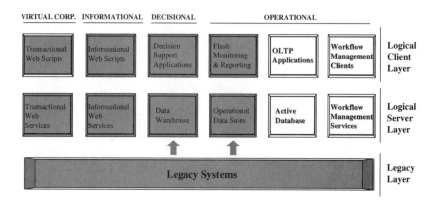

Figure 1–12   Process Implementation: Architectural View

tems as quickly as possible. If unlucky, the IT professional will find the data needed for the report are scattered throughout different legacy systems. An even unluckier may find that the processing required to produce the report will have a toll on the operations of the enterprise.

These delays are not only frustrating both for the decision-maker and the IT professional, they are dangerous for the enterprise. The information that eventually reaches the decision-maker may be inconsistent, inaccurate, or worse, obsolete.

The Recommended Approach

Decision support applications (or OLAP) that obtain data from the data warehouse are recommended for this particular need. The data warehouse holds transformed and integrated enterprise-wide operational data appropriate for strategic decision-making, as shown in Figure 1–13. The data warehouse also contains data obtained from external sources, whenever this data is relevant to decision-making.

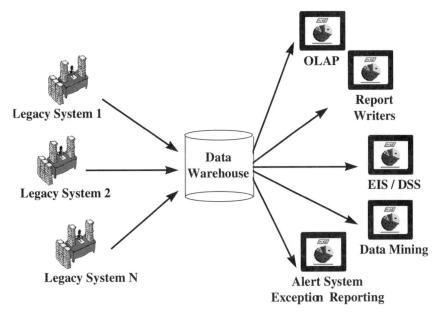

Figure 1–13   Decision Support

Decision support applications analyze and make data warehouse information available in formats that are readily understandable by
decision-makers. Figure 1–14 highlights how this approach fits into
the Enterprise Architecture.

Hyperdata Distribution

The Need

Past informational requirements were met by making data available in
physical form through reports, memos, and company manuals. This
practice resulted in an overflow of documents providing much data
and not enough information.

Paper-based documents also have the disadvantage of becoming dated.
Enterprises encountered problems in keeping different versions of related items synchronized. There was a constant need to update, repub-
lish, and redistribute documents.

INFO*MOTION*
DECISION SUPPORT

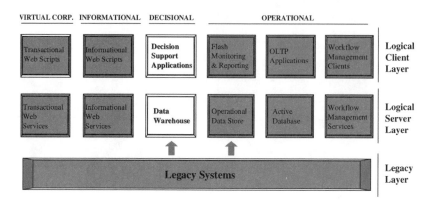

Figure 1–14   Decision Support: Architectural View

In response to this problem, enterprises made data available to users over a network to eliminate the paper. It was hoped that users could selectively view the data that they needed whenever they needed it. This approach likewise proved to be insufficient because users still had to navigate through a sea of data to locate the specific item of information that was needed.

The Recommended Approach

Users need the ability to browse through nonlinear presentations of data. Web technology is particularly suitable to this need because of its extremely flexible and highly visual method of organizing information (see Figure 1–15).

Web technology allows users to display charts and figures; navigate through large amounts of data; visualize the contents of database files; seamlessly navigate across charts, data, and annotation; and organize charts and figures in a hierarchical manner. Users are therefore able to locate information with relative ease.

Figure 1–16 highlights how this approach fits into the Enterprise Architecture.

Chapter **1** I The Enterprise IT Architecture

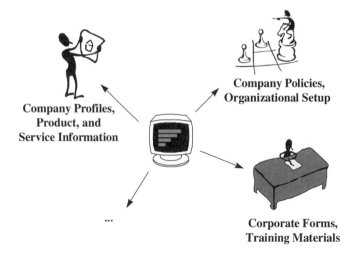

Figure 1–15   Hyperdata Distribution

INFO*MOTION*
HYPERDATA DISTRIBUTION

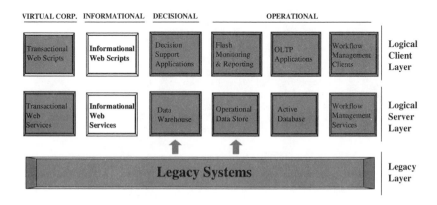

Figure 1–16   Hyperdata Distribution: Architectural View

Virtual Corporation

The Need

A virtual corporation is an enterprise that has extended its business processes to encompass both its key customers and suppliers. Its business processes are newly redesigned; its product development or service delivery are accelerated to better meet customer needs and preferences; its management practices promote new alignments between management and labor, as well as new linkages between enterprise, supplier and customer. A new level of cooperation and openness is created and encouraged between the enterprise and its key business partners.

The Recommended Approach

Partnerships at the enterprise level translate into technological links between the enterprise and its key suppliers or customers (see Figure 1–17). Information required by each party is identified, and steps are taken to ensure that this data crosses organizational boundaries properly.

Some organizations seek to establish a higher level of cooperation with their key business partners by jointly redesigning their business processes to provide greater value to the customer.

Internet and web technologies are well suited to support redesigned, transactional processes, thanks to decreasing Internet costs, improved

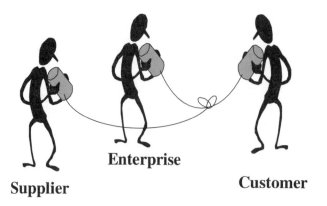

Supplier   **Enterprise**   **Customer**

Figure 1–17   Virtual Corporation

INFO*MOTION*
VIRTUAL CORPORATION

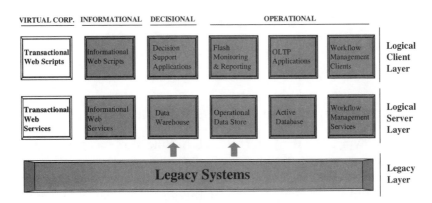

Figure 1–18   Virtual Corporation: Architectural View

security measures, improved user-friendliness, and navigability. Figure 1–18 highlights how this approach fits into the Enterprise Architecture.

▶ Migration Strategy: How Do We Move Forward?

The strategies presented in the previous section enable organizations to move from their current technology architectures into the Info*Motion* Enterprise Architecture. This section describes the tasks for any migration effort.

Review the Current Enterprise Architecture

As simplistic as this may sound, the starting point is a review of the current Enterprise Architecture. It is important to have an idea of what we have now before we can plan for where we want to be.

The IT department or division should have this information readily available, although it may not necessarily be expressed in terms of the architectural components identified above. A short and simple exercise of mapping the current architecture of your enterprise to the architecture described above should quickly highlight any gaps in the current architecture.

Identify Information Architecture Requirements

Knowing that the Enterprise IT Architecture has gaps is not sufficient. It is important to know whether these can be considered real gaps when viewed within the context of the enterprise's requirements. Gaps should cause concern only if the absence of an architectural component prevents the IT infrastructure from meeting present requirements or from supporting long-term strategies.

For example, if transactional web scripts are not critical to your enterprise given its current needs and strategies, there should be no cause for concern.

Develop a Migration Plan Based on Requirements

It is not advisable for an enterprise to use this list of architectural gaps to justify a dramatic overhaul of its IT infrastructure; such an undertaking would be expensive and would cause unnecessary disruption of business operations.

Instead, the enterprise would do well to develop a migration plan that consciously maps coming IT projects to the InfoMotion Enterprise Architecture.

The Natural Migration Path

While developing the migration plan, the enterprise should consider the natural migration path that the InfoMotion architecture implies, as illustrated in Figure 1–19.

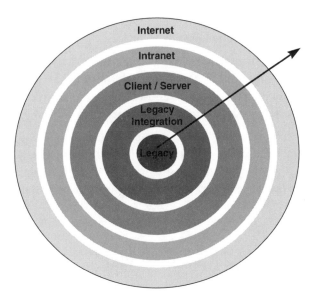

Figure 1–19 Natural Migration Roadmap

- At the very core of the Enterprise Architecture is the Legacy layer. For most companies, this core layer is where the majority of technology investments have been made. It should also be the starting point of any architecture migration effort, i.e., the enterprise should start from this core technology before focusing its attention on newer forms or layers of technology.
- The Legacy Integration layer insulates the rest of the Enterprise Architecture from the growing obsolescence of the Legacy layer. It also provides the succeeding technology layers with a more stable foundation for future evolution.
- Each of the succeeding technology layers (i.e., Client/Server, Intranet, Internet) builds upon its predecessors.
- At the outermost layer, the public Internet infrastructure itself supports the operations of the enterprise.

The Customized Migration Path

Depending on the priorities and needs of the enterprise, one or more of the migration scenarios described in the previous section will be helpful starting points. The scenarios provide generic roadmaps that address typical architectural needs.

The migration plan, however, must be customized to address the specific needs of the enterprise. Each project defined in the plan must individually contribute to the enterprise in the short term, while laying the groundwork for achieving long-term enterprise and IT objectives.

By incrementally migrating its IT infrastructure (one component and one project at a time), the enterprise will find itself slowly but surely moving towards a modern, resilient Enterprise Architecture, with minimal and acceptable levels of disruption in operations.

Monitor and Update the Migration Plan

The migration plan must be monitored, and the progress of the different projects fed back into the planning task. One must not lose sight of the fact that a modern Enterprise Architecture is a moving target; new technology renders continuous evolution of the Enterprise Architecture inevitable.

▶ In Summary

An enterprise has longevity in the business arena only when its products and services are perceived by its customers to be of value.

Likewise, Information Technology has value in an enterprise only when its cost is outweighed by its ability to increase and guarantee quality, improve service, cut costs or reduce cycle time, as depicted in Figure 1–20.

The Enterprise Architecture is the foundation for all Information Technology efforts. It therefore must provide the enterprise with the ability to:

$$\text{Value} = \frac{\text{Quality x Service}}{\text{Cost x Cycle Time}}$$

Figure 1–20   The Value Equation

- distill information of value from the data which surrounds it, which it continuously generates (information/data); and
- get that information to the right people and processes at the right time (motion).

These requirements form the basis for the Info*Motion* equation, shown in Figure 1–21.

$$\text{Info}\textit{Motion} = \frac{\textbf{Information}}{\textbf{Data}} \times \textbf{Motion}$$

Figure 1–21   The Info*Motion* Equation

By identifying distinct architectural components and their interrelationships, the Info*Motion* Enterprise Architecture increases the capability of the IT infrastructure to meet present business requirements while positioning the enterprise to leverage emerging trends, such as data warehousing, in both business and technology. Figure 1–22 reprises the Info*Motion* Enterprise Architecture, the elements of which we have discussed.

INFOMOTION
ENTERPRISE ARCHITECTURE

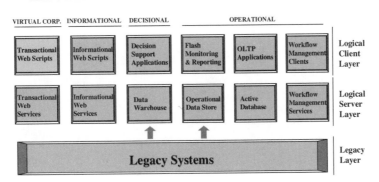

Figure 1–22   The Info*Motion* Architecture

Data Warehouse Concepts

In this chapter, we look briefly at how computing has changed its focus from operational to decisional concerns. We also define data warehousing concepts, and cite the typical reasons for building data warehouses.

▶ Gradual Changes in Computing Focus

In retrospect, it is easy to see how computing has shifted its focus from operational to decisional concerns. The differences in operational and decisional information requirements presented new challenges that old computing practices could not meet. Below, we elaborate on how this change in computing focus became the impetus for the development of data warehousing technologies.

Early Computing Focused on Operational Requirements

The Business Cycle (depicted in Figure 2–1) shows us that any enterprise must operate at three levels: operational (i.e., the day-to-day running of the business); tactical (i.e., the definition of policy and the monitoring of operations); and strategic (i.e., the definition of organization's vision, goals and objectives).

In Chapter 1, we noted that much of the effort and money in computing has focused on meeting the *operational* business requirements of enterprises. After all, without the OLTP applications that record thousands, even millions, of discrete transactions each day, it would not be possible for any enterprise to meet customer needs while enforcing business policies consistently. Nor would it be possible for an enterprise to grow without significantly expanding its manpower base.

With operational systems deployed and day-to-day information needs being met by the OLTP systems, the focus of computing has over the recent years shifted naturally to meeting the *decisional* business requirements of an enterprise. Figure 2–1 illustrates the business cycle as we view it today.

Decisional Requirements Cannot Be Fully Anticipated

Unfortunately, it is not possible for IT professionals to anticipate the information requirements of an enterprise's decision-makers for the

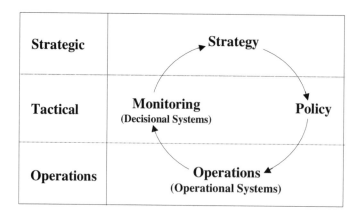

Figure 2–1   The Business Cycle

simple reason that their information needs and report requirements change as the business situation changes.

Decision-makers themselves cannot be expected to know their information requirements ahead of time; they review enterprise data from different perspectives and at different levels of detail to find and address business problems as the problems arise. Decision-makers also need to look through business data to identify opportunities that can be exploited. They examine performance trends to identify business situations that can provide competitive advantage, improve profits, or reduce costs. They analyze market data and make the tactical as well as strategic decisions that determine the course of the enterprise.

Operational Systems Fail to Provide Decisional Information

Since these information requirements cannot be anticipated, operational systems (which correctly focus on recording and completing different types of business transactions) are unable to provide decision-makers with the information they need. As a result, business managers fall back on the time-consuming, and often frustrating, process of going through operational inquiries or reports already supported by operational systems in an attempt to find or derive the information they really need. Alternatively, IT professionals are pressured to produce an ad hoc report from the operational systems as quickly as possible.

It will not be unusual for the IT professional to find that the data needed to produce the report are scattered throughout different operational systems and must first be carefully integrated. Worse, it's likely that the processing required to extract the data from each operational system will demand so much of the system resources that the IT professional must wait until nonoperational hours before running the queries required to produce the report.

These delays are not only time-consuming and frustrating both for the IT professionals and the decision-makers, they are dangerous for the enterprise. When the report is finally produced, the data may be inconsistent, inaccurate, or obsolete. There is also the very real possibility that this new report will trigger the request for another ad hoc report.

Decisional Systems Have Evolved to Meet Decisional Requirements

Over the years, decisional systems have been developed and implemented in the hope of meeting these information needs. Some enterprises have actually succeeded in developing and deploying data warehouses within their respective organizations, long before the term *data warehouse* even became fashionable.

Most decisional systems, however, have failed to deliver on their promises. This book introduces data warehousing technologies and shares lessons learned from the successes and failures of those who have been on the "bleeding edge."

▶ The Data Warehouse Defined

What is a data warehouse? William H. Inmon in *Building the Data Warehouse* (QED Technical Publishing Group, 1992, ISBN: 0-89435-404-3) defines a data warehouse as "a collection of integrated, subject-oriented databases designed to supply the information required for decision-making."

A more thorough look at the above definition yields the following observations.

Integrated

A data warehouse contains data extracted from the many operational systems of the enterprise, possibly supplemented by external data. For example, a typical banking data warehouse will require the integration of data drawn from the deposit systems, loan systems, and the general ledger, just to name three.

Each of these operational systems records different types of business transactions and enforces the policies of the enterprise regarding these transactions. If each of the operational systems has been custom built or an integrated system was not implemented as a solution, then it is unlikely that these systems are integrated. Thus, Customer A in the deposit system and Customer B in the loan system may be one and the same person—but there is no automated way for anyone in the bank to know this. Customer relationships are managed informally through relationships with bank officers.

A data warehouse brings together data from the various operational systems to provide an integrated view of the customer and the full scope of his or her relationship with the bank.

Subject Oriented

Traditional operational systems focus on the data requirements of a department or division, producing the much-criticized "stovepipe" systems of most enterprises. With the advent of business process reengineering, enterprises began espousing process-centered teams and case workers. Modern operational systems, in turn, shifted their focus to the operational requirements of an entire business process and aim to support the execution of the business process from start to finish.

A data warehouse goes beyond traditional information views by focusing on enterprise-wide subjects such as customers, sales, and profits. These subjects span both organizational and process boundaries and require information from multiple sources to provide a complete picture.

Databases

Although the term *data warehousing technologies* is used to refer to the gamut of technology components that are required to plan, develop, manage, implement, and use a data warehouse, the term *data warehouse* itself refers to a large, read-only repository of data.

At the very heart of every data warehouse lie the large databases that store the integrated data of the enterprise, obtained from both internal and external data sources. The term *internal data* refers to all data that are extracted from the operational systems of the enterprise. External data are data provided by third-party organizations, including business partners, customers, government bodies, and organizations that choose to make a profit by selling their data (e.g., credit bureaus).

Also stored in the databases are the metadata that describe the contents of the data warehouse. A more thorough discussion of metadata their role in data warehousing is provided in Chapter 13.

Required for Decision-Making

Unlike the databases of operational systems, which are often normalized to preserve and maintain data integrity, a data warehouse is designed and structured in a denormalized manner to better support the usability of the data warehouse. Users are better able to examine, derive, summarize, and analyze data at various levels of detail, over different periods of time, when using a denormalized data structure.

The database is denormalized to mimic a business user's dimensional view of the business. For example, while a finance manager is interested in the profitability of the various products of a company, a product manager will be more interested in the sales of the product in the various sales regions. In data warehousing parlance, users need to "slice and dice" through different areas of the database at different levels of detail to obtain the information they need. In this manner, a decision-maker can start with a high-level view of the business, then drill down to get more detail on the areas that require his attention, or vice versa.

Each Unit of Data Is Relevant to a Point in Time

Every data warehouse will inevitably have a Time dimension; each data item (also called facts or measures) in the data warehouse is time-stamped to support queries or reports that require the comparison of figures from prior months or years.

The time-stamping of each fact also makes it possible for decision-makers to recognize trends and patterns in customer or market behavior over time.

A Data Warehouse Contains Both Atomic and Summarized Data

Data warehouses hold data at different levels of detail. Data at the most detailed level, i.e., the atomic level, are used to derive the summarized of aggregated values. Aggregates (presummarized data) are stored in the warehouse to speed up responses to queries at higher levels of granularity.

If the data warehouse stores data only at summarized levels, its users will not be able to drill down on data items to get more detailed information. However, the storage of very detailed data results in larger space requirements.

▶ The Dynamic, Ad Hoc Report

The most ideal scenario for enterprise decision-makers (and for IT professionals) is to have a repository of data and a set of tools that will allow decision-makers to create their own set of dynamic reports. The term *dynamic report* refers to a report that can be quickly modified by its user to present either greater or less detail, without any additional programming required. Dynamic reports are the only kind of reports that provide true, ad hoc reporting capabilities. Figure 2–2 presents an example of a dynamic report.

For Current Year, 2Q

Sales Region	Targets ('000s)	Actuals ('000s)
Asia	24,000	25,550
Europe	10,000	12,200
North America	**8,000**	**2,000** ◤
Africa	5,600	6,200
...	...	...

Figure 2–2   The Dynamic Report—Summary View

For Current Year, 2Q

Sales Region	Country	Targets ('000s)	Actuals ('000s)
Asia	Philippines	14,000	15,050
	Hong Kong	10,000	10,500
Europe	France	4,000	4,050
	Italy	6,000	8,150
North America	United States	1,000	1,500
	Canada	**7,000**	**500**
Africa	Egypt	5,600	6,200

Figure 2–3   The Dynamic Report—Detailed View

A decision-maker should be able to start with a short report that summarizes the performance of the enterprise. When the summary calls attention to an area that bears closer inspection, the decision-maker should be able to point to that portion of the report, then obtain greater detail on it dynamically, on an as-needed basis, with no further programming. Figure 2–3 presents a detailed view of the summary shown in Figure 2–2.

By providing business users with the ability to dynamically view more or less of the data on an ad hoc, as-needed basis, the data warehouse eliminates delays in getting information and removes the IT professional from the report-creation loop.

▶ The Purposes of a Data Warehouse

At this point, it is helpful to summarize the typical reasons enterprises undertake data warehousing initiatives.

To Provide Business Users with Access to Data

The data warehouse provides access to integrated enterprise data previously locked away in unfriendly, difficult-to-access environments. Business users can now establish, with minimal effort, a secure connection to the warehouse through their desktop PC. Security is enforced either by the warehouse front-end application, by the server database, or both.

Because of its integrated nature, a data warehouse spares business users from the need to learn, understand, or access operational data in their native environments and data structures.

To Provide One Version of the Truth

The data in the data warehouse are consistent and quality assured before being released to business users. Since a common source of information is now used, the data warehouse puts to rest all debates about the veracity of data used or cited in meetings. The data warehouse becomes the common information resource for decisional purposes throughout the organization.

Note that "one version of the truth" is often possible only after much discussion and debate about the terms used within the organization. For example, the term *customer* can have different meanings to different people—it is not unusual for some people to refer to prospective clients as "customers," while others in the same organization may use the term "customers" to mean only actual, current clients.

While these differences may seem trivial at first glance, the subtle nuances that exist depending on the context may result in misleading numbers and ill-informed decisions. For example, when the Western Region sales manager asks for the number of customers, he probably means the "number of customers from the Western Region," not the "number of customers served by the entire company."

To Record the Past Accurately

Many of the figures and numbers that managers receive have little meaning unless compared to historical figures. For example, reports that compare the company's performance now against its performance last year are quite common. Reports that show the company's performance for the same month over the past three years are likewise of interest to decision-makers.

The operational systems will not be able to meet this kind of information need, and for a good reason. A data warehouse should be used to record the past accurately, leaving the OLTP systems free to focus on correctly recording current transactions and balances. Actual historical values are not stored on the operational system nor derived by adding or subtracting transaction values against the latest balance. Instead, historical data are loaded and integrated with other data in the warehouse for quick access.

To Slice and Dice Through Data

As stated earlier in this chapter, dynamic reports allow users to view warehouse data from different angles, at different levels of detail. Business users with the means and the ability to slice and dice through warehouse data can actively meet their own information needs.

The ready availability of different data views also improves business analysis by reducing the time and effort required to collect, format, and distill information from data.

To Separate Analytical and Operational Processing

Decisional processing and operational information processing have totally divergent architectural requirements. Attempts to meet both decisional and operational information needs through the same system or through the same system architecture merely increase the brittleness of the IT architecture and will create system maintenance nightmares.

Data warehousing disentangles analytical from operational processing by providing a separate system architecture for decisional implementations. This makes the overall IT architecture of the enterprise more resilient to changing requirements.

To Support the Reengineering of Decisional Processes

At the end of each BPR initiative come the projects required to establish the technological and organizational systems to support the newly reengineered business process.

Although reengineering projects have traditionally focused on operational processes, data warehousing technologies make it possible to reengineer decisional business processes as well. Data warehouses, with their focus on meeting decisional business requirements, are the ideal systems for supporting reengineered decisional business processes.

▶ A Word About Data Marts

A discussion of data warehouses is not complete without a note on data marts. Unlike data warehouses, which contain large quantities of data from key operational systems in an enterprise, a data mart typically contains only a subset of the data that would have been stored in an enterprise data warehouse. Data mart data are selected to meet the specific needs of a subset of the organization. It is not unusual to find a data mart developed and implemented for a department, a division, or a geographical location.

Data marts are often preferred by enterprises as a first step to building a data warehouse, since these can be used as a "proof of concept." Initial success with the data mart can be used to convince skeptics in the enterprise and loosen the enterprise's purse strings.

A number of misconceptions exist about data marts and their relationships to data warehouses. We discuss two of those misconceptions below.

Misconception: Data Warehouses and Data Marts Cannot Coexist

There are parties who strongly advocate the deployment of data marts as opposed to the deployment of data warehouses. They correctly point out the difficulties of building an enterprisewide data warehouse in one large project and lead unsuspecting organizations down the "data mart vs. data warehouse" path.

What many do not immediately realize is that data warehouses and data marts can coexist within the same organization; the correct approach is "data mart AND data warehouse." We discuss this subject more thoroughly in the "Warehousing Architectures" section of Chapter 5.

Misconception: Data Marts Can Be Built Independently of One Another

Some enterprises find it easier to deploy multiple data marts independently of one another. At first glance, such an approach is indeed easier since there are no integration issues. Different groups of users are involved with each data mart, which implies fewer conflicts about the use of terms and about business rules. Each data mart is free to exist within its own isolated world, and all the users are happy.

Unfortunately, what enterprises fail to realize until much later is that by deploying one isolated data mart after another, the enterprise has actually created new islands of automation. And while at the onset these data marts are certainly easier to develop, the task of maintaining many unrelated data marts is exceedingly complex and will create data management, synchronization, and consistency issues. Each data mart presents its own version of "the truth" and will quite naturally provide information that conflicts with the reports from other data marts.

Multiple data marts are definitely appropriate within an organization, but these should be implemented only under the integrating framework of an enterprise-wide data warehouse. Each data mart is developed as an extension of the data warehouse and is fed by the data warehouse. The data warehouse enforces a consistent set of business rules and ensures the consistent use of terms and definitions.

▶ A Word About Operational Data Stores

Data warehouse discussions will also naturally lead to Operational Data Stores, which at first glance may appear no different from data warehouses.

Although both technologies support decisional information needs of enterprise decision-makers, the two are distinctly different and are deployed to meet different types of decisional information needs.

Definition of Operational Data Stores

In *Building the Operational Data Store* (John Wiley & Sons, 1996, ISBN: 0-471-12822-8), W. H. Inmon, C. Imhoff, and G. Battas define an Operational Data Store as "the architectural construct where collective integrated operational data is stored." ODS can also be defined as a collection of integrated databases designed to support operational monitoring. Unlike the databases of OLTP applications (that are operational or function oriented), the Operational Data Store contains subject-oriented, enterprise-wide data. However, unlike data warehouses, the data in Operational Data Stores are volatile, current, and detailed. The ODS provides an integrated view of the data in the operational systems.

Table 2–1 compares the data warehouse with the Operational Data Store.

Table 2–1 Data Warehouses vs. Operational Data Stores

	DW	ODS
Purpose	Strategic Decision Support	Operational Monitoring
Similarities	Integrated Data Subject-Oriented	Integrated Data Subject-Oriented
Differences	Static Data Historical Data Summarized Data	Volatile Data Current Data More Detailed

Data are transformed and integrated into a consistent, unified whole as they are obtained from legacy and other operational systems to provide business users with an integrated and current view of operations. Data in the Operational Data Store are constantly refreshed so that the resulting image reflects the latest state of operations.

Flash Monitoring and Reporting Tools

As mentioned in Chapter 1, flash monitoring and reporting tools are like a dashboard that provides meaningful online information on the operational status of the enterprise. This service is achieved by the use of ODS data as inputs to the flash monitoring and reporting tools, to provide business users with a constantly refreshed, enterprise-wide view of operations without creating unwanted interruptions or additional load on transaction-processing systems. Figure 2–4 diagrams how this scheme works.

Relationship of Operational Data Stores to Data Warehouse

Enterprises with Operational Data Stores find themselves in the enviable position of being able to deploy data warehouses with considerable ease. Since operational data stores are integrated, many of the issues related to extracting, transforming, and transporting data from legacy systems have been addressed by the ODS, as illustrated in Figure 2–5.

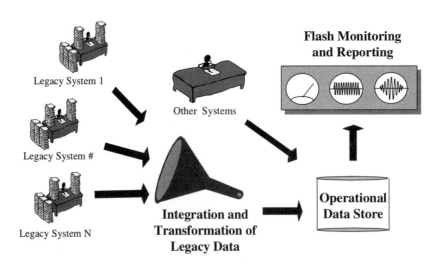

Figure 2–4   Operational Monitoring

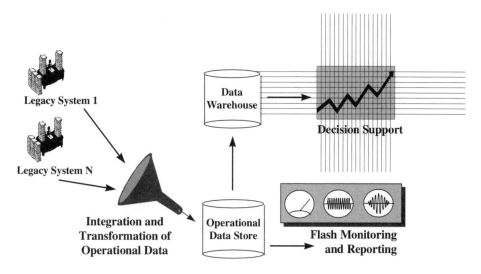

Figure 2–5   The Operational Data Store Feeds the Data Warehouse

The data warehouse is populated by means of regular snapshots of the data in the Operational Data Store. However, unlike the ODS, the data warehouse maintains the historical snapshots of the data for comparisons across different time frames. The ODS is free to focus only on the current state of operations and is constantly updated in real time.

▶ Data Warehouse Cost-Benefit Analysis / Return on Investment

Senior management typically requires a cost-benefit analysis (CBA) or a study of return on investment (ROI) prior to embarking on a data warehousing initiative. Although the task of calculating ROI for data warehousing initiatives is unique to each enterprise, it is possible to classify the type of benefits and costs that are associated with data warehousing.

Benefits

Data warehousing benefits can be expected from the following areas:

- **Redeployment of staff assigned to old decisional systems.** The cost of producing today's management reports is typically undocumented and unknown within an enterprise. The quantification of such costs in terms of staff hours and erroneous data may yield surprising results. Benefits of this nature, however, are typically minimal, since warehouse maintenance and enhancements require staff as well. At best, staff will be redeployed to more productive tasks.

- **Improved productivity of analytical staff due to availability of data.** Analysts go through several steps in their day-to-day work: locating data, retrieving data, analyzing data to yield information, presenting information, and recommending a course of action. Unfortunately, much of the time (sometimes up to 40 percent) spent by enterprise analysts on a typical day is devoted to locating and retrieving data. The availability of integrated, readily accessible data (in the data warehouse) should significantly reduce the time that analysts spend with data collection tasks and increase the time they have available to actually analyze the data they have collected. This leads either to shorter decision cycle times or improvements in the quality of the analysis.

- **Business improvements resulting from analysis of warehouse data.** The most significant business improvements in warehousing result from the analysis of warehouse data, especially if the easy availability of information yields insights heretofore unknown to the enterprise. The goal of the data warehouse is to meet decisional information needs; it therefore follows naturally that the greatest benefits of warehousing are obtained when decisional information needs are actually met and sound business decisions are made both at the tactical and strategic level. Understandably, such benefits are the most significant and, therefore, the most difficult to project and the most difficult to quantify.

Costs

Data warehousing costs typically fall into one of four categories. These are:

- **Hardware.** This item refers to the costs associated with setting up the hardware and operating environment required by the data warehouse. In many instances, this setup may require the acquisition of new equipment or the upgrade of existing equipment. Larger warehouse implementations naturally imply higher hardware costs.
- **Software.** This item refers to the costs of purchasing the licenses to use software products that automate the extraction, cleansing, loading, retrieval, and presentation of warehouse data.
- **Services.** This item refers to services provided by systems integrators, consultants, and trainers during the course of a data warehouse project. Enterprises typically rely more on the services of third parties in early warehousing implementations, when the technology is still quite new to the enterprise.
- **Internal staff costs.** This item refers to costs incurred by assigning internal staff to the data warehousing effort, as well as costs associated with training internal staff on new technologies and techniques.

ROI Considerations

The costs and benefits associated with data warehousing vary significantly from one enterprise to another. The differences are chiefly influenced by

- the current state of technology within the enterprise;
- the culture of the organization in terms of decision-making styles and attitudes towards technology; and
- the company's position in its chosen market vs. its competitors.

The effect of data warehousing on the tactical and strategic management of an enterprise is often likened to cleaning the muddy windshield of a car. It is difficult to quantify the value of driving a car with a cleaner windshield. Similarly, it is difficult to quantify the value of managing your organization with better information and insight.

Lastly, it is important to note that data warehouse justification is often complicated by the fact that much of the benefit may take some time to realize and therefore is difficult to quantify in advance.

▶ In Summary

Data warehousing technologies have evolved as a result of the unsatisfied decisional information needs of enterprises. With the increased stability of operational systems, information technology professionals have increasingly turned their attention to meeting the decisional requirements of the enterprise.

A data warehouse, according to Bill Inmon, is a collection of integrated, subject-oriented databases designed to supply the information required for decision-making. Each data item in the data warehouse is relevant to some moment in time.

A discussion of data warehouses is incomplete without a word on data marts. A data mart has traditionally been defined as a subset of the enterprise-wide data warehouse. Many enterprises, upon realizing the complexity involved in deploying a data warehouse, will opt to deploy data marts instead. Although data marts are able to meet the immediate needs of a targeted group of users, the enterprise should shy away from deploying multiple, unrelated data marts. The presence of such islands of information will only result in data management and synchronization problems.

A discussion of data warehouses is likewise incomplete without a discussion of Operational Data Stores. Like data warehouses, Operational Data Stores are integrated and subject-oriented. However, an ODS is always current and is constantly updated (ideally in real time). The Operational Data Store is the ideal data source for a data warehouse, since it already contains integrated operational data as of a given point in time.

Although data warehouses have proven to have significant returns on investment, particularly when they are meeting a specific, targeted business need, it is extremely difficult to quantify the expected benefits of a data warehouse. The costs are easier to calculate, as these break down simply into hardware, software, services, and in-house staffing costs.

Part 2

People

Although a number of people are involved in a single data warehousing project, there are three key roles that carry enormous responsibilities. Negligence in carrying out any of these three roles can easily derail a well-planned data warehousing initiative. This section of the book therefore focuses on the Project Sponsor, the Chief Information Officer, and the Project Manager and seeks to answer the questions frequently asked by individuals who have accepted the responsibilities that come with these roles.

- **Project Sponsor.** Every data warehouse initiative has a Project Sponsor—a high-level executive who provides strategic guidance, support, and direction to the data warehousing project. The Project Sponsor ensures that project objectives are aligned with enterprise objectives, resolves organizational issues, and usually obtains funding for the project.
- **Chief Information Officer (CIO).** The CIO is responsible for the effective deployment of information technology resources and staff to meet the strategic, decisional, and operational information requirements of the enterprise. Data warehousing, with its accompanying array of new technology and its dependence on operational systems, naturally makes strong demands on the physical and human resources under the jurisdiction of the CIO, not only during design and development but also during maintenance and subsequent evolution.
- **Project Manager.** The warehouse Project Manager is responsible for all technical activities related to implementing a data warehouse. Ideally, an IT professional from the enterprise fulfills this critical role. It is not unusual, however, for this role to be outsourced for early or pilot projects, because of the newness of warehousing technologies and techniques.

The Project Sponsor

Before the Project Sponsor becomes comfortable with the data warehousing effort, quite a number of his or her questions and concerns will have to be addressed. This chapter attempts to provide answers to questions frequently asked by Project Sponsors.

▶ How Will a Data Warehouse Affect our Decision-Making Processes?

It is naïve to expect an immediate change to the decision-making processes in an organization when a data warehouse first goes into production. End users will initially be occupied more with learning how to use the data warehouse than with changing the way they obtain information and make decisions. It is also likely that the first set of predefined reports and queries supported by the data warehouse will differ little from existing reports.

Decision-makers will experience varying levels of initial difficulty with the use of the data warehouse; proper usage assumes a level of desktop computing skills, data knowledge, and business knowledge.

- **Desktop computing skills.** Not all business users are familiar and comfortable with the desktop computers, and it is unrealistic to expect all the business users in an organization to make direct, personal use of the front-end warehouse tools. On the other hand, there are power users within the organization who enjoy using computers, love spreadsheets, and will quickly push the tools to the limit with their queries and reporting requirements.
- **Data knowledge.** It is critical that business users be familiar with the contents of the data warehouse before they make use of it. In many cases, this requirement entails extensive communication on two levels. First, the scope of the warehouse must be clearly communicated to properly manage user expectations about the type of information they can retrieve, particularly in the earlier rollouts of the warehouse. Second, business users who will have direct access to the data warehouse must be trained on the use of the selected front-end tools and on the meaning of the warehouse contents.
- **Business knowledge.** Warehouse users must have a good understanding of the nature of their business and of the types of business issues that they need to address. The answers that the warehouse will provide are only as good as the questions that are directed to it.

As end users gain confidence both in their own skills and in the veracity of the warehouse contents, data warehouse usage and overall support of the warehousing initiative will increase. Users will begin to "outgrow" the canned reports and will move to a more ad hoc, analytical style when using the data warehouse.

As the data scope of the warehouse increases and additional standard reports are produced from the warehouse data, decision-makers will start feeling overwhelmed by the number of standard reports that they receive. Decision-makers will gradually want to lessen their dependence on the regular reports and instead will want to start relying on exception reporting or highlighting, and alert systems.

- **Exception reporting or highlighting.** Instead of scanning regular reports one line item at a time, decision-makers will want to receive exception reports that enumerate only the items that meet their definition of "exceptions." For example, instead of receiving sales reports per region for all regions within the company, a sales executive may instead prefer to receive sales reports for areas where actual sales figures are either 10 percent more or less than the budgeted figures.

- **Alert systems.** Alert systems also follow the same principle, that of highlighting or bringing to the fore areas or items that require managerial attention and action. However, instead of reports, decision-makers will receive notification of exceptions through other means, for example, an e-mail message.

As the warehouse gains acceptance, decision-making styles will evolve from the current practice of waiting for regular reports from IT or MIS to using the data warehouse to understand the current status of operations and, further, to using the data warehouse as the basis for strategic decision-making. At the most sophisticated level of usage, a data warehouse will allow senior management to understand and drive the business changes needed by the enterprise.

▶ How Does a Data Warehouse Improve My Financial Processes? Marketing? Operations?

A successful enterprise-wide data warehouse effort will improve financial, marketing and operational processes through the simple availability of integrated data views. Previously unavailable perspectives of the enterprise will increase understanding of cross-functional operations. The integration of enterprise data results in standardized terms across organizational units (e.g., a uniform definition of *customer* and *profit*). A common set of metrics for measuring performance will emerge from the data warehousing effort. Communication among these different groups will also improve.

Financial Processes

Consolidated financial reports, profitability analysis, and risk monitoring improve the financial processes of an enterprise, particularly in financial service institutions, such as banks. The very process of consolidation requires the use of a common vocabulary and increased understanding of operations across different groups in the organization.

While financial processes will improve because of the newly available information, it is important to note that the warehouse can provide information based only on available data. For example, one of the most popular banking applications for data warehousing is profitability analysis. Unfortunately, enterprises may encounter a rude shock when it becomes apparent that revenues and costs are not tracked at the same level of detail within the organization. Banks frequently track their expenses at the level of branches or organization units but wish to compute profitability on a per customer basis. With profit figures at the customer level and costs at the branch level, there is no direct way to compute profit. As a result, enterprises may resort to formulas that allow them to compute or derive cost and revenue figures at the same level for comparison purposes.

Marketing

Data warehousing supports marketing organizations by providing a comprehensive view of each customer and his many relationships with the enterprise. Over the years, marketing efforts have shifted in focus. Customers are no longer viewed as individual accounts but instead are viewed as individuals with multiple accounts. This change in perspective provides the enterprise with cross-selling opportunities.

The notion of customers as individuals also makes possible the segmentation and profiling of customers to improve target-marketing efforts. The availability of historical data makes it possible to identify trends in customer behavior, hopefully with positive results in revenue.

Operations

By providing enterprise management with decisional information, data warehouses have the potential of greatly affecting the operations of an enterprise by highlighting both problems and opportunities that heretofore went undetected.

Strategic or tactical decisions based on warehouse data will naturally affect the operations of the enterprise. It is in this area that the greatest return on investment and, therefore, greatest improvement can be found.

When Is a Data Warehouse Project Justified?

As we mentioned in Chapter 2, return on investment (ROI) from data warehousing projects varies from organization to organization and is quite difficult to quantify prior to a warehousing initiative.

However, we can identify a common list of problems encountered by enterprises as a result of unintegrated customer data and lack of historical data. A properly deployed data warehouse can solve the problems, as discussed below.

Lack of Information Sharing

- Divisions or departments have the same customers but do not share information with each other.
- As a result, cross-selling opportunities are missed, and improved customer understanding is lost. Customers are annoyed by requests for the same information by different units within the same enterprise.

Solving this problem results in the following benefits: better customer management decisions can be made; customers are treated as individuals; new business opportunities can be explored.

Different Groups Produce Conflicting Reports

- Data in different operational systems provide different information on the same subject. The inconsistent use of terms results in different business rules for the same item.
- Thus, facts and figures are inconsistently interpreted, and different versions of the "truth" exist within the enterprise. Decision-makers have to rely on conflicting data and may lose credibility with customers, suppliers, or partners.
- Solving this problem results in the following benefits: a consistent view of enterprise operations becomes available; better, informed decisions can be made.

Tedious Report Creation Process

- Critical reports take too long to produce. Data gathering is ad hoc, inconsistent, and manually performed. There are no formal rules to govern the creation of these reports.
- As a result, business decisions based on these reports may be bad decisions. Business analysts within the organization spend more time collecting data instead of analyzing data. Competitors with more sophisticated means of producing similar reports have a considerable advantage.
- Solving this problem results in the following benefits: the report creation process is dramatically streamlined, and the time required to produce the same reports is significantly reduced. More time can be spent on analyzing the data, and decision-makers do not have to work with "old" data.

Reports Are Not Dynamic, and Do Not Support an Ad Hoc Usage Style

- Managerial reports are not dynamic and often do not support the ability to drill down for further detail.
- As a result, when a report highlights interesting or alarming figures, the decision-maker is unable to zoom in and get more detail.
- When this problem is solved, decision-makers can obtain more detail as needed. Analysis for trends and causal relationships are possible.

Reports That Require Historical Data Are Difficult to Produce

- Customer, product, and financial histories are not stored in operational systems. Conversely, attempts to store historical data in operational systems result in unwieldy data structures.
- As a result, decision-makers are unable to analyze trends over time. The enterprise is unable to anticipate events and behave proactively or aggressively. Customer demands come as a surprise, and the enterprise must scramble to react.

- Decision-makers can increase or strengthen relationships with current customers. Marketing campaigns can be predictive in nature, based on historical data.

Aside from solving the problems above, other reasons commonly used to justify a data warehouse initiative are the following:

- **Support of enterprise strategy.** The data warehouse is a key supporting factor in the successful execution of one or more parts of the enterprise's strategy, including enhanced revenue or cost control initiatives.
- **Enterprise emphasis on customer and product profitability.** Increase the focus and efficiency of the enterprise by gaining a better understanding of its customers and products.
- **Perceived need outside the IT group.** Data warehousing is sought and supported by business users who demand integrated data for decision-making. A true business need, not technological experimentation, drives the initiative.
- **Integrated data.** The enterprise lacks a repository of integrated and historical data that are required for decision-making.
- **Cost of current efforts.** The current cost of producing standard, regular managerial reports is typically hidden within an organization. A study of these costs can yield unexpected results that help justify the data warehouse initiative.
- **The competition is doing it.** Just because competitors are going into data warehousing does not mean an enterprise should plunge headlong into it. However, knowing that the competition is applying data warehousing technology should make any manager stop and see whether data warehousing is something that his own organization needs.

What Expenses Are Involved?

The costs associated with developing and implementing a data warehouse typically fall into the categories described below.

Hardware

Warehousing hardware can easily account for up to 50 percent of the costs in a data warehouse pilot project. A separate machine or server is often recommended for data warehousing so as not to burden operational IT environments. The operational and decisional environments may be connected via the enterprise's network, especially if automated tools have been scheduled to extract data from operational systems or if replication technology is used to create copies of operational data.

Enterprises heavily dependent on mainframes for their operational systems can look to powerful client/server platforms for their data warehouse solutions.

Hardware costs are generally higher at the start of the data warehousing initiative due to the purchase of new hardware. However, data warehouses grow quickly, and subsequent extensions to the warehouse may quickly require hardware upgrades.

A good way to cut down on the early hardware costs is to invest in server technology that is highly scalable. As the warehouse grows both in volume and in scope, subsequent investments in hardware can be made as needed.

Software

Software refers to all the tools required to create, set up, configure, populate, manage, use, and maintain the data warehouse. The data warehousing tools currently available from a variety of vendors are staggering in their features and price range (Chapter 11 provides an overview of these tools).

Each enterprise will be best served by a combination of tools, the choice of which is determined or influenced not only by the features of the software but also by the current computing environment of the operational systems, as well as the intended computing environment of the warehouse.

Software costs can easily account for a quarter to a third of the overall data warehousing cost in a pilot project.

Services

Services from consultants or system integrators are often required to manage and integrate the disparate components of the data warehouse. The use of system integrators, in particular, is appealing to enterprises that prefer to use the "best of breed" of hardware and software products and have no wish to assume the responsibility for integrating the various components.

The use of consultants is also popular, particularly with early warehousing implementations, when the enterprise is just learning about data warehousing technologies and techniques.

Service-related costs can account for roughly 30 percent to 35 percent of the overall cost of a pilot project but may drop as the enterprise decreases its dependence on external resources.

Internal Staff

Internal staff costs refer to costs incurred as a result of assigning enterprise staff to the warehousing project. The staff could otherwise have been assigned to other activities.

The heaviest demands are on the time of the IT staff who have the task of planning, designing, building, populating, and managing the warehouse. The participation of end users, typically analysts and managers, is also crucial to a successful warehousing effort.

The Project Sponsor, the CIO, and the Project Manager will also be heavily involved because of the nature of their roles in the warehousing initiative.

Summary of Typical Costs

The external costs of a typical data warehouse pilot project of three to six months can range anywhere from US$0.8M to US$2M, depending on the combination of hardware, software, and services required.

Table 3–1 provides an indicative breakdown of the external costs of a warehousing pilot project where new hardware is purchased.

Table 3–1   Typical External Cost Breakdown for a Data Warehouse Pilot
(Amounts expressed in US$)

Item	Min.	Min. as % of Total	Max.	Max. as % of Total
Hardware	400,000	49.26	1,000,000	51.81
Software	132,000	16.26	330,000	17.10
Services	280,000	34.48	600,000	31.09
Totals	*812,000*		*1,930,000*	

Note that the costs listed above do not yet consider any infrastructure improvements or upgrades (e.g., network cabling or upgrades) that may be required to properly integrate the warehousing environment into the rest of the enterprise IT architecture.

▶ What Are the Risks?

The typical risks encountered on data warehousing projects fall into the following categories:

- **Organizational.** These risks relate either to the project team structure and composition or to the culture of the enterprise.
- **Technological.** These risks relate to the planning, selection, and use of warehousing technologies. Technological risks also arise from the existing computing environment, as well as the manner by which warehousing technologies are integrated into the existing enterprise IT architecture.
- **Project management.** These risks are true of most technology projects but are particularly dangerous in data warehousing because of the scale and scope of warehousing projects.
- **Data warehouse design.** Data warehousing requires a new set of design techniques that differ significantly from the well-accepted practices in OLTP system development.

Organizational

Wrong Project Sponsor

The project sponsor must be a business executive, not an IT executive. Considering its scope and scale, the warehousing initiative should be business driven; otherwise, the organization will view the entire effort as a technology experiment.

A strong Project Sponsor is required to address and resolve organizational issues before these have a chance to derail the project (e.g., lack of user participation, disagreements regarding definition of data, political disputes). The Project Sponsor must be someone who will be a user of the warehouse, someone who can publicly assume responsibility for the warehousing initiative, and someone with sufficient clout.

This role *cannot* be delegated to a committee. Unfortunately, many an organization will choose to establish a data warehouse steering committee to take on the collective responsibility of this role. If such a committee is established, the head of the committee may by default become the Project Sponsor.

End-User Community Not Involved

The end-user community provides the data warehouse implementation team with the detailed business requirements. Unlike OLTP business requirements, which tend to be exact and transaction based, data warehousing requirements are moving targets and are subject to constant change.

Despite this, the intended warehouse end users should be interviewed to provide an understanding of the types of queries and reports (query profiles) they require. By talking to the different users, the warehousing team also gains a better understanding of the IT literacy of the users (user profiles) they will be serving and will better understand the types of data access and retrieval tools that each user will be more likely to use. The end-user community also provides the team with the security requirements (access profiles) of the warehouse.

These business requirements are critical inputs to the design of the data warehouse.

Senior Management Expectations Not Managed

Because of the costs, data warehousing almost always requires a go-signal from senior management, often obtained after a long, protracted ROI presentation.

In their bid to obtain senior management support, warehousing supporters must be careful not to overstate the benefits of the data warehouse, particularly during requests for budgets and business case presentations. Raising senior management expectations beyond manageable levels is one sure way to court extremely embarrassing and highly visible disasters.

End-User Community Expectations Not Managed

Aside from managing senior management expectations, the warehousing team must, in the same manner, manage the expectations of their end users.

Warehouse analysts must bear in mind that the expectations of end users are immediately raised when their requirements are first discussed. The warehousing team must constantly manage these expectations by emphasizing the phased nature of data warehouse implementation projects and by clearly identifying the intended scope of each data warehouse rollout.

End users should also be reminded that the reports they will get from the warehouse are heavily dependent on the availability and quality of the data in the enterprise's operational systems.

Political Issues

Attempts to produce integrated views of enterprise data are likely to raise political issues. For example, different units have been known to wrestle for "ownership" of the warehouse, especially in organizations where access to information is associated with political power. In other enterprises, the various units want to have as little to do with warehousing as possible, for fear of having warehousing costs allocated to their units.

Understandably, the unique combination of culture and politics within each enterprise will exert its own positive and negative influences on the warehousing effort.

Logistical Overhead

A number of tasks in data warehousing require coordination with multiple parties, not only within the enterprise, but with external suppliers and service providers as well. A number of factors increase the logistical overhead in data warehousing, among them:

- **Formality.** Highly formal organizations generally have higher logistical overhead because of the need to comply with pre-established methods for getting things done.
- **Organizational hierarchies.** Elaborate chains of command likewise may cause delays or may require greater coordination efforts to achieve a given result.
- **Geographical dispersion.** Logistical delays also arise from geographical distribution, as in the case of multibranch banks, nationwide operations or international corporations. Multiple, stand-alone applications with no centralized data store have the same effect. Moving data from one location to another without the benefit of a network or a transparent connection is difficult and will add to logistical overhead.

Technological

Inappropriate Use of Warehousing Technology. A data warehouse is an inappropriate solution for enterprises that need operational integration on a real-time, online basis. An ODS is the ideal solution to needs of that nature.

Multiple unrelated data marts are likewise not the appropriate architecture for meeting enterprise decisional information needs. All data warehouse and data mart projects should remain under a single architectural framework.

Poor Data Quality of Operational Systems. When the data quality of the operational systems is suspect, the team will, by necessity, devote much of their time and effort to data scrubbing and data quality checking. Poor data quality also adds to the difficulties of extracting, transforming, and loading data into the warehouse.

The importance of data quality cannot be overstated. Warehouse end users will not make use of the warehouse if the information they retrieve is wrong or of dubious quality. The *perception* of lack of data quality, whether such a perception is true or not, is all that is required to derail a data warehousing initiative.

Inappropriate End-User Tools. The wide range of end-user tools provides data warehouse users with different levels of functionality and requires different levels of IT sophistication from the user community.

Providing senior management users with the inappropriate tools is one of the quickest ways to kill enthusiasm for the data warehouse effort. Likewise, power users will quickly become disenchanted with simple data access and retrieval tools.

Overdependence on Tools to Solve Data Warehousing Problems. The data warehouse solution should not be built around tools or sets of tools. Most of the warehousing tools (e.g., extraction, transformation, migration, data quality, and metadata tools) are far from mature at this point.

Unfortunately, enterprises are frequently on the receiving end of sales pitches that promise to solve all the various problems (data quality/ extraction/replication/loading) that plague warehousing efforts through the selection of the right tool or, even, hardware platform.

What enterprises soon realize in their first warehousing project is that much of the effort in a warehousing project still cannot be automated.

Manual Data Capture and Conversion Requirements. The extraction process is highly dependent on the extent to which data are available in the appropriate electronic format. In cases where the required data simply do not exist in any of the operational systems, a warehousing team may find itself resorting to the strongly discouraged practice of using data capture screens to obtain data through manual encoding operations. Unfortunately, a data warehouse quite simply cannot be filled up through manual data encoding!

Conversion transforms electronically stored data to the appropriate format or granularity. Underestimating the requirements to obtain and transform data into the correct format may lead to slipped schedules and unmanaged expectations regarding the data that will be available in the warehouse.

Technical Architecture and Networking

Study and monitor the impact of the data warehouse development and usage on the network infrastructure. Assumptions about batch windows, middleware, extract mechanisms, etc., should be verified to avoid nasty surprises midway into the project.

Project Management

Defining Project Scope Inappropriately

The mantra for data warehousing should be: start small and build incrementally. Organizations that prefer the big-bang approach quickly find themselves on the path to certain failure. Monolithic projects are unwieldy and difficult to manage, especially when the warehousing team is new to the technology and techniques.

In contrast, the phased, iterative approach has consistently proven itself to be effective, not only in data warehousing but also in most information technology initiatives. Each phase has a manageable scope, requires a smaller team, and lends itself well to a coaching and learning environment. The lessons learned by the team on each phase are a form of direct feedback into subsequent phases.

Underestimating Project Time Frame

Estimates in data warehousing projects often fail to devote sufficient time to the extraction, integration, and transformation tasks. Unfortunately, it is not unusual for this area of the project to consume anywhere between 60 percent to 80 percent of a team's time and effort. Figure 3–1 illustrates the distribution of efforts.

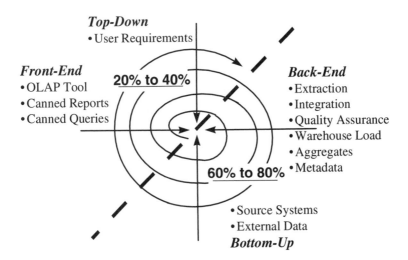

Figure 3–1 Typical Effort Distribution on a Warehousing Project

The project team should therefore work on stabilizing the back-end of the warehouse as quickly as possible. The front-end tools are useless if the warehouse itself is not yet ready for use.

Underestimating Project Overhead

Time estimates in data warehousing projects often fail to consider delays due to logistics. Keep an eye on the lead time for hardware delivery, especially if the machine is yet to be imported into the city or country. Quickly determine the acquisition time for middleware or warehousing tools. Watch out for logistical overhead (as discussed on page 62–63).

Allocate sufficient time for team orientation and training prior to and during the course of the project to ensure that everyone remains aligned. Devote sufficient time and effort to creating and promoting effective communication within the team.

Losing Focus

The data warehousing effort should be focused entirely on delivering the essential minimal characteristics (EMCs) of each phase of the implementation. It is easy for the team to be distracted by requests for nonessential or low-priority features (i.e., nice-to-have data or functionality). These should be ruthlessly deferred to a later phase; otherwise, valuable project time and effort will be frittered away on nonessential features, to the detriment of the warehouse scope or schedule.

Not Looking Beyond the First Data Warehouse Rollout

A data warehouse needs to be strongly supported and nurtured (also known as "care and feeding") for at least a year after its initial launch. End users will need continuous training and support, especially if new users are gradually granted access to the warehouse. Collect warehouse usage and query statistics to get an idea of warehouse acceptance and to obtain inputs for database optimization and tuning. Plan subsequent phases or rollouts of the warehouse, taking into account the lessons learned from the first rollout. Allocate, acquire, or train the appropriate resources for support activities.

Data Warehouse Design

Using OLTP Database Design Strategies for the Data Warehouse. Enterprises that venture into data warehousing for the first time may make the mistake of applying OLTP database design techniques to their data warehouse. Unfortunately, data warehousing requires design strategies that are very different from the design strategies for transactional, operation systems.

For example, OLTP databases are fully normalized and are designed to consistently store operational data, one transaction at a time. In direct contrast, a data warehouse requires database designs that even business users find directly usable. Dimensional or star schemas with highly denormalized dimension tables on relational technology require different design techniques and different indexing strategies. Data warehousing may also require the use of hypercubes or multidimensional database technology for certain functions and users.

Choosing the Wrong Level of Granularity. The warehouse contains both atomic (extremely detailed) and summarized (high-level) data. To get the most value out of the system, the most detailed data required by users should be loaded into the data warehouse. The degree to which users can slice and dice through the data warehouse is entirely dependent on the granularity of the facts. Too high a grain makes detailed reports or queries impossible to produce. Too low a grain unnecessarily increases the space requirements (and the cost) of the data warehouse.

Not Defining Strategies to Key Database Design Issues. The suitability of the warehouse design significantly impacts the size, performance, integrity, future scalability, and adaptability of the warehouse. Outline (or high-level) warehouse designs may overlook the demands of slowly changing dimensions, large dimensions, and key generation requirements, among others.

▶ Risk-Mitigating Approaches

The above risks are best addressed through the people and mechanisms described below.

- *The Right Project Sponsor and Project Manager.* Having the appropriate leaders setting the tone, scope, and direction of a data warehousing initiative can spell the difference between failure and success.

- *Appropriate architecture.* The enterprise must verify that a data warehouse is the appropriate solution to its needs. If the need is for operational integration, then an Operational Data Store is more appropriate.

- *Phased approach.* The entire data warehousing effort must be phased so that the warehouse can be iteratively extended in a cost-justified and prioritized manner. A number of prioritized areas should be delivered first; subsequent areas are implemented in incremental steps. Work on nonurgent components is deferred.

- *Cyclical refinement.* Obtain feedback from users as each rollout or phase is completed, and as users make use of the data warehouse and the front-end tools. Any feedback should serve as inputs to subsequent rollouts. With each new rollout, users are expected to specify additional requirements and gain a better understanding of the types of queries that are now available to them.

- *Evolutionary life cycle.* Each phase of the project should be conducted in a manner that promotes evolution, adaptability, and scalability. An overall data warehouse architecture should be defined when a high-level understanding of user needs has been obtained and the phased implementation path has been studied.

- *Completeness of data warehouse design.* The data warehouse design must address slowly changing dimensions, aggregation, key generalization, heterogeneous facts and dimensions, and minidimensions. These dimensional modeling concerns are addressed in Chapter 12.

▶ Is My Organization Ready for a Data Warehouse?

Although there are no hard-and-fast rules for determining when your organization is ready to launch a data warehouse initiative, the following positive signs are good clues.

Decision-Makers Feel the Need for Change

A successful data warehouse implementation will have a significant impact on the enterprise's decision-making processes, which in turn will have significant impact on the operations of the enterprise. The performance measures and reward mechanisms are likely to change, and they bring about corresponding changes to the processes and the culture of the organization.

Individuals who have an interest in preserving the status quo are likely to resist the data warehousing initiative, once it becomes apparent that such technologies enable organizational change.

Users Clamor for Integrated Decisional Data

A data warehouse is likely to get strong support from both the IT and user community if there is a strong and unsatisfied demand for integrated decisional data (as opposed to integrated operational data). It will be foolish to try using data warehousing technologies to meet operational information needs.

IT professionals will benefit from a long-term, architected solution to users' information needs, and users will benefit from having information at their fingertips.

The Operational Systems Are Fairly Stable

An IT department, division, or unit that continuously fights fires on unstable operational systems will quickly deprioritize the data warehousing effort. Organizations will almost always defer the warehousing effort in favor of operational concerns—after all, the enterprise has survived without a data warehouse for years; another few months will not hurt.

When the operational systems are up in production and are fairly stable, there are internal data sources for the warehouse and a data warehouse initiative will be given higher priority.

Staff Can Be Assigned to the Project

Although significant portions of the data warehouse effort can be outsourced to external parties, there are key roles that must be fulfilled by the enterprise's internal staff. The demands on the time of end users and IT staff for a data warehouse project are as heavy as (or perhaps are heavier than) the demands of an operational system development project.

Once the data warehouse is up, sufficient resources are also required to support its users and its continued evolution.

There Is Adequate Funding

A data warehouse project cannot afford to fizzle out in the middle of the effort due to a shortage of funds. Be aware of long-term funding requirements beyond the first data warehouse rollout before starting on the pilot project.

▶ How Do I Measure the Results?

Data warehousing results come in different forms and can, therefore, be measured in one or more of the following ways.

New Reports/Queries Support. Results are seen clearly in the new reports and queries that are now readily available but would have been difficult to obtain without the data warehouse.

The extent to which these reports and queries actually contribute to more informed decisions and the translation of these informed decisions to bottom-line benefits may not be as easy to trace, however.

Turnaround Time. Results are also evident in the less time it now takes to obtain information on the subjects covered by the warehouse. Senior managers can also get the information they need directly, thus improving the security and confidentiality of such information.

Turnaround time for decision-making is dramatically reduced. In the past, decision-makers in meetings either had to make an uninformed decision or table a discussion item because they lacked information. The ability of the data warehouse to quickly provide needed information speeds up the decision-making process.

Timely Alerts and Exception Reporting. The data warehouse proves its worth each time it sounds an alert or highlights an exception in enterprise operations. Early detection makes it possible to avert or correct potentially major problems and allows decision-makers to exploit business situations with small or immediate windows of opportunity.

Number of Active Users. The number of active users provides a concrete measure for the usage and acceptance of the warehouse.

Frequency of Use. The number of times a user actually logs on to the data warehouse within a given time period (e.g., weekly) shows how often the warehouse is used by any given users. Frequent usage is a strong indication of warehouse acceptance and usability. An increase in usage indicates that users are asking questions more frequently. Tracking the time of day when the data warehouse is frequently used will also indicate peak usage hours.

Session Times. The length of time a user spends each time he logs on to the data warehouse shows how much the data warehouse contributes to his job.

Query Profiles. The number and types of queries users make provide an idea of how sophisticated the users have become. As the queries become more sophisticated, users will most likely request additional functionality or increased data scope.

This metric also provides the warehouse database administrator (DBA) with valuable insight as to the types of stored aggregates or summaries that can further optimize query performance. It also indicates which tables in the warehouse are frequently accessed. Conversely, it also allows the warehouse DBA to identify tables that are hardly used and therefore are candidates for purging.

Change Requests. An analysis of users' change requests can provide insight into how well users are applying the data warehouse technology. Unlike most IT projects, a high number of data warehouse change requests is a good sign; it implies that users are discovering more and more how warehousing can contribute to their jobs.

Business Changes. The immediate results of data warehousing are fairly easy to quantify. However, true warehousing ROI comes from business changes and decisions that have been made possible by information obtained from the warehouse. These, unfortunately, are not as easy to quantify and measure.

▶ In Summary

The importance of the Project Sponsor in a data warehousing initiative cannot be overstated. The project sponsor is the highest-level business representative of the warehousing team and therefore must be a visionary, respected, and decisive leader.

At the end of the day, the Project Sponsor is responsible for the success of the data warehousing initiative within the enterprise.

4

The CIO

The Chief Information Officer (CIO) is responsible for the effective deployment of information technology resources and staff to meet the strategic, decisional, and operational information requirements of the enterprise.

Data warehousing, with its accompanying array of new technologies and its dependence on operational systems, naturally makes strong demands on the technical and human resources under the jurisdiction of the CIO.

For this reason, it is natural for the CIO to be strongly involved in any data warehousing effort. This chapter attempts to answer the typical questions of CIOs who participate in data warehousing initiatives.

▶ How Do I Support the Data Warehouse?

After the data warehouse goes into production, different support services are required to ensure that the implementation is not derailed. These support services fall into the categories described below.

Regular Warehouse Load

The data warehouse needs to be constantly loaded with additional data. The amount of work required to load data into the warehouse on a regular basis depends on the extent to which the extraction, transformation, and loading processes have been automated, as well as the load frequency required by the warehouse.

The frequency of the load depends on the user requirements, as determined during the data warehouse design activity. The most frequent load possible with a data warehouse is once a day, although it is not unusual to find organizations that load their warehouses once a week, or even once a month.

The regular loading activities fall under the responsibilities of the warehouse support team, who almost invariably report to directly or indirectly to the CIO.

Applications

After the data warehouse and related data marts have been deployed, the IT department or division may turn its attention to the development and deployment of Executive Systems or custom applications that run directly against the data warehouse or the data marts. These applications are developed or targeted to meet the needs of specific user groups.

Any in-house application development will likely be handled by internal IT staff; otherwise, such projects should be outsourced under the watchful eye of the CIO.

Warehouse DB Optimization

Apart from the day-to-day database administration support of production systems, the warehouse DBA must also collect and monitor new sets of query statistics with each rollout or phase of the data warehouse.

The data structure of the warehouse is then refined or optimized on the basis of these usage statistics, particularly in the area of stored aggregates and table indexing strategies.

User Assistance or Help Desk

As with any information system in the enterprise, a User Assistance Desk or Help Desk can provide users with general information, assistance, and support. An analysis of the help requests received by the Help Desk provides insight on possible subjects for follow-on training with end users.

In addition, the Help Desk is an ideal site for publicizing the status of the system after every successful load.

Training

Provide more training as more end users gain access to the data warehouse. Aside from covering the standard capabilities, applications, and tools that are available to the users, the warehouse training should also clearly convey what data are available in the warehouse.

Advanced training topics may be appropriate for more advanced users. Specialized work groups or one-on-one training may be appropriate as follow-on training, depending on the type of questions and help requests that the Help Desk receives.

Preparation for Subsequent Rollouts

All internal preparatory work for subsequent rollouts must be performed while support activities for prior rollouts are underway. This activity may create resource contention and therefore should be carefully managed.

▶ How Will My Data Warehouse Evolve?

One of the toughest decisions any data warehouse planner has to make is to decide when to evolve the system with new data and when to wait for the user base, IT organization, and business to catch up with the latest release of the warehouse.

Warehouse evolution is not only a technical and management issue, it is also a political issue. The IT organization must continually either:

- market or sell the warehouse for continued funding and support of existing capabilities; or
- attempt to control the demand for new capabilities.

Each new extension of the data warehouse results in increased complexity in terms of data scope, data management, and warehouse optimization. In addition, each rollout of the warehouse is likely to be in different stages and therefore to have different support needs.

For example, an enterprise may find itself busy with the planning and design of the third phase of the warehouse, while deployment and training activities are underway for the second phase, and Help Desk Support is available for the first phase. The CIO will undoubtedly face the unwelcome task of making critical decisions regarding resource assignments.

In general, data warehouse evolution takes place in one or more of the following areas:

- **Data.** Evolution in this area typically results in an increase in scope (although a decrease is not impossible). The extraction subsystem will require modification in cases where the source systems are modified or new operational systems are deployed.
- **Users.** New users will be given access to the data warehouse, or existing users will be trained on advanced features. This implies new or additional training requirements, the definition of new users and access profiles, and the collection of new usage statistics. New security measures may also be required.
- **IT organization.** New skill sets are required to build, manage, and support the data warehouse. New types of support activities will be needed.
- **Business.** Changes in the business result in changes in the operations, monitoring needs, and performance measures used by the organization. The business requirements that drive the data warehouse change as the business changes.
- **Application functionality.** New functionality can be added to existing OLAP tools, or new tools can be deployed to meet end-user needs.

▶ Who Should Be Involved in a Data Warehouse Project?

Every data warehouse project has a team of people with diverse skills and roles. The involvement of internal staff during the warehouse development is critical to the warehouse maintenance and support tasks once the data warehouse is in production. Not all the roles in a data warehouse project can be outsourced to third parties; of the typical roles listed below, internal enterprise staff should fulfill the roles listed in bold face:

- **Steering Committee**
- **User Reference Group**
- **Warehouse Driver**
- Warehouse Project Manager
- Business Analysts
- Warehouse Data Architect
- Metadata Administrator
- Warehouse DBA
- **Source System DBA and System Administrator**
- **Project Sponsor (see Chapter 3)**

The same person may play more than one role.

Every data warehouse project has a team of people with diverse skills and roles. Below is a list of typical roles in a data warehouse project. Note that the same person may play more than one role.

Steering Committee

The Steering Committee is composed of high-level executives representing each major type of user requiring access to the data warehouse. The Project Sponsor is a member of the committee; in most cases, the sponsor heads the committee. The Steering Committee should already be formed by the time data warehouse implementation starts; however, the existence of a Steering Committee is not a prerequisite for data warehouse planning. During implementation, the Steering Committee receives regular status reports from the project team and intervenes to redirect project efforts whenever appropriate.

User Reference Group

Representatives from the user community (typically middle-level managers and analysts) provide critical inputs to data warehousing projects by specifying detailed data requirements, business rules, predefined queries, and report layouts. User representatives also test the outputs of the data warehousing effort.

It is not unusual for end-user representatives to spend up to 80 percent of their time on the project, particularly during the requirements analysis and data warehouse design activities. Toward the end of a rollout, up to 80 percent of the representatives' time may be required again for testing the usability and correctness of warehouse data.

End users also participate in regular meetings or interviews with the warehousing team throughout the life of each rollout (up to 50 percent involvement).

Warehouse Driver

The Warehouse Driver reports to the steering committee, ensures that the project is moving in the right direction, and is responsible for meeting project deadlines.

The Warehouse Driver is a business manager but is responsible for defining the data warehouse strategy (with the assistance of the warehouse project manager) and for planning and managing the data warehouse implementation from the business side of operations.

The Warehouse Driver also communicates the warehouse objectives to other areas of the enterprise. This individual normally serves as the coordinator in cases where the implementation team has cross-functional team members. It is therefore not unusual for the Warehouse Driver to be the liaison to the User Reference Group.

Warehouse Project Manager

The Project Manager is usually an individual who is very well versed in technology and in managing technology projects. This person's technical skills strongly complement the business acumen of the Warehouse Driver.

The Project Manager normally reports to the Warehouse Driver and jointly defines the data warehouse strategy with the Warehouse Driver. It is not unusual, though, to find organizations where the Warehouse Driver and Project Manager jointly manage the project. In such cases, the Project Manager is actually a Technical Manager.

The Project Manager is responsible for implementing the project plans and acts as coordinator on the technology side of the project, particularly when the project involves several vendors. The warehouse Project Manager keeps the Warehouse Driver updated on the technical aspects of the project but isolates the Warehouse Driver from the technical details.

Business Analyst(s)

The analysts act as liaisons between the User Reference Group and the more technical members of the project team. Through interviews with members of the User Reference Group, the analysts identify, document, and model the current business requirements and usage scenarios.

Analysts play a critical role in managing end-user expectations, since most of the contact between the User Reference Group and the warehousing team takes place through the analysts. Analysts represent the interests of the end users in the project and therefore have the responsibility of ensuring that the resulting implementation will meet end-user needs.

Warehouse Data Architect

The warehouse data architect develops and maintains the warehouse's enterprise-wide view of the data. This individual analyzes the information requirements specified by the user community and designs the data structures of the data warehouse accordingly.

The workload of the architect is heaviest at the start of each rollout, when most of the design decisions are made. The workload tapers off as the rollout gets underway.

The warehouse data architect has an increasingly critical role as the warehouse evolves. Each successive rollout that extends the warehouse must respect an overall integrating architecture—and the responsibility for the integrating architecture falls squarely on the warehouse data architect. Data mart deployments that are fed by the warehouse should likewise be considered part of the architecture to avoid the data administration problems created by multiple, unrelated data marts.

Metadata Administrator

The metadata administrator defines metadata standards and manages the metadata repository of the warehouse. The workload of the Metadata Administrator is quite high both at the start and toward the end of each warehouse rollout. Workload is high at the start primarily due to metadata definition and setup work. Workload toward the end of a rollout increases as the schema, the aggregate strategy, and the metadata repository contents are finalized.

Metadata play an important role in data warehousing projects and therefore warrant the separate discussion in Chapter 13.

Warehouse DBA

The warehouse database administrator works closely with the Warehouse Data Architect. The workload of the warehouse DBA is typically heavy throughout a data warehouse project. Much of this individual's time will be devoted to setting up the warehouse schema at the start of each rollout. As the rollout gets underway, the warehouse DBA takes on the responsibility of loading the data, monitoring the performance of the warehouse, refining the initial schema, and creating dummy data for testing the decision support front-end tools. Toward the end of the rollout, the warehouse DBA will be busy with database optimization tasks as well as aggregate table creation and population.

As expected, the warehouse DBA and the metadata administrator work closely together. The warehouse DBA is responsible for creating and populating metadata tables within the warehouse in compliance with the standards that have been defined by the metadata administrator.

Source System Database Administrators (DBAs) and System Administrators (SAs)

These IT professionals play extremely critical roles in the data warehousing effort. Among their typical responsibilities are:

- **Identify best extraction mechanisms.** Given their familiarity with the current computing environment, source system DBAs and SAs are often asked to identify the data transfer and extraction mechanisms best suited for their respective operational systems.
- **Contribute to source-to-target field mapping.** These individuals are familiar with the data structures of the operational systems and are therefore the most qualified to contribute to or finalize the mapping of source system fields to warehouse fields.
- **Data quality assessment.** In the course of their day-to-day operations, the DBAs and SAs encounter data quality problems and are therefore in a position to highlight areas that require special attention during data cleansing and transformation.

Depending on the status of the operational systems, these individuals may spend the majority of their time on the above activities during the course of a rollout.

Conversion and Extraction Programmer(s)

The programmers write the extraction and conversion programs that pull data from the operational databases. They also write programs that integrate, convert, and summarize the data into the format required by the data warehouse. Their primary resource persons for the extraction programs will be the source system DBAs and SAs.

If data extraction, transformation, and transportation tools are used, these individuals are responsible for setting up and configuring the selected tools and ensuring that the correct data records are retrieved for loading into the warehouse.

Technical and Network Architect

The technical and network architect ensures that the technical architecture defined for the data warehouse rollout is suitable for meeting the stated requirements. This individual also ensures that the technical and network architecture of the data warehouse is consistent with the existing enterprise infrastructure.

The network architect coordinates with the project team on the extensions to the enterprise's network infrastructure required to support the data warehouse and constantly monitors the warehouse's impact on network capacity and throughput.

Trainer

The trainer develops all required training materials and conducts the training courses for the data warehousing project. The warehouse project team will require some data warehousing training, particularly during early or pilot projects. Toward the end of each rollout, end users of the data warehouse will also require training on the warehouse contents and on the tools that will be used for analysis and reporting.

▶ What Is the Team Structure Like?

Figure 4–1 illustrates a typical project team structure for a data warehouse project. Note that there are many other viable alternative team structures. Also, unless the team is quite large and involves many contracted parties, a formal team structure may not even be necessary.

The team structure will evolve once the project has been completed. Day-to-day maintenance and support of the data warehouse will call for a different organizational structure—sometimes one that is more permanent.

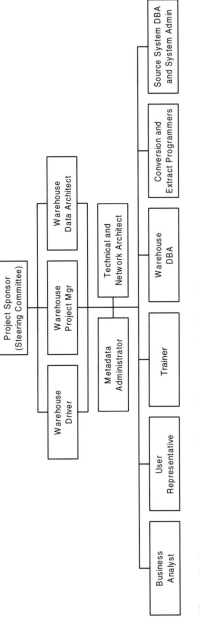

Figure 4–1 Typical Project Team Structure for Development

83

Resource contention will arise when a new rollout is underway and resources are required for both warehouse development and support.

▶ What New Skills Will My People Need?

IT professionals and end-users will both require new but different skill sets, as described below.

IT Professionals

Data warehousing places new demands on the IT professionals of an enterprise. New skill sets are required, particularly in the following areas:

- **New database design skills.** Traditional database design principles do not work well with a data warehouse. Dimensional modeling concepts break many of the OLTP design rules. Also, the large size of warehouse tables requires database optimization and indexing techniques that are appropriate for very large database (VLDB) implementations.
- **Technical capabilities.** New technical skills are required, especially in enterprises where new hardware or software is purchased (e.g., new hardware platform, new RDBMS, etc.). System architecture skills are required for warehouse evolution, and networking management and design skills are required to ensure the availability of network bandwidth for warehousing requirements.
- **Familiarity with tools.** In many cases, data warehousing works better when tools are purchased and integrated into one solution. IT professionals must become familiar with the various warehousing tools that are available and must be able to separate the wheat from the chaff. IT professionals must also learn to use, and learn to work around, the limitations of the tools they select.
- **Knowledge of the business.** Thorough understanding of the business and of how the business will utilize data are critical in a

data warehouse effort. IT professionals cannot afford to focus on technology only. Business analysts, in particular, have to understand the business well enough to properly represent the interests of end users. Business terms have to be standardized, and the corresponding data items in the operational systems have to be found or derived.

- **End-user support.** Although IT professionals have constantly provided end-user support to the rest of the enterprise, data warehousing puts the IT professional in direct contact with a special kind of end user: senior management. Their successful day-to-day use of the data warehouse (and the resulting success of the warehousing effort) depends greatly on the end-user support that they receive.

The IT professional's focus changes from meeting operational user requirements to helping users satisfy their own information needs.

End Users

Gone are the days when end users had to wait for the IT department to release printouts or reports or to respond to requests for information. End users can now directly access the data warehouse and can tap it for required information, looking up data themselves.

This advance assumes that end users have acquired the following skills:

- **Desktop computing.** End users must be able to use OLAP tools (under a graphical user interface environment) to gain direct access to the warehouse. Without desktop computing skills, end users will always rely on other parties to obtain the information they require.
- **Business knowledge.** The answers that the data warehouse provides are only as good as the questions that it receives. End users will not be able to formulate the correct questions or queries without a sufficient understanding of their own business environment.
- **Data knowledge.** End users must understand the data that is available in the warehouse and must be able to relate the warehouse data to their knowledge of the business.

Apart from the above skills, data warehousing is more likely to succeed if end users are willing to make the warehouse an integral part of the management and decision-making process of the organization. The warehouse support team must help end users overcome a natural tendency to revert to "business as usual" after the warehouse is rolled out.

▶ How Does Data Warehousing Fit into My IT Architecture?

As discussed in Chapter 1, the data warehouse is an entirely separate architectural component, distinct from the operational systems. Each time a new architectural component is added or introduced, the enterprise architect must consciously study its impact on the rest of the IT architecture and ensure that

- the IT architecture does not become brittle as a result of this new component; and
- the new architectural components are isolated from the obsolescence of legacy applications.

A data warehouse places new demands on the technical infrastructure of the enterprise. The following factors determine the technical environment required.

- **User requirements.** The user requirements largely determine the scope of the warehouse, i.e., the requirements are the basis for identifying the source systems and the required data items.
- **Location of the source systems and the warehouse.** If the source systems and the data warehouse are not in the same location, the extraction of data from operational systems into the warehouse may present difficulties with regard to logistics or network communications. In actual practice, the initial extraction is rarely 100 percent correct—some fine-tuning will be required because of errors in the source-to-target field mapping, misunderstood requirements, or changes in requirements. Easy, immediate access to both the source systems and the warehouse make it easier to modify and correct the data extraction, transforma-

tion, and loading processes. The availability of easy access to both types of computing environments depends on the current technical architecture of the enterprise.

- **Number and location of warehouse users.** The number of users that may access the warehouse concurrently implies a certain level of network traffic. The location of each user will also be a factor in determining how users will be granted access to the warehouse data. For example, if the warehouse users are dispersed over several remote locations, the enterprise may decide to use secure connections through the public Internet infrastructure to deliver the warehouse data.

- **Existing enterprise IT architecture.** The existing enterprise IT architecture defines or sets the limits on what is technically feasible and practical for the data warehouse team.

- **Budget allocated to the data warehousing effort.** The budget for the warehousing effort determines how much can be done to upgrade or improve the current technical infrastructure in preparation for the data warehouse.

It is always prudent to first study and plan the technical architecture (as part of defining the data warehouse strategy) before the start of any warehouse implementation project.

▶ How Many Vendors Do I Need to Talk to?

A warehousing project, like any IT project, will require a combination of hardware, software, and services, which may not all be available from one vendor. Some enterprises choose to isolate themselves from the vendor selection and liaison process by hiring a systems integrator, who subcontracts work to other vendors. Other enterprises prefer to deal with each vendor directly, and therefore assume the responsibility of integrating the various tools and services they acquire.

Vendor Categories

Although some vendors have products or services that allow them to fit in more than one of the vendor categories below, most if not all vendors are particularly strong in only one of the categories discussed below.

- **Hardware or operating system vendors.** Data warehouses require powerful server platforms to store the data and to make these data available to multiple users. All the major hardware vendors offer computing environments that can be used for data warehousing.

- **Middleware/data extraction and transformation tool vendors.** These vendors provide software products that facilitate or automate the extraction, transportation, and transformation of operational data into the format required for the data warehouse.

- **RDBMS vendors.** These vendors provide the relational database management systems that are capable of storing up to terabytes of data for warehousing purposes. These vendors have been introducing more and more features (e.g., advanced indexing features) that support VLDB implementations.

- **Consultancy and integration services supplier.** These vendors provide services either by taking on the responsibility of integrating all components of the warehousing solution on behalf of the enterprise, by offering technical assistance on specific areas of expertise, or by accepting outsourcing work for the data warehouse development or maintenance.

- **Front-end/OLAP/decision support/data access and retrieval tool vendors.** These vendors offer products that access, retrieve, and present warehouse data in meaningful and attractive formats. Data mining tools, which actively search for previously unrecognized patterns in the data, also fall into this category.

Enterprise Options

The number of vendors that an enterprise will work with depends on the approach the enterprise wishes to take. There are three main alternatives when it comes to building a data warehouse. An enterprise can:

- **Build its own.** The enterprise can build the data warehouse, using a custom architecture. A "best of breed" policy is applied to the selection of warehouse components and vendors. The data warehouse team accepts responsibility for integrating all the distinct selected products from multiple vendors.

- **Use a framework.** Nearly all data warehousing vendors present a warehousing framework to influence and guide the data warehouse market. Most of these frameworks are similar in scope and substance, with differences greatly influenced by the vendor's core technology or product. Vendors have also opportunistically established alliances with one another and are offering their product combinations as the closest thing to an "off the shelf" warehousing solution.
- **Use an anchor supplier (hardware, software, or service Vendor).** Enterprises may also select a supplier for a product or service as its key or anchor vendor. The anchor supplier's products or services are then used to influence the selection of other warehousing products and services.

▶ What Should I Look for in a Data Warehouse Vendor?

The following sections provide evaluation criteria for the different components that make up a data warehouse solution. Different weighting should be applied to each criterion, depending on its importance to the organization.

Solution Framework

The following evaluation criteria can be applied to the overall warehousing solution:

- **Relational data warehouse.** The data warehouse resides on a Relational DBMS. (Multidimensional databases are not an appropriate platform for an enterprise data warehouse, although they may be used for data marts with power-user requirements.)
- **Scalability.** The warehouse solution can scale up in terms of disk space, processing power, and warehouse design as the ware-

house scope increases. This scalability is particularly important if the warehouse is expected to grow at a rapid rate.

- **Front-end independence.** The design of the data warehouse is independent of any particular front-end tool. This independence leaves the warehouse team free to mix and match different front-end tools according to the needs and skills of warehouse users. Enterprises can easily add more sophisticated front-ends (such as data mining tools) at a later time.

- **Architectural integrity.** The proposed solution does not make the overall system architecture of the enterprise brittle; rather, it contributes to the long-term resiliency of the IT architecture.

- **Preservation of prior investments.** The solution leverages as much as possible prior software and hardware investments and existing skill sets within the organization.

Project and Integration Consultancy Services

The following evaluation criteria can be applied to consultants and system integrators:

- **Star join schema.** Warehouse designers use a dimensional modeling approach based on a star join schema. This form of modeling results in database designs that are navigable by business users and are resilient to evolving business requirements.

- **Source data audit.** A thorough physical and logical data audit is performed prior to implementation, to identify data quality issues within source systems and propose remedial steps. Source system quality issues are the number-one cause of data warehouse project delays. The data audit also serves as a reality check to determine if the required data are available in the operational systems of the enterprise.

- **Decisional requirements analysis.** Perform a thorough decisional requirements analysis activity with the appropriate end-user representatives prior to implementation to identify detailed decisional requirements and their priorities. This analysis must serve as the basis for key warehouse design decisions.

- **Methodology.** The consultant team specializes in data warehousing and uses a data warehousing methodology based on the current state-of-the-art. Avoid consultants who apply unsuitable OLTP methodologies to the development of data warehouses.

- **Appropriate fact record granularity.** The fact records are stored at the lowest granularity necessary to meet current decisional requirements without precluding likely future requirements. The wrong choice of grain can dramatically reduce the usefulness of the warehouse by limiting the degree to which users can slice and dice through data.

- **Operational Data Store.** The consultant team is capable of implementing on Operational Data Store layer beneath the data warehouse if one is necessary for operational integrity. The consultant team is cognizant of the key differences between Operational Data Store and warehousing design issues, and it designs the solution accordingly.

- **Knowledge transfer.** The consultant team views knowledge transfer as a key component of a data warehousing initiative. The project environment encourages coaching and learning for both IT staff and end users. Business users are encouraged to share their in-depth understanding and knowledge of the business with the rest of the warehousing team.

- **Incremental rollouts.** The overall project approach is driven by risks and rewards, with clearly defined phases (rollouts) that incrementally extend the scope of the warehouse. The scope of each rollout is strictly managed to prevent schedule slippage.

Front-End/OLAP/Decision Support/Data Access and Retrieval Tools

The following evaluation criteria can be applied to front-end/OLAP/decision support/data access and retrieval tools:

- **Multidimensional views.** The tool supports pivoting, drill-up, and drill-down and displays query results as spreadsheets, graphs, and charts.

- **Usability.** The tool works under the GUI environment and has features that make it user-friendly (e.g., the ability to open and run an existing report with one or two clicks of the mouse).

- **Star schema aware.** Applicable only to Relational OLAP tools. The tool recognizes a star schema database and takes advantage of the schema design.
- **Tool sophistication.** The tool is appropriate for the intended user. Not all users are comfortable with desktop computing, and Relational OLAP tools can meet most user requirements. Multi-dimensional databases are highly sophisticated and are more appropriate for power users.
- **Delivery lead time.** The product vendor can deliver the product within the required time frame.
- **Planned functionality for future releases.** Since this area of data warehousing technologies is constantly evolving and maturing, it is helpful to know the enhancements or features that the tool will eventually have in its future releases. The planned functionality should be consistent with the above evaluation criteria.

Middleware/Data Extraction and Transformation Tools

The following evaluation criteria can be applied to middleware and extraction and transformation tools:

- **Price/performance.** The product performs well in a price/performance/maintenance comparison with other vendors of similar products.
- **Extraction and transformation steps supported.** The tool supports or automates one or more of the basic steps to extracting and transforming data. These steps are reading source data, transporting source data, remapping keys, creating load images, generating or creating stored aggregates, logging load exceptions, generating indexes, quality assurance checking, alert generation, and backup and recovery.
- **Delivery lead time.** The product vendor can deliver the product within the required time frame.

Most tools in this category are very expensive. Seriously consider writing in-house versions of these tools as an alternative, especially if your source and target environments are homogeneous.

Relational Database Management Systems

The following evaluation criteria can be applied to an RDBMS:

- **Preservation of prior investments.** The warehouse solution leverages as much as possible prior software and hardware investments and existing skill sets within the organization. Note however, that data warehousing does require additional database management techniques because of the size and scale of the database.
- **Financial stability.** The product vendor has proven to be a strong and visible player in the relational database market, and its financial performance indicates growth or stability.
- **Data warehousing features.** The product has or will have features that support data warehousing requirements (e.g., bit-mapped indexes for large tables, aggregate navigation).
- **Star schema aware.** The product's query optimizer recognizes the star schema and optimizes the query accordingly. Note that most query optimizers strongly support only OLTP-type queries. Unfortunately, although these optimizers are appropriate for transactional environments, they may actually slow down the performance on decisional queries.
- **Warehouse metadata.** The tool supports the use of warehouse metadata for aggregate navigation, query statistics collection, etc.
- **Price/performance.** The product performs well in a price/performance comparison with other vendors of similar products.

Hardware or Operating System Platforms

The following evaluation criteria can be applied to hardware and operating system platforms:

- **Scalability.** The warehouse solution can scale up in terms of space and processing power. This scalability is particularly important if the warehouse is projected to grow at a rapid rate.
- **Financial stability.** The product vendor has proven to be a strong and visible player in the hardware segment, and its financial performance indicates growth or stability.

- **Price/performance.** The product performs well in a price/performance comparison with other vendors of similar products.
- **Delivery lead time.** The product vendor can deliver the hardware or an equivalent service unit within the required time frame. If the unit is not readily available within the same country, there may be delays due to importation logistics.
- **Reference sites.** The hardware vendor has a reference site that is using a similar unit for the same purpose. The warehousing team can either arrange a site visit or interview representatives from the site visit. Alternatively, an onsite test of the unit can be conducted, especially if no reference is available.
- **Availability of support.** Support for the hardware and its operating system is available, and support response times are within the acceptable down time for the warehouse.

How Does Data Warehousing Affect My Existing Systems?

Existing operational systems are the source of internal warehouse data. Extractions can take place only during the batch windows of the operational systems, typically after office hours. If batch windows are sufficiently large, warehouse-related activities will have little or no disruptive effects on normal, day-to-day operations.

Improvement Areas in Operational Systems

Data warehousing, however, does highlight areas in existing systems where improvements can be made to operational systems, particularly in two areas:

- **Missing data items.** Decisional information needs almost always require the collection of data that are currently outside the scope of the existing systems. If possible, the existing system are extended to support the collection of such data. The team will have to study alternatives to data collection if the operational systems cannot be modified (for example, if the operational system is an application package whose warranties will be void if modifications are made).

- **Insufficient data quality.** The data warehouse efforts may also identify areas where the data quality of the operational systems can be improved. This is especially true for data items that are used to uniquely identify customers, such as social security numbers.

The data warehouse implementation team should continuously provide constructive feedback regarding the operational systems. Easy improvements can be quickly implemented, and improvements that require significant effort and resources can be prioritized during IT planning.

By ensuring that each rollout of a data warehouse phase is always accompanied by a review of the existing systems, the warehousing team can provide valuable inputs to plans for enhancing operational systems.

▶ Data Warehousing and Its Impact on Other Enterprise Initiatives

By its enterprise-wide nature, a data warehousing initiative will naturally have an impact on other enterprise initiatives, two of which are discussed below.

How Does Data Warehousing Tie In with BPR?

Data warehousing refers to the gamut of activities that support the decisional information requirements of the enterprise. BPR is "the radical redesign of strategic and value-added processes—and the systems, policies, and organizational structures that support them—to optimize the work flows and productivity in an organization."

Most BPR projects have focused on the optimization of operational business processes. Data warehousing, on the other hand, focuses on optimizing the decisional (or decision-making) processes within the enterprise. It can be said that data warehousing is the technology enabler for reengineering decisional processes.

The ready availability of integrated data for corporate decision-making also has implications for the organizational structure of the enterprise. Most organizations are structured or designed to collect, summarize, report, and direct the status of operations (i.e., there is an operational monitoring purpose). The availability of integrated data at different levels of detail may encourage a flattening of the organization structure.

Data warehouses also provide the enterprise with the measures for gauging competitive standing. The use of the warehouse leads to insights as to what drives the enterprise. These insights may quickly lead to business process reengineering initiatives in the operational areas.

How Does Data Warehousing Tie In with Intranets?

The term *intranet* refers to the use of Internet technologies for internal corporate networks. Intranets have been touched as cost-effective, client/server solutions to enterprise computing needs. Intranets are also popular due to the universal, easy-to-learn, easy-to-use front-end, i.e., the web browser.

The web-publishing nature of the Internet, and the browser's metaphor of searching for information, are consistent with the data warehouse's querying metaphor. The availability of many web-based tools that draw their data from relational database structures has naturally encouraged the use of web technology as a means for delivering warehouse data to end-users.

A data warehouse with a web-enabled front-end therefore provides enterprises with interesting options for intranet-based solutions.

With the introduction of technologies that enable secure connections over the public Internet infrastructure, enterprises now also have a cost-effective way of distributing or delivering warehouse data to users in multiple locations.

▶ When Is a Data Warehouse Not Appropriate?

Not all organizations are ready for a data warehousing initiative. Below are two instances when a data warehouse is simply inappropriate.

When the Operational Systems Are Not Ready

The data warehouse is populated with information primarily from the operational systems of the enterprise. A good indicator of operational system readiness is the amount of IT effort focused on operational systems.

A number of telltale signs indicate a lack of readiness. These include the following:

- **Many new operational systems are planned for development or are in the process of being deployed.** Much of the enterprise's IT resources will be assigned to this effort and will therefore not be available for data warehousing projects.
- **Many of the operational systems are legacy applications that require much firefighting.** The source systems are brittle or unstable and are candidates for replacement. IT resources are also directed at fighting operational system fires.
- **Many of the operational systems require major enhancements and must be overhauled.** If the operational systems require major enhancements, then chances are these systems do not sufficiently support the day-to-day operations of the enterprise. Again, IT resources will be directed to enhancement or replacement efforts. Furthermore, deficient operational systems almost always fail to capture all the data required to meet the decisional information needs of business managers.

Regardless of the reason for a lack of operational system readiness, the bottom line is simple: an *enterprise-wide* data warehouse is out of the question due to the lack of adequate source systems. However, this does not preclude a phased data warehousing initiative, as illustrated in Figure 4–2.

The enterprise may opt for an interleaved deployment of systems. A series of projects can be conducted, where a project to deploy an opera-

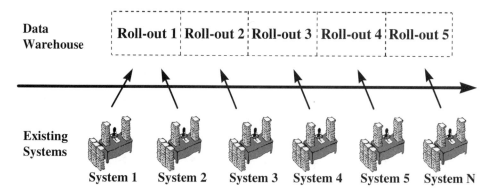

Figure 4–2 Data Warehouse Rollout Strategy

tional system is followed by a project that extends the scope of the data warehouse to encompass the newly stabilized operational system.

The main focus of the majority of IT staff remains on deploying the operational systems. However, a data warehouse scope extension project is initiated as each operational system stabilizes. This project extends the data warehouse scope with data from each new operational system.

Note, however, that this approach may create unrealistic end-user expectations, particularly during earlier rollouts. The scope and strategy should therefore be communicated clearly and consistently to all users. Most, if not all, business users will understand that enterprise-wide views of data are not possible while most of the operational systems are not feeding the warehouse.

When the Need Is Operational Integration

Despite its ability to provide integrated data for *decisional* information needs, a data warehouse does not in any way contribute to meeting the *operational* information needs of the enterprise. Data warehouses are refreshed at best on a daily basis. They do not integrate data quickly enough or often enough for operational management purposes.

If the enterprise needs operational integration, then the typical data warehouse deployment (as shown in Figure 4–3) is insufficient.

Instead, the enterprise needs an Operational Data Store and its accompanying front-end applications. As mentioned in Chapter 1, flash mon-

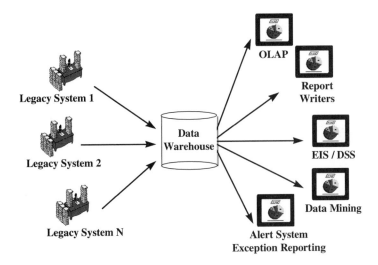

Figure 4–3 Traditional Data Warehouse Architecture

itoring and reporting tools are often likened to a dashboard that is constantly refreshed to provide operational management with the latest information about enterprise operations. Figure 4–4 illustrates the Operational Data Store architecture.

When the intended users of the system are operational managers and when the requirements are for an integrated view of constantly refreshed operational data, an Operational Data Store is the appropriate solution.

Enterprises that have implemented Operational Data Stores will find it natural to use the Operational Data Store as one of the primary source systems for their data warehouse. Thus, the Data Warehouse contains a series (i.e., layer upon layer) of ODS snapshots, where each layer corresponds to data as of a specific point in time.

▶ How Do I Manage or Control a Data Warehouse Initiative?

There are several ways to manage or control a data warehouse project. Note that most of the techniques described below are useful in any technology project.

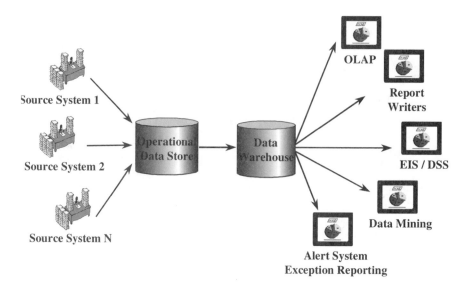

Figure 4–4   The Data Warehouse and the Operational Data Store

Milestones. Clearly defined milestones provide project management and the Project Sponsor with regular checkpoints to track the progress of the data warehouse development effort. Milestones should be far enough apart to show real progress, but not so far apart that senior management becomes uneasy or loses focus and commitment. In general, one data warehouse rollout should be treated as one project, lasting anywhere between three to six months.

Incremental Rollouts, Incremental Investments. Avoid biting off more than you can chew; projects that are gigantic leaps forward are more likely to fail. Instead, break up the data warehouse initiative into incremental rollouts. By doing so, you give the warehouse team manageable but ambitious targets and clearly defined deliverables.

Applying a phased approach also has the added benefit of allowing the Project Sponsor and the warehousing team to set priorities and manage end-user expectations. The benefits of each rollout can be measured separately, and the data warehouse is justified on a phase-per-phase basis.

A phased approach, however, requires an overall architect so that each phase also lays the foundation for subsequent warehousing efforts, and earlier investments remain intact.

Clearly Defined Rollout Scopes. To the maximum extent possible, clearly define the scope of each rollout to set the expectations of both senior management and warehouse end-users. Each rollout should deliver useful functionality. As in most development projects, the project manager will be walking the fine line between increasing the scope to better meet user needs and ruthlessly controlling the scope to meet the rollout deadline.

Individually Cost-Justified Rollouts. The scope of each rollout determines the corresponding rollout cost. Each rollout should be cost-justified on its own merits to ensure appropriate return on investment. However, this practice should not preclude long-term architectural investments that do not have an immediate return in the same rollout.

Plan to Have Early Successes. Data warehousing is a long-term effort that must have early and continuous successes that justify the length of the journey. Focus early efforts on areas that can deliver highly visible success, and that success will increase organizational support.

Plan to be Scalable. Initial successes with the data warehouse will result in a sudden demand for increased data scope, increased functionality, or both! The warehousing environment and design must both be scalable to deal with increased demand as needed.

Reward your Team. Data warehousing is hard work, and teams need to know their work is appreciated. A motivated team is always an asset in long-term initiatives.

▶ In Summary

The Chief Information Officer (CIO) has the unenviable task of juggling the limited IT resources of the enterprise. He or she makes the resource assignment decisions that determine the skill sets of the various IT project teams.

Unfortunately, data warehousing is just one of the many projects on the CIO's plate. If the enterprise is still in the process of deploying operational system, data warehousing will naturally be at a lower priority.

CIOs also have the difficult responsibility of evolving the enterprise's IT architecture. They must ensure that the addition of each new system, and the extension of each existing system, contributes to the stability and resiliency of the overall IT architecture.

Fortunately, data warehouse and operational data store technologies allow CIOs to migrate reporting and analytical functionality from legacy or operational environments, thereby creating a more robust and stable computing environment for the enterprise.

The Project Manager

The warehouse Project Manager is responsible for any and all technical activities related to planning, designing, and building a data warehouse. Under ideal circumstances, this role is fulfilled by internal IT staff. It is not unusual, however, for this role to be outsourced, especially for early or pilot projects, because warehousing technologies and techniques are so new.

▶ How Do I Roll Out a Data Warehouse Initiative?

If you are starting a data warehouse initiative, there are three main things to keep in mind. Always start with a planning activity. Always implement a pilot project as your "proof of concept." And, always extend the functionality of the warehouse in an iterative manner.

Start with a Data Warehouse Planning Activity

The scope of a data warehouse varies from one enterprise to another. The desired scope and scale are typically determined by the information requirements that drive the warehouse design and development. These requirements, in turn, are driven by the business context of the enterprise—the industry, the fierceness of competition, and the state of the art in industry practices.

Regardless of the industry, however, it is advisable to start a data warehouse initiative with a short planning activity. The Project Manager should launch and manage the activities listed below.

Decisional Requirements Analysis. Start with an analysis of the decision support needs of the organization. The warehousing team must understand the user requirements and attempt to map these to the data sources available. The team also designs potential queries or reports that can meet the stated information requirements.

Note that unlike system development projects for OLTP applications, the information needs of decisional users cannot be pinned down and are frequently changing. The Requirements Analysis team should therefore gain enough of an understanding of the business to be able to anticipate likely changes to end-user requirements.

Decisional Source System Audit. Conduct an audit of all potential sources of data. This crucial and very detailed task verifies that data sources exist to meet the decisional information needs identified during requirements analysis. There is no point in designing a warehouse schema that cannot be populated because of a lack of source data.

Similarly, there is no point in designing reports or queries when data are not available to generate them. Log all data items that are currently not supported or provided by the operational systems and submit these to the CIO as inputs for IT planning.

Logical and Physical Warehouse Schema Design (Preliminary). The results of requirements analysis and source system audit serve as inputs to the design of the warehouse schema. The schema details all fact and dimension tables and fields, as well as the data sources for each warehouse field. The preliminary schema produced as part of the warehousing planning activity will be progressively refined with each roll-out of the data warehouse.

The goal of the team is to design a data structure that will be resilient enough to meet the constantly changing information requirements of warehouse end-users.

Other Concerns. The three tasks described above should also provide the warehousing team with an understanding of:

- the required warehouse architecture;
- the appropriate phasing and rollout strategy; and
- the ideal scope for a pilot implementation.

The data warehouse plan must also evaluate the need for an ODS layer between the operational systems and the data warehouse.

You can find additional information on the above activities in Part III, *Process*.

Implement a Proof-of-Concept Pilot

Start with a pilot implementation as the first rollout for data warehousing. Pilot projects have the advantage of being small and manageable, thereby providing the organization with a data warehouse "proof of concept" that has a good chance of success.

Determine the functional scope of a pilot implementation based on two factors:

- **The degree of risk the enterprise is willing to take.** The project difficulty increases as the number of source systems, users, and locations increases. Politically sensitive areas of the enterprise are also very high risk.
- **The potential for leveraging the pilot project.** Avoid constructing a "throwaway" prototype for the pilot project. The pilot warehouse must have actual value to the enterprise. Figure 5–1 is a matrix for assessing the pilot project.

Avoid high-risk projects with very low reward possibilities. Ideally, the pilot project has low or manageable risk factors but has a highly visible impact on the way decisions are made in the enterprise. An early

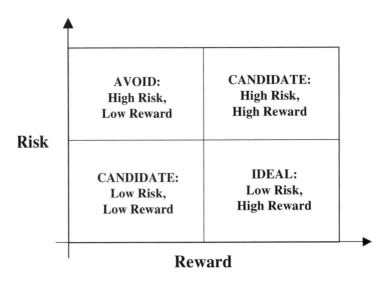

Figure 5–1   Selecting Pilot Projects: Risk vs. Reward

and high-profile success will increase the grassroots support of the warehousing initiative.

Extend Functionality Iteratively

Once the warehouse pilot is in place and is stable, implement subsequent rollouts of the data warehouse to continuously layer new functionality or extend existing warehousing functionality on a cost-justifiable, prioritized basis, illustrated by the diagram in Figure 5–2.

Top-Down. Drive all rollouts by a top-down study of user requirements. Note that decisional requirements are subject to constant change; the team will never be able to fully document and understand the requirements, simply because the requirements change as the business situation changes. Don't fall into the trap of wanting to analyze everything to extreme detail (i.e., analysis paralysis).

Bottom-Up. While some team members are working top-down, other team members are working bottom-up. The results of the bottom-up study serve as the reality check for the rollout—some of the top-down requirements will quickly become unrealistic, given the state and con-

Chapter **5** I The Project Manager

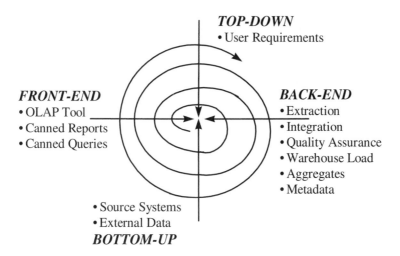

Figure 5–2   Iterative Extension of Functionality, i.e., Evolution

tents of the intended source systems. End users should be quickly informed of limitations imposed by source system data to properly manage their expectations.

Back-End. Each rollout or iteration extends the back-end (i.e., the server component) of the data warehouse. Warehouse subsystems are created or extended to extract, transform, clean, and integrate more data. Warehouse data structures are extended to support a larger scope of data. Aggregate records are computed and loaded. Metadata records are populated as required.

Front-End. The front-end (i.e., client component) of the warehouse is also extended by deploying the existing data access and retrieval tools to more users and by deploying new tools (e.g., data mining tools, new decision support applications) to warehouse users. The availability of more data implies that new reports and new queries can be defined.

▶ How Important Is the Hardware Platform?

Although the mainframe environment is also used as a data warehouse platform, data warehousing hardware discussions typically revolve around two main types of hardware technologies: symmetric multiprocessing (SMP) and massively parallel processing (MPP) servers.

SMPs. Symmetric multiprocessing (SMP) hardware has multiple processors that share one memory (see Figure 5–3). This type of architecture is often referred to as the "Shared Everything" architecture. When additional computing power is required, additional CPUs are added to the machine (although there is a limit to the number) or several SMP machines are clustered together.

MPPs. In contrast, massively parallel processing (MPP) hardware supports multiple nodes, where each node has one or more processors, each with its own memory (see Figure 5–4). Additional nodes can be added to increase processing power.

The choice between SMP and MPP is influenced by a number of factors, including the complexity of the query environment, the price/performance ratio, the proven processing capacity of the hardware platform with the target RDBMS, the anticipated warehouse applications, and the foreseen increases in warehouse size and users.

For example, complex queries that involve multiple table joins might realize better performance with an MPP configuration. MPPs, though, are generally more expensive. Clustered SMPs may provide a highly scalable implementation with better price/performance benefits.

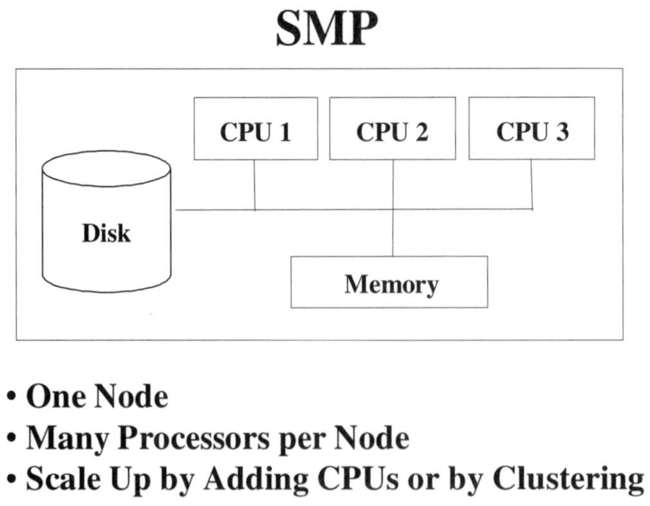

SMP

- **One Node**
- **Many Processors per Node**
- **Scale Up by Adding CPUs or by Clustering**

Figure 5–3   SMP Hardware Configuration

MPP

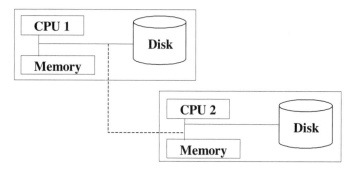

- **Many Nodes**
- **One or More Processors per**
- **Each Node Has its Own Memory**
- **Scale Up by Adding A Node**

Figure 5–4   MPP Hardware Configuration

▶ What Technologies Are Involved?

Several types of technologies are used to make data warehousing possible. These technology types are enumerated briefly below. You can find more information in Part 4, *Technology*.

- **Source systems.** The operational systems of the enterprise are the most likely source systems for a data warehouse. The warehouse may also make use of external data sources from third parties.

- **Middleware, extraction, transportation and transformation technologies.** These tools extract and reorganize data from the various source systems. These tools vary greatly in terms of complexity, features, and price. The ideal tools for the enterprise are heavily dependent on the computing environment of the source systems and the intended computing environment of the data warehouse.

- **Data quality tools.** These tools identify or correct data quality errors that exist in the raw source data. Most tools of this type are used to call the warehouse team's attention to potential quality problems. Unfortunately, much of the data cleansing process is still manual; it is also tedious due to the volume of data involved.

- **Warehouse storage.** Database management systems (DBMS) are used to store the warehouse data. DBMS products are generally classified as relational (e.g., Oracle, Informix, Sybase) or multi-dimensional (e.g., Essbase, BrioQuery, Express Server).
- **Metadata management.** These tools create, store, and manage the warehouse metadata.
- **Data access and retrieval tools.** These are tools used by warehouse end users to access, format, and disseminate warehouse data in the form of reports, query results, charts, and graphs. Other data access and retrieval tools actively search the data warehouse for patterns in the data (i.e., data mining tools). Decision Support Systems and Executive Information Systems also fall into this category.
- **Data modeling tools.** These tools are used to prepare and maintain an information model of both the source databases and the warehouse database.
- **Warehouse management tools.** These tools are used by warehouse administrators to create and maintain the warehouse (e.g., create and modify warehouse data structures, generate indexes).
- **Data warehouse hardware.** This refers to the data warehouse server platforms and their related operating systems.

Figure 5–5 depicts the typical warehouse software components and their relationships to one another.

▶ Do I Still Use Relational Databases for Data Warehousing?

Although there were initial doubts about the use of relational database technology in data warehousing, experience has shown that there is actually no other appropriate database management system for an enterprise-wide data warehouse.

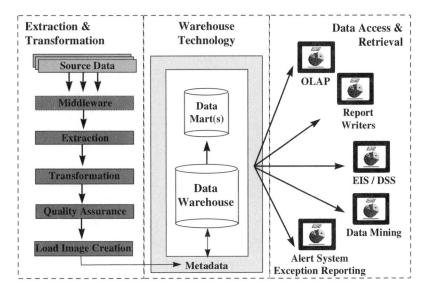

Figure 5–5   Data Warehouse Components

MDDBs. The confusion about relational databases arises from the proliferation of OLAP products that make use of a multidimensional database (MDDB). MDDBs store data in a "hypercube" i.e., a multidimensional array that is paged in and out of memory as needed, as illustrated in Figure 5–6.

RDBMS. In contrast, relational databases store data as tables with rows and columns that do not map directly to the multidimensional view that users have of data. Structured Query Language (SQL) scripts are used to retrieve data from RDBMSes.

Two Rival Approaches

Although these two approaches are apparent "rivals," the apparent competition between MDDB and relational database (RDB) technology presents enterprises with interesting architectural alternatives for implementing data warehousing technology. It is not unusual to find enterprises making use of both technologies, depending on the requirements of the user community.

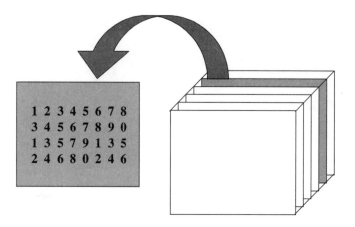

Figure 5-6 MDDB Data Structures

From an architectural perspective, the enterprise can get the best of both worlds through the careful use of both technologies in different parts of the warehouse architecture.

- **Enterprise data warehouses.** These have a tendency to grow significantly beyond the size limit of most MDDBs and are therefore typically implemented with relational database technology. Only relational database technology is capable of storing up to terabytes of data while still providing acceptable load and query performance.
- **Data marts.** A data mart is typically a subset of the enterprise data warehouse. These subsets are determined either by geography (i.e., one data mart per location) or by user group. Data marts, due to their smaller size, may take advantage of multidimensional databases for better reporting and analysis performance.

Warehousing Architectures

Below, we present how the relational and multi-dimensional database technologies can be used together for data warehouse and data mart implementation.

RDBMSes in Warehousing Architectures. Data warehouses are built on relational database technology. Online Analytical Processing (OLAP) tools are then used to interact directly with the relational data warehouse or with a relational data mart (see Figure 5–7). Relational OLAP (ROLAP) tools recognize the relational nature of the database but still present their users with multidimensional views of the data.

MDDBs in Warehousing Architectures. Alternatively, data is extracted from the relational data warehouse and placed in multidimensional data structures to reflect the multidimensional nature of the data (see Figure 5–8). Multidimensional OLAP (MOLAP) tools run against the multidimensional server, rather than against the data warehouse.

Tiered Data Warehousing Architectures. The enterprise is free to mix and match these two database technologies, depending on the scale and size of the data warehouse, as illustrated in Figure 5–9.

It will not be unusual to find an enterprise with the following tiered data warehousing architecture:

- ROLAP tools, which run directly against relational databases, are used whenever the queries are fairly simple and when the administration overhead that comes with multidimensional tools is not justified for a particular user base.
- Multidimensional databases are used for data marts, and specific multidimensional front-end applications query the contents of the MDDB. Data marts may also use relational database technology, in which case, users make use of ROLAP front-ends.

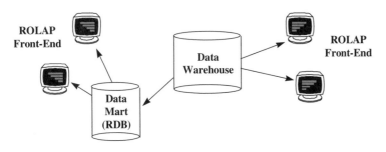

Figure 5–7 Relational Databases

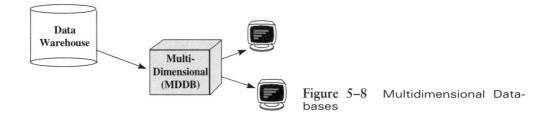

Figure 5–8 Multidimensional Databases

Trade-Offs: MDDB vs. RDBMS

Consider the following factors when choosing between the multidimensional and relational approaches:

Size. Multidimensional databases are generally limited by size, although the size limit has been increasing gradually over the years. In the mid-1990s, 10 gigabytes of data in a hypercube already presented problems and unacceptable query performance. Some multidimensional products today are able to handle up to 100 gigabytes of data. Despite this improvement, however, large data warehouses are still

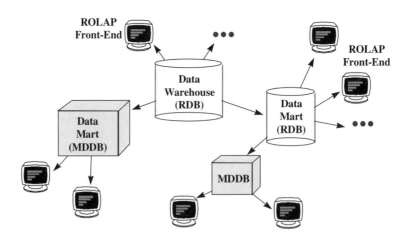

Figure 5–9   Tiered Data Warehousing Architecture

Chapter **5** I The Project Manager

better served by relational front-ends running against high-performing and scalable relational databases.

Volatility of Source Data. Highly volatile data are better handled by relational technology. Multidimensional data in hypercubes generally take long to load and update. Thus, the time required to constantly load and update the multidimensional data structure may prevent the enterprise from loading new data as often as desired.

Aggregate Strategy. Multidimensional hypercubes support aggregations better, although this advantage will disappear as relational databases improve their support of aggregate navigation. Drilling up and down on RDBMSes generally take longer than on MDDBs as well. However, due to their size limitation, MDDBs will not be suited to warehouses or data marts with very detailed data.

Investment Protection. Most enterprises have already made significant investments in relational technology (e.g., RDBMS assets) and skill sets. The continued use of these tools and skills for another purpose provides additional return on investment and lowers the technical risk for the data warehousing effort.

Ability to Manage Complexity. A multidimensional DBMS adds a layer to the overall systems architecture of the warehouse. Sufficient resources must be allocated to administer and maintain the MDDB layer. If the administrative overhead is not or cannot be justified, an MDDB will not be appropriate.

Type of Users. Power users generally prefer the range of functionality available in multidimensional OLAP tools. Users that require broad views of enterprise data require access to the data warehouse and therefore are best served by a relational OLAP tool.

Recently, many of the large database vendors have announced plans to integrate their multi-dimensional and relational database products. In this scenario, end-users make use of the multi-dimensional front-end tools for all their queries. If the query requires data that are not available in the MDDB, the tools will retrieve the required data from the larger relational database. Dubbed as a "drill-through" feature, this innovation will certainly introduce new data warehousing architectures.

▶ How Long Does a Data Warehousing Project Last?

Data warehousing is a long, daunting task; it requires significant, prolonged effort on the part of the enterprise and may have the unpleasant side effect of highlighting problem areas in operational systems. Like any task of great magnitude, the data warehousing effort must be partitioned into manageable chunks, where each piece is managed as an individual project or rollout.

Data warehouse rollouts after the pilot warehouse must fit together within an overall strategy. Define the strategy at the start of the data warehousing effort. Constantly update (at least once a year) the data warehouse strategy as new requirements are understood, new operational systems are installed, and new tools become available.

In cases where the enterprise also has an Operational Data Store initiative, the ODS and warehousing projects must be synchronized. The data warehouse should take advantage of the ODS as a source system as soon as possible.

Figure 5–10 depicts how the entire decisional systems effort can be interleaved.

Each data warehouse rollout should be scoped to last anywhere between three to six months, with a team of about 6 to 12 people working on it full time. Part-time team members can easily bring the total

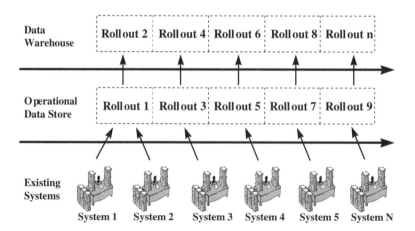

Figure 5–10   Interleaved Operational, ODS, and Warehouse Projects

number of participants to more than 20. Sufficient resources must be allocated to support each rollout.

How Is a Data Warehouse Different from Other IT Projects?

Since much of computing has focused on meeting operational information needs, IT professionals have a natural tendency to apply the same methodologies, approaches or techniques to data warehousing projects. Unfortunately, data warehousing projects differ from other IT projects in a number of ways, as discussed below.

A Data Warehouse Project is Not a Package Implementation Project

A data warehouse project requires a number of tools and software utilities that are available from multiple vendors. At present, there is still no single suite of tools that can automate the entire data warehousing effort.

Most of the major warehouse vendors, however, are now attempting to provide off-the-shelf solutions for warehousing projects by bundling their warehousing products with that of other warehousing partners. This solution limits the potential tool integration problems of the warehousing team.

A Data Warehouse Never Stops Evolving; It Changes with the Business

Unlike OLTP systems that are subject only to changes related to the process or area of the business they support, a data warehouse is subject to changes to the decisional information requirements of decision-makers. In other words, it is subject to any changes in the business context of the enterprise.

Also, unlike OLTP systems, a successful data warehouse will result in more questions from business users. Change requests for the data warehouse are a positive indication that the warehouse is being used.

Data Warehouses Are Huge

Without exaggeration, enterprise-wide data warehouses are *huge*. A pilot data warehouse can easily be more than 10 gigabytes in size. A data warehouse in production for a little over a year can easily reach 1 terabyte, depending on the granularity and the volume of data. Databases of this size require different database optimization and tuning techniques.

Project Progress and Effort Are Highly Dependent on Accessibility and Quality of Source System Data

The progress of a data warehouse project is highly dependent on where the operational data resides. Enterprises that make use of proprietary application packages will find themselves dealing with locked data. Enterprises with data distributed over different locations with no easy access will also encounter difficulties.

Similarly, the quality of the existing data plays a major role in the project. Data quality problems consistently remain at the top of the list of data warehouse issues. Unfortunately, none of the available tools can automate away the problem of data quality. Although tools can help identify problem areas, these problems can be only be resolved manually.

▶ What Are the Critical Success Factors of a Data Warehousing Project?

A number of factors influence the progress and success of data warehousing projects. While the list below does not claim to be complete, it highlights areas of the warehousing project that the project manager is in a position to actively control or influence.

- **Proper planning.** Define a warehousing strategy and expect to review it after each warehouse rollout. Bear in mind that IT resources are still required to manage and administer the warehouse once it is in production. Stay coordinated with any scheduled maintenance work on the warehouse source systems.

- **Iterative development and change management.** Stay away from the big-bang approach. Divide the warehouse initiative into manageable rollouts, each to last anywhere between three to six months. Constantly collect feedback from users. Identify lessons learned at the end of each project and feed these into the next iteration.

- **Access to and involvement of key players.** The Project Sponsor, the CIO, and the Project Manager must all be actively involved in setting the direction of the warehousing project. Work together to resolve the business and technical issues that will arise on the project. Choose the project team members carefully, taking care to ensure that the project team roles that must be performed by internal resources are staffed accordingly.

- **Training and communication.** If data warehousing is new to the enterprise or if new team members are joining the warehousing initiative, set aside enough time for training the team members. The roles of each team member must be communicated clearly to set role expectations.

- **Vigilant issue management.** Keep a close watch on project issues and ensure their speedy resolution. The Project Manager should be quick to identify the negative consequences on the project schedule if issues are left unresolved. The Project Sponsor should intervene and ensure the proper resolution of issues, especially if these are clearly causing delays, or deal with highly politicized areas of the business.

- **Warehousing approach.** One of the worst things a Project Manager can do is to apply OLTP development approaches to a warehousing project. Apply a system development approach that is tailored to data warehousing; avoid OLTP development approaches that have simply been repackaged into warehousing terms.

- **Demonstration with a pilot project.** The ideal pilot project is a high-impact, low-risk area of the enterprise. Use the pilot as a proof-of-concept to gain champions within the enterprise and to refute the opposition.

- **Focus on essential minimal characteristics.** The scope of each project or rollout should be ruthlessly managed to deliver the essential minimal characteristics for that rollout. Don't get carried away by spending time on the bells and whistles, especially with the front-end tools.

▶ In Summary

The Project Manager is responsible for all technical aspects of the project on a day-to-day basis. Since up to 80 percent of any data warehousing project can be devoted to the back-end of the warehouse, the role of Project Manager can easily be one of the busiest on the project.

Despite the fact that business users now drive the warehouse development, a huge part of any data warehouse project is still technology centered. The critical success factors of typical technology projects therefore still apply to data warehousing projects. Bear in mind, however, that data warehousing projects are more susceptible to organizational and logistical issues than the typical technology project.

Part 3

Process

Although there have been attempts to use traditional software development methodologies from the OLTP arena for data warehouse development, warehousing practitioners generally agree that an iterative development approach is more suited to warehouse development than are traditional waterfall approaches.

This section of the book presents an iterative warehousing approach for enterprises about to embark on a data warehousing initiative. The approach begins with the definition of a data warehouse strategy, then proceeds to define the way to set up warehouse management and support processes.

The latter part of the approach focuses on the tasks required to plan and implement one rollout (i.e., one phase) of the warehouse. Repeat these tasks for each phase of the warehouse development.

Warehousing Strategy

Define the data warehouse strategy as part of the information technology strategy of the enterprise. The traditional Information Strategy Plan (ISP) addresses operational computing needs thoroughly but may not give sufficient attention to decisional information requirements. A data warehouse strategy remedies this by focusing on the decisional needs of the enterprise.

We start this chapter by presenting the components of a Data Warehousing strategy. We follow with a discussion of the tasks required to define a strategy for your enterprise.

▶ Strategy Components

At a minimum, the data warehouse strategy should include the following elements.

- *Preliminary data warehouse rollout plan.* Not all of the user requirements can be met in one data warehouse project—such a project would necessarily be large, and dangerously unmanageable. It is more realistic to prioritize the different user requirements and assign them to different warehouse rollouts. Doing so allows the enterprise to divide the warehouse development into phased, successive rollouts, where each rollout focuses on meeting an agreed set of requirements.

The iterative nature of such an approach allows the warehousing team to extend the functionality of the warehouse in a manageable manner. The phased approach lowers the overall risk of the data warehouse project, while delivering increasing functionality to the users.

- *Preliminary data warehouse architecture.* Define the overall data warehouse architecture for the pilot and subsequent warehouse rollouts to ensure the scalability of the warehouse. Whenever possible, define the initial technical architecture of each rollout.

  By consciously thinking through the data warehouse architecture, warehouse planners can determine the various technology components (e.g., MDDB, RDBMS, tools) that are required for each rollout.

- *Short-listed data warehouse environment and tools.* There are a number of tools and warehousing environments from which to choose. Create a short-list for the tools and environments that appear to meet your warehousing needs. A standard set of tools will lessen tool integration problems and will minimize the learning required of both the warehousing team and the warehouse users.

Below are the tasks required to create the enterprise's warehousing strategy. Note that the tasks described below can typically be completed in three to five weeks, depending on the availability of resource persons and the size of the enterprise.

▶ Determine Organizational Context

An understanding of the organization helps to establish the context of the project and may highlight aspects of the corporate culture that may ease or complicate the warehousing project. Answers to organizational background questions are typically obtained from the Project Sponsor, the CIO, or the Project Manager assigned to the warehousing effort.

Typical organizational background questions include:

- **Who is the Project Sponsor for this project?** The Project Sponsor sets the scope of the warehousing project. He or she also plays a crucial role in establishing the working relationship among warehousing team members, especially if third parties are involved. Note that easy access to warehousing data may also be limited to the organizational scope that is within the control or authority of the Project Sponsor.
- **What are the IS or IT groups in the organization? Which are involved in the data warehousing effort?** Since data warehousing is very much a technology-based endeavor, the IS or IT groups within the organization will always be involved in any warehousing effort. It is often insightful to understand the bulk of the work currently performed within the IS or IT departments. If the IS or IT groups are often fighting fires or are very busy deploying operational systems, data warehousing is unlikely to be high on the list of IT priorities.
- **What are the roles and responsibilities of the individuals who have been assigned to this effort?** It is helpful to define the roles and responsibilities of the various individuals involved in the data warehousing project. This practice sets common, realistic expectations and improves understanding and communication within the team. In cases where the team is composed of external parties (especially where several vendors are involved), a clear definition of roles becomes critical.

▶ Conduct Preliminary Survey of Requirements

Obtain an inventory of the requirements of business users through individual and group interviews with the end-user community. Whenever possible, obtain layouts of the current management reports (and their planned enhancements).

The requirements inventory represents the breadth of information that the warehouse is expected to eventually provide. Note that while it is important to get a clear picture of the extent of requirements, it is not necessary to detail all the requirements in depth at this point. The objective is to understand the user needs enough to prioritize the requirements. This is a critical input for identifying the scope of each data warehouse rollout.

Interview Categories and Sample Questions

The following questions, arranged by category, should be useful as a starting point for the interviews with intended end users of the warehouse.

- **Functions.** What is the mission of your group or unit? How do you go about fulfilling this mission? How do you know if you've been successful with your mission? What are the key performance indicators and critical success factors?
- **Customers.** How do you group or classify your customers? Do these groupings change over time? Does your grouping affect how you treat your customers? What kind of information do you track for each type of client? What demographic information do you use, if any? Do you need to track customer data for each customer?
- **Profit.** At what level do you measure profitability in your group? Per agent? Per customer? Per product? Per region? At what level of detail are costs and revenues tracked in your organization? How do you track costs and revenues now? What kind of profitability reports do you use or produce now?
- **Systems.** What systems do you use as part of your job? What systems are you aware of in other groups that contain information you require? What kind of manual data transformations do you have to perform when data are unavailable?
- **Time.** How many months or years of data do you need to track? Do you analyze performance across years? At what level of detail do you need to see figures? Daily? Weekly? Monthly? Quarterly? Yearly? Do you need month-to-date or year-to-date computations? For which figures? How soon do you need to see data (e.g., do you need yesterday's data today?) How soon after week-end, month-end, quarter-end, and year-end do you need to see the previous period's figures?

- **Queries and reports.** What reports do you use now? What information do you actually use in each of the reports you now receive? Can we obtain samples of these reports? How often are these reports produced? Do you get them soon enough, frequently enough? Who makes these reports for you? What reports do you produce for other people?

- **Product.** What products do you sell, and how do you classify them? Do you have a product hierarchy? Do you analyze data for all products at the same time, or do you analyze one product type at a time? How do you handle changes in product hierarchy and product description?

- **Geography.** Does your company operate in more than one location? Do you divide your market into geographical areas? Do you track sales per geographic region?

Interviewing Tips

Many of the interviewing tips enumerated below may seem like common sense. Nevertheless, interviewers are encouraged to keep the following points in mind:

- **Avoid making commitments about warehouse scope.** It will not be surprising to find that some of the queries and reports requested by interviewees cannot be supported by the data that currently reside in the operational databases. Interviewers should keep this in mind and communicate this potential limitation to their interviewees. The interviewers cannot afford to make commitments regarding the warehouse scope at this time.

- **Keep the interview objective in mind.** The objective of these interviews is to create an inventory of requirements. There is no need to get a detailed understanding of the requirements at this point.

- **Don't overwhelm the interviewees.** The interviewing team should be small; two people are the ideal number—one to ask questions, another to take notes. Interviewees may be intimidated if a large group of interviewers shows up.

- **Record the session if the interviewee lets you.** Most interviewees will not mind if interviewers bring along a tape recorder to record the session. Transcripts of the session may later prove helpful.

- **Change the interviewing style depending on the interviewee.** Middle-managers are more likely to deal with actual reports and detailed information requirements. Senior executives are more likely to dwell on strategic information needs. Change the interviewing style as needed by adapting the type of questions to the type of interviewee.

- **Listen carefully.** Listen to what the interviewee has to say. The sample interview questions are merely a starting point—follow-up questions have the potential of yielding interesting and critical information. Take note of the terms that the interviewee uses. Popular business terms such as "profit" may have different meanings or connotations within the enterprise.

- **Obtain copies of reports, whenever possible.** The reports will give the warehouse team valuable information about source systems (which system produced the report), as well as business rules and terms. If a person manually makes the reports, the team may benefit from talking to this person.

▶ Conduct Preliminary Source System Audit

Obtain an inventory of potential warehouse data sources through individual and group interviews with key personnel in the IT organization. While the CIO no doubt has a broad, high-level view of the systems in the enterprise, the best resource persons for the source system audit are the DBAs and system administrators who maintain the operational systems.

Typical background interview questions, arranged by categories, for the IT department include:

- **Current architecture.** What is the current technology architecture of the organization? What kind of systems, hardware, DBMS, network, end-user tools, development tools, and data access tools are currently in use?

- **Source system relationships.** Are the source systems related in any way? Does one system provide information to another? Are the systems integrated in any manner? In cases where multiple systems each have customer and product records, which one serves as the "master" copy?

- **Network facilities.** Is it possible to use a single terminal or PC to access the different operational systems, from all locations?
- **Data quality.** How much cleaning, scrubbing, deduplication, and integration do you suppose will be required? What areas (tables or fields) in the source systems are currently known to have poor data quality?
- **Documentation.** How much documentation is available for the source systems? How accurate and up-to-date are these manuals and reference materials? Try to obtain the following information whenever possible: copies of manuals and reference documents, database size, batch window, planned enhancements, typical backup size, backup scope and backup medium, data scope of the system (e.g., important tables and fields), system codes and their meanings, and keys generation schemes.
- **Possible extraction mechanisms.** What extraction mechanisms are possible with this system? What extraction mechanisms have you used before with this system? What extraction mechanisms will not work?

▶ Identify External Data Sources (If Applicable)

The enterprise may also make use of external data sources to augment the data from internal source systems. Examples of external data that can be used are:

- Data from credit agencies
- Zip code or mail code data
- Statistical or census data
- Data from industry organizations
- Data from publications and news agencies

Although the use of external data presents opportunities for enriching the data warehouse, it may also present difficulties because of differences in granularity. For example, the external data may not be readily available at the level of detail required by the data warehouse and may require some transformation or summarization.

Verify assumptions about the external databases before planning to use these as data sources in warehousing projects.

Define Warehouse Rollouts (Phased Implementation)

Divide the data warehouse development into phased, successive rollouts. Note that the scope of each rollout will have to be finalized as part of the planning for that rollout. The availability and quality of source data will play a critical role in finalizing that scope.

As stated earlier, applying a phased approach for delivering the warehouse should lower the overall risk of the data warehouse project while delivering increasing functionality and data to more users. It also helps manage user expectations through the clear definition of scope for each rollout.

Figure 6–1 is a sample table listing all requirements identified during the initial round of interviews with end users. Each requirement is assigned a priority level. An initial complexity assessment is made, based

No.	Requirement	Priority	Complexity	Users	Roll-Out No.
1	Customer Profitability	High	High	Customer Service	1
2	Product Market Share	High	Medium	Product Manager	1
3	Weekly Sales Trends	Medium	Low	VP, Sales	2
...	...	...	...	...	...

Figure 6–1   Sample Rollout Definition

on the estimated number of source systems, early data quality assessments, and the computing environments of the source systems. The intended user group is also identified.

More factors can be listed to help determine the appropriate rollout number for each requirement. The rollout definition is finalized only when it has been approved by the Project Sponsor.

▶ Define Preliminary Data Warehouse Architecture

Define the preliminary architecture of each rollout based on the approved rollout scope. Explore the possibility of using a mix of relational and multidimensional databases and tools, as illustrated in Figure 6–2.

At a minimum, the preliminary architecture should indicate the following:

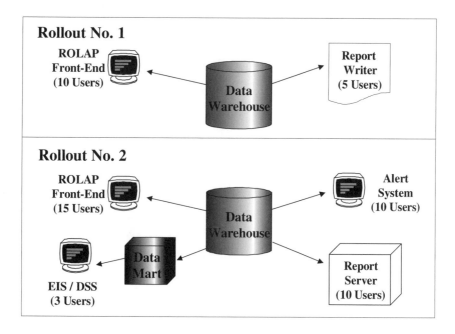

Figure 6–2   Sample Preliminary Architecture per Rollout

- **Data warehouses and data mart.** Define the intended deployment of data warehouses and data marts for each rollout. Indicate how the different databases are related (i.e., how the databases feed one another). The warehouse architecture must ensure that the different data marts are not deployed in isolation.
- **Number of users.** Specify the intended number of users for each data access and retrieval tool (or front-end) for each rollout.
- **Location.** Specify the location of the data warehouse, the data marts, and the intended users for each rollout. This has implications on the technical architecture requirements of the warehousing project.

▶ Evaluate Development and Production Environments and Tools

Enterprises can choose from several environments and tools for the data warehouse initiative. Select the combination of tools that best meets the needs of the enterprise. At present, no single vendor provides

No.	Tool Category	Short-listed Tools	Evaluation Criteria	Weights (%)	Preliminary Scores
1	Data Access and Retrieval	Tool A	Criterion 1 Criterion 2 Criterion 3	30% 30% 40%	78%
		Tool B	Criterion 1 Criterion 2 Criterion 3	30% 30% 40%	82%
		Tool C	Criterion 1 Criterion 2 Criterion 3	30% 30% 40%	84%
2	RDBMS				

Figure 6–3   Sample Tool Short-List

an integrated suite of warehousing tools. There are, however, clear leaders for each tool category.

Eliminate all unsuitable tools, and produce a short-list from which each rollout or project will choose its tool set (see Figure 6–3). Alternatively, select and standardize on a set of tools for all warehouse rollouts.

▶ In Summary

A data warehouse strategy at a minimum contains:

- a preliminary data warehouse rollout plan, which indicates how the development of the warehouse is to be phased;
- a preliminary data warehouse architecture, which indicates the likely physical implementation of the warehouse rollouts; and
- short-listed options for the warehouse environment and tools.

The approach for arriving at these strategy components may vary from one enterprise to another; the approach presented in this chapter is one that has consistently proven to be effective.

Expect the data warehousing strategy to be updated annually each warehouse rollout provides new learning and as new tools and technologies become available.

Chapter 7

Warehouse Management and Support Processes

Warehouse management and support processes are designed to address aspects of planning and managing a data warehouse project that are critical to the successful implementation and subsequent extension of the data warehouse. Unfortunately, these aspects are all too often overlooked in initial warehousing deployments.

These processes are defined to assist the project manager and warehouse driver during warehouse development projects.

▶ Define Issue Tracking and Resolution Process

During the course of a project, it is inevitable that a number of business and technical issues will surface. The project will quickly be delayed by unresolved issues if an issue tracking and resolution process is not in place. Of particular importance are business issues that involve more than one group of users. These issues typically include disputes over the definition of business terms and the financial formulas that govern the transformation of data.

An individual on the project team should be designated to track and follow up the resolution of each issue as it arises. Extremely urgent issues (i.e., issues that may cause project delays if left unresolved) or issues with strong political overtones can be brought to the attention of the Project Sponsor, who must use his or her clout to expedite the resolution process.

Figure 7–1 shows a sample issue log that tracks all the issues that arise during the course of the project.

The following issue tracking guidelines will prove helpful:

- **Issue description.** State the issue briefly in two to three sentences. Provide a more detailed description of the issue as a separate paragraph. If there are possible resolutions to the issue, include these in the issue description. Identify the consequences of leaving this issue open, particularly any impact on the project schedule.
- **Urgency.** Indicate the priority level of the issue: high, medium, or low. Low-priority issues that are left unresolved may later become high priority. The team may have agreed on a resolution rate depending on the urgency of the issue. For example, the team can agree to resolve high-priority issues within three days, medium-priority issues within a week, and low-priority issues within two weeks.
- **Raised by.** Identify the person who raised the issue. If the team is large or does not meet on a regular basis, provide information on how to contact the person (e.g., telephone number, e-mail

No.	Issue Description	Urgency	Raised By	Assigned To	Date Opened	Date Closed	Resolved By	Resolution Description
1	Conflict over definition of "Customer"	High	MWH	MCD	Feb 03	Feb 05	CEO	Use CorPlan's definition
2	Currency exchange rates are not tracked in GL	High	MCD	RGT	Feb 04	-	-	-

Figure 7–1 Sample Issue Log

address). The people who are resolving the issue may require additional information or details that only the issue originator can provide.

- **Assigned to.** Identify the person on the team who is responsible for resolving the issue. Note that this person does not necessarily have the answer. However, he or she is responsible for tracking down the person who can actually resolve the issue. He or she also follows up on issues that have been left unresolved.

- **Date opened.** This is the date when the issue was first logged.

- **Date closed.** This is the date when the issue was finally resolved.

- **Resolved by.** The person who resolved the issue. Note that this person must have the required authority within the organization to resolve issues. User representatives typically resolve business issues. The CIO or a designated representative typically resolves technical issues. The Project Sponsor typically resolves issues related to project scope.

- **Resolution description.** State briefly the resolution of this issue in two or three sentences. Provide a more detailed description of the resolution in a separate paragraph. If subsequent actions are required to implement the resolution, these should be stated clearly and resources should be assigned to implement them. Identify target dates for implementation.

Issue logs formalize the issue resolution process. They also serve as a formal record of key decisions made throughout the project.

In some cases, the team may opt to augment the log with yet another form—one form for each issue. This typically happens when the issue descriptions and resolution descriptions are quite long. In this case, only the brief issue statement and brief resolution descriptions are recorded in the issue log.

▶ Perform Capacity Planning

Warehouse capacity requirements come in the following forms: space required, machine processing power, network bandwidth, and number of concurrent users. These requirements increase with each rollout of the data warehouse.

During the stage of defining the warehouse strategy, the team will not have the exact information for these requirements. However, as the warehouse rollout scopes are finalized, the capacity requirements will likewise become more defined.

Review the following capacity planning requirements basing your review on the scope of each rollout.

Space Requirements. Space requirements are determined by the following:

- schema design, expected volume, and expected growth rate;
- indexing strategy used;
- backup and recovery strategy;
- aggregation strategy;
- staging and deduplication area required; and
- metadata space requirements.

Machine Processing Power. MPP (massively parallel processing) and SMP (symmetric multiprocessing) machines are the ideal hardware platform for data warehousing. Choose a configuration that is scalable and that meets the minimum processing requirements.

Network Bandwidth. The network bandwidth must not be allowed to slow down the warehouse extraction and warehouse performance. Verify all assumptions about the network bandwidth before proceeding with each rollout.

▶ Define Warehouse Purging Rules

Purging rules specify when data are to be removed from the data warehouse. Keep in mind that most companies are interested only in tracking their performance over the last three to five years. In cases where a longer retention period is required, the end users will quite likely require only high-level summaries for comparison purposes. They will not be as interested in the detailed or atomic data.

Define the mechanisms for archiving or removing older data from the data warehouse. Check for any legal, regulatory, or auditing requirements that may warrant the storage of data in other media prior to actual purging from the warehouse. Acquire the software and devices that are required for archiving.

▶ Define Security Measures

Keep the data warehouse secure to prevent the loss of competitive information either to unforeseen disasters or to unauthorized users. Define the security measures for the data warehouse, taking into consideration both physical security (i.e., where the data warehouse is physically located), as well as user-access security.

Additional precautions are required if either the warehouse data or warehouse reports are available to users through an intranet or over the public Internet infrastructure.

▶ Define Backup and Recovery Strategy

Define the backup and recovery strategy for the warehouse, taking into consideration the following factors:

- **Data to be backed up.** Identify the data that must be backed up on a regular basis. This gives an indication of the regular backup size. Aside from warehouse data and metadata, the team might also want to back up the contents of the staging or deduplication areas of the warehouse.
- **Batch window of the warehouse.** Backup mechanisms are now available to support the backup of data even when the system is online, although these are expensive. If the warehouse does not need to be online 24 hours a day, 7 days a week, determine the maximum allowable down time for the warehouse (i.e., determine its batch window). Part of that batch window is allocated to the regular warehouse load and, possibly, to report generation and other similar batch jobs. Determine the maximum time period available for regular backups and backup verification.
- **Maximum acceptable time for recovery.** In case of disasters that result in the loss of warehouse data, the backups will have to be

restored in the quickest way possible. Different backup mechanisms imply different time frames for recovery. Determine the maximum acceptable length of time for the warehouse data and metadata to be restored, quality assured, and brought online.

- **Acceptable costs for backup and recovery.** Different backup mechanisms imply different costs. The enterprise may have budgetary constraints that limit its backup and recovery options.

Also consider the following when selecting the backup mechanism:

- **Archive format.** Use a standard archiving format to eliminate potential recovery problems.
- **Automatic backup devices.** Without these, the backup media (e.g., tapes) will have to be changed by hand each time the warehouse is backed up.
- **Parallel data streams.** Commercially available backup and recovery systems now support the backup and recovery of databases through parallel streams of data into and from multiple removable storage devices. This technology is especially helpful for the large databases typically found in data warehouse implementations.
- **Incremental backups.** Some backup and recovery systems also support incremental backups to reduce the time required to back up daily. Incremental backups archive only new and updated data.
- **Offsite backups.** Remember to maintain offsite backups to prevent the loss of data due to site disasters such as fires.
- **Backup and recovery procedures.** Formally define and document the backup and recovery procedures. Perform recovery practice runs to ensure that the procedures are clearly understood.

▶ Set Up Collection of Warehouse Usage Statistics

Warehouse usage statistics are collected to provide the data warehouse designer with inputs for further refining the data warehouse design and to track general usage and acceptance of the warehouse.

Define the mechanism for collecting these statistics, and assign resources to monitor and review these regularly.

▶ In Summary

The capacity planning process and the issue tracking and resolution process are critical to the successful development and deployment of data warehouses, especially during early implementations.

The other management and support processes become increasingly important as the warehousing initiative progresses further.

Data Warehouse Planning

The data warehouse planning approach presented in this chapter describes the activities related to planning one rollout of the data warehouse. The activities discussed below build on the results of the warehouse strategy formulation described in Chapter 6.

Data warehouse planning further details the preliminary scope of one warehouse rollout by obtaining detailed user requirements for queries and reports, creating a preliminary warehouse schema design to meet the user requirements, and mapping source system fields to the warehouse schema fields. By so doing, the team gains a thorough understanding of the effort required to implement that one rollout.

A planning project typically lasts between five to eight weeks, depending on the scope of the rollout. The progress of the team varies, depending (among other things) on the participation of enterprise resource persons, the availability and quality of source system documentation, and the rate at which project issues are resolved.

Upon completion of the planning effort, the team moves into data warehouse implementation for the planned rollout. The activities for data warehouse implementation are discussed in Chapter 9.

▶ Assemble and Orient Team

Identify all parties who will be involved in the data warehouse implementation and brief them about the project. Distribute copies of the warehouse strategy as background material for the planning activity.

Define the team setup if a formal project team structure is required. Take the time and effort to orient the team members on the rollout scope, and explain the role of each member of the team. This approach allows the project team members to set realistic expectations about skill sets, project workload, and project scope.

Assign project team members to specific roles, taking care to match skill sets to role responsibilities. When all assignments have been completed, check for unavoidable training requirements due to skill-role mismatches (i.e., the team member does not possess the appropriate skill sets to properly fulfill his or her assigned role).

If required, conduct training for the team members to ensure a common understanding of data warehousing concepts. It is easier for everyone to work together if all have a common goal and an agreed approach for attaining it. Describe the schedule of the planning project to the team. Identify milestones or checkpoints along the planning project timeline. Clearly explain dependencies between the various planning tasks.

Considering the short time frame for most planning projects, conduct status meetings at least once a week with the team and with the Project Sponsor. Clearly set objectives for each week. Use the status meeting as the venue for raising and resolving issues.

▶ Conduct Decisional Requirements Analysis

Decisional Requirements Analysis is one of two activities that can be conducted in parallel during Data Warehouse Planning; the other activity being Decisional Source System Audit (described in the next section). The object of Decisional Requirements Analysis is to gain a thorough understanding of the information needs of decision-makers.

Decisional Requirements Analysis Is Working Top-Down

Decisional requirements analysis represents the top-down aspect of data warehousing. Use the warehouse strategy results as the starting point of the decisional requirements analysis; a preliminary analysis should have been conducted as part of the warehouse strategy formulation.

Review the intended scope of this warehouse rollout as documented in the warehouse strategy document. Finalize this scope by further detailing the preliminary decisional requirements analysis. It will be necessary to revisit the user representatives. The rollout scope is typically expressed in terms of the queries or reports that are to be supported by the warehouse by the end of this rollout. The Project Sponsor must review and approve the scope to ensure that management expectations are set properly.

Document any known limitations about the source systems (e.g., poor data quality, missing data items). Provide this information to source system auditors for their confirmation. Verified limitations in source system data are used as inputs to finalizing the scope of the rollout—if the data are not available, they cannot be loaded into the warehouse.

Take note that the scope strongly influences the implementation time frame for this rollout. Too large a scope will make the project unmanageable. As a general rule, limit the scope of each project or rollout so that it can be delivered in three to six months by a full-time team of 6 to 12 team members.

Conducting Warehouse Planning
without a Warehouse Strategy

It is not unusual for enterprises to go directly into warehouse planning without previously formulating a warehouse strategy. This typically happens when a group of users is clearly driving the warehouse initiative and are more than ready to participate in the initial rollout as user representatives. More often than not, these users have already taken the initiative to list and prioritize their information requirements.

In this type of situation, a number of tasks from the strategy formulation will have to be conducted as part of the planning for the first warehouse rollout. These tasks are as follows:

- **Determine organizational context.** An understanding of the organization is always helpful in any warehousing project, especially since organizational issues may completely derail the warehouse initiative.
- **Define data warehouse rollouts.** Although business users may have already predefined the scope of the first rollout, it helps the warehouse architect to know what lies ahead in subsequent rollouts.
- **Define data warehouse architecture.** Define the data warehouse architecture for the current rollout (and if possible, for subsequent rollouts).
- **Evaluate development and production environment and tools.** The strategy formulation was expected to produce a short-list of tools and computing environments for the warehouse. This evaluation will be finalized during planning by the actual selection of both environments and tools.

▶ Conduct Decisional Source System Audit

The decisional source system audit is a survey of all information systems that are current or potential sources of data for the data warehouse.

A preliminary source system audit during warehouse strategy formulation should provide a complete inventory of data sources. Identify all possible source systems for the warehouse if this information is currently unavailable.

```
• Source Systems
• External Data
BOTTOM-UP
```

Data Sources Can Be Internal or External

Data sources are primarily internal. The most obvious candidates are the operational systems that automate the day-to-day business transactions of the enterprise. Note that aside from transactional or operational processing systems, one often-used data source is the enterprise general ledger, especially if the reports or queries focus on profitability measurements.

If external data sources are also available, these may be integrated into the warehouse.

DBAs and IT Support Staff Are the Best Resource Persons

The best resource persons for a decisional source system audit of internal systems are the database administrators (DBAs), system administrators (SAs) and other IT staff who support each internal system that is a potential source of data. With their intimate knowledge of the systems, they are in the best position to gauge the suitability of each system as a warehouse data source.

These individuals are also more likely to be familiar with any data quality problems that exist in the source systems. Clearly document any known data quality problems, as these have a bearing on the data extraction and cleansing processes that the warehouse must support.

Known data quality problems also provide some indication of the magnitude of the data cleanup task.

In organizations where the production of managerial reports has already been automated (but not through an architected data warehouse), the DBAs and IT support staff can provide very valuable insight about the data that are presently collected. These staff members can also provide the team with a good idea of the business rules that are used to transform the raw data into management reports.

Conduct individual and group interviews with the IT organization to understand the data sources that are currently available. Review all available documentation on the candidate source systems. This is without doubt one of the most time-consuming and detailed tasks in data warehouse planning, especially if up-to-date documentation of the existing systems is not readily available.

As a consequence, the whole-hearted support of the IT organization greatly facilitates this entire activity.

Obtain the following documents and information if these have not yet been collected as part of the data warehouse strategy definition:

- **Enterprise IT architecture documentation.** This refers to all documentation that provides a bird's-eye view of the IT architecture of the enterprise, including but not limited to:
  - System architecture diagrams and documentation—A model of all the information systems in the enterprise and their relationships to one another.
  - Enterprise data model—A model of all data that currently stored or maintained by the enterprise. This may also indicate which systems support which data item.
  - Network architecture—A diagram showing the layout and bandwidth of the enterprise network, especially for the locations of the project team and the user representatives participating in this rollout.
- **User and technical manuals of each source system.** This refers to data models and schemas for all existing information systems that are candidate data sources. If extraction programs are used for ad hoc reporting, obtain documentation of these extraction programs as well. Obtain copies of all other available system documentation, whenever possible.

- **Database sizing.** For each source system, identify the type of database used, the typical backup size, as well as the backup format and medium. It is helpful to also know what data are actually backed up on a regular basis. This is particularly important if historical data are required in the warehouse and such data are available only in backups.

- **Batch window.** Determine the batch windows for each of the operational systems. Identify all batch jobs that are already performed during the batch window. Any data extraction jobs required to feed the data warehouse must be completed within the batch windows of each source system without affecting any of the existing batch jobs already scheduled. Under no circumstances will the team want to disrupt normal operations on the source systems.

- **Future enhancements.** What application development projects, enhancements, or acquisition plans have been defined or approved for implementation in the next 6 to 12 months, for each of the source systems? Changes to the data structure will affect the mapping of source system fields to data warehouse fields. Changes to the operational systems may also result in the availability of new data items or the loss of existing ones.

- **Data scope.** Identify the most important tables of each source system. This information is ideally available in the system documentation. However, if definitions of these tables are not documented, the DBAs are in the best position to provide that information. Also required are business descriptions or definitions of each field in each important table, for all source systems.

- **System codes and keys.** Each of the source systems no doubt uses a set of codes for the system will be implementing key generation routines as well. If these are not documented, ask the DBAs to provide a list of all valid codes and a textual description for each of the system codes that are used. If the system codes have changed over time, ask the DBAs to provide all system code definitions for the relevant time frame. All key generation routines should likewise be documented. These include rules for assigning customer numbers, product numbers, order numbers, invoice numbers, etc. Check whether the keys are reused (or recycled) for new records over the years. Reused keys may cause errors during deduplication and must therefore be thoroughly understood.

- **Extraction mechanisms.** Check if data can be extracted or read directly from the production databases. Relational databases such as Oracle or Sybase are open and should be readily accessible. Application packages with proprietary database management software, however, may present problems, especially if the data structures are not documented. Determine how changes made to the database are tracked, perhaps through an audit log. Determine also if there is a way to identify data that have been changed or updated. These are important inputs to the data extraction process.

▶ Design Logical and Physical Warehouse Schema

Design the data warehouse schema that can best meet the information requirements of this rollout. Two main schema design techniques are available:

- **Normalization.** The database schema is designed using the normalization techniques traditionally used for OLTP applications;
- **Dimensional modeling.** This technique produces denormalized, star schema designs consisting of fact and dimension tables. A variation of the dimensional star schema also exists (i.e., snowflake schema).

There are ongoing debates regarding the applicability or suitability of both these modeling techniques for data warehouse projects, although dimensional modeling has certainly been gaining popularity in recent years. Dimensional modeling has been used successfully in large data warehousing implementations across multiple industries. The popularity of this modeling technique is also evident from the number of databases and front-end tools that now support optimized performance with star schema designs (e.g., Oracle RDBMS 8, R/OLAP XL).

A discussion of dimensional modeling techniques is provided in Chapter 12.

▶ Produce Source-to-Target Field Mapping

The Source-To-Target Field Mapping documents how fields in the operational (source) systems are transformed into data warehouse fields. Under no circumstances should this mapping be left vague or open to misinterpretation, especially for financial data. The mapping allows non-team members to audit the data transformations implemented by the warehouse.

```
←——————————

BACK-END
• Extraction
• Integration
• QA
• DW Load
• Aggregates
• Metadata
```

Many-to-Many Mappings

A single field in the data warehouse may be populated by data from more than one source system. This is a natural consequence of the data warehouse's role of integrating data from multiple sources.

The classic examples are Customer Name and Product Name. Each operational system will typically have its own customer and product records. A data warehouse field called Customer Name or Product Name will therefore be populated by data from more than one system.

Conversely, a single field in the operational systems may need to be split into several fields in the warehouse. There are operational systems that still record addresses as lines of text, with field names like Address Line 1, Address Line 2, etc. These can be split into multiple address fields such as Street Name, City, Country, and Mail/Zip Code. Other examples are numeric figures or balances that have to be allocated correctly to two or more different fields.

To eliminate any confusion as to how data are transformed as the data items are moved from the source systems to the warehouse database, create a source-to-target field mapping that maps each source field in each source system to the appropriate target field in the data warehouse schema. Also, clearly document all business rules that govern how data values are integrated or split up. This is required for each field in the source-to-target field mapping.

The source-to-target field mapping is critical to the successful development and maintenance of the data warehouse. This mapping serves as the basis for the data extraction and transformation subsystems. Figure 8–1 shows an example of this mapping.

Revise the data warehouse schema on an as-needed basis if the field-to-field mapping yields missing data items in the source systems. These missing data items may prevent the warehouse from producing one or more of the requested queries or reports. Raise these types of scope issues as quickly as possible to the Project Sponsor.

		TARGET	No.	1	2	3	4	5	6	7	.
			Schema	R 1	R 1	R 1	R 1	R 1	R 1	R 1	.
SOURCE			Table	TT1	TT1	TT1	TT2	TT2	TT2	TT2	.
No.	System	Table	Fields	TF1	TF2	TF3	TF4	TF5	TF6	TF7	.
1	SS1	ST1	SF1								.
2	SS1	ST1	SF2								.
3	SS1	ST1	SF3								.
4	SS1	ST1	SF4								.
5	SS1	ST2	SF5								.
6	SS1	ST2	SF6								.
7	SS2	ST2	SF7								.
8	SS2	ST3	SF8								.
9	SS2	ST3	SF9								.
10	SS2	ST3	SF10								.

... ...

SOURCE: SS1 = Source System 1, ST 1 = Source Table 1, SF1 = Source Field 1
TARGET: R1 = Rollout 1, TT1 = Target Table 1, TF1 = Target Field 1

Figure 8–1   Sample Source-to-Target Field Mapping

Historical Data and Evolving Data Structures

If users require the loading of historical data into the data warehouse, two things must be determined quickly:

- **Changes in schema.** Determine if the schemas of all source systems have changed over the relevant time period. For example, if the retention period of the data warehouse is two years and data from the past two years have to be loaded into the warehouse, the team must check for possible changes in source system schemas over the past two years. If the schemas have changed over time, the task of extracting the data immediately becomes more complicated. Each different schema may require a different source-to-target field mapping.
- **Availability of historical data.** Determine also if historical data are available for loading into the warehouse. Backups during the relevant time period may not contain the required data items. Verify assumptions about the availability and suitability of backups for historical data loads.

These two tedious tasks will be more difficult to complete if documentation is out of date or insufficient and if none of the IT professionals in the enterprise today are familiar with the old schemas.

▶ Select Development and Production Environment and Tools

Finalize the computing environment and tool set for this rollout based on the results of the development and production environment and tools study during the data warehouse strategy definition. If an exhaustive study and selection had been performed during the strategy definition stage, this activity becomes optional.

If, on the other hand, the warehouse strategy was not formulated, the enterprise must now evaluate and select the computing environment and tools that will be purchased for the warehousing initiative. This activity may take some time, especially if the evaluation process requires extensive vendor presentations and demonstrations, as well as site visits. This activity is therefore best performed early on to allow for sufficient time to study and select the tools. Sufficient lead times are also required for the delivery (especially if importation is required) of the selected equipment and tools.

▶ Create Prototype for This Rollout

Using the short-listed or final tools and production environment, create a prototype of the data warehouse.

> **FRONT-END**
> - **OLAP Tool**
> - **Canned Reports**
> - **Canned Queries**
> ⟶

A prototype is typically created and presented for one or more of the following reasons:

- **To assist in the selection of front-end tools.** It is sometimes possible to ask warehousing vendors to present a prototype to the evaluators as part of the selection process. However, such prototypes will naturally not be very specific to the actual data and reporting requirements of the rollout.

- **To verify the correctness of the schema design.** The team is better served by creating a prototype using the logical and physical warehouse schema for this rollout. If possible, use actual data from the operational systems for the prototype queries and reports. If the user requirements (in terms of queries and reports) can be created using the schema, then the team has concretely verified the correctness of the schema design.

- **To verify the usability of the selected front-end tools.** The warehousing team can invite representatives from the user community to actually use the prototype to verify the usability of the selected front-end tools.

- **To obtain feedback from user representatives.** The prototype is often the first concrete output of the planning effort. It provides users with something tangible that they can see and touch. It allows users to experience for the first time the kind of computing environment they will have when the warehouse is up. Such an experience typically triggers a lot of feedback (both positive and negative) from users. It may even cause users to articulate previously unstated requirements. Regardless of the type of feedback, however, it is always good to hear what the users have to say as early as possible. This provides the team more time to adjust the approach or the design accordingly.

During the prototype presentation meeting, the following should be made clear to the business users who will be viewing or using the prototype:

- **Objective of the prototype meeting.** State the objectives of the meeting clearly to properly orient all participants. If the objective is to select a tool set, then the attention and focus of users should be directed accordingly.
- **Nature of data used.** If actual data from the operational systems are used with the prototype, make it clear to all business users that the data have not yet been integrated or cleansed or transformed. Users should understand that the data have not yet been quality assured. If dummy or test data are used, then this should be clearly communicated as well. Users who are concerned with the correctness of the prototype data have unfortunately sidetracked many prototype presentations.
- **Prototype scope.** If the prototype does not yet mimic all the requirements identified for this rollout, then say so. Don't wait for the users to explicitly ask whether the team has considered (or forgotten!) the requirements they had specified in earlier meetings or interviews.

▶ Create Implementation Plan for This Rollout

With the scope now fully defined and the source-to-target field mapping fully specified, it is now possible to draft an implementation plan for this rollout. Consider the following factors when creating the implementation plan:

- **Number of source systems, and their related extraction mechanisms and logistics.** The more source systems there are, the more complex the extraction and integration processes will be. Also, source systems with open computing environments present fewer complications with the extraction process than do proprietary systems.

- **Number of decisional business processes supported.** The larger the number of decisional business processes supported by this rollout, the more users there are who will want to have a say about the data warehouse contents, the definition of terms, and the business rules that must be respected.

- **Number of subject areas involved.** This is a strong indicator of the rollout size. The more subject areas there are, the more fact tables will be required. This implies more warehouse fields to map to source systems and, of course, a larger rollout scope.

- **Estimated database size.** The estimated warehouse size provides an early indication of the loading, indexing, and capacity challenges of the warehousing effort. The database size allows the team to estimate the length of time it takes to load the warehouse regularly (given the number of records and the average length of time it takes to load and index each record).

- **Availability and quality of source system documentation.** A lot of the team's time will be wasted on searching for or misunderstanding the data that are available in the source systems. The availability of good-quality documentation will significantly improve the productivity of source system auditors and technical analysts.

- **Data quality issues and their impact on the schedule.** Unfortunately, there is no direct way to estimate the impact of data quality problems on the project schedule. Any attempts to estimate the delays often produce unrealistically low figures, much to the consternation of warehouse project managers. Early knowledge and documentation of data quality issues will help the team anticipate problems. Also, data quality is very much a user responsibility that cannot be left to IT to solve. Without sufficient user support, data quality problems will continually be a thorn in the side of the warehouse team.

- **Required warehouse load rate.** A number of factors external to the warehousing team (particularly batch windows of the operational systems and the average size of each warehouse load) will affect the design and approach used by the warehouse implementation team.

- **Required warehouse availability.** The warehouse itself will also have batch windows. The maximum allowed down time for the warehouse also influences the design and approach of the warehousing team. A fully available warehouse (24 hours × 7 days) requires an architecture that is completely different from that required by a warehouse that is available only 12 hours a day, 5 days a week. These different architectural requirements naturally result in differences in cost and implementation time frame.

- **Lead time for delivery and setup of selected tools, development, and production environment.** Project schedules sometimes fail to consider the length of time required to setup the development and production environments of the warehousing project. While some warehouse implementation tasks can proceed while the computing environments and tools are on their way, significant progress cannot be made until the correct environment and tool sets are available.

- **Time frame required for IT infrastructure upgrades.** Some IT infrastructure upgrades (e.g., network upgrade or extension) may be required or assumed by the warehousing project. These dependencies should be clearly marked on the project schedule. The warehouse Project Manager must coordinate with the infrastructure Project Manager to ensure that sufficient communication exists between all concerned teams.

- **Business sponsor support and user participation.** There is no way to overemphasize the importance of Project Sponsor support and end user participation. No amount of planning by the warehouse Project Manager (and no amount of effort by the warehouse project team) can make up for the lack of participation by these two parties.

- **IT support and participation.** Similarly, the support and participation of the database administrators and system administrators will make a tremendous difference to the overall productivity of the warehousing team.

- **Required vs. existing skill sets.** The match (or mismatch) of personnel skill sets and role assignments will likewise affect the productivity of the team. If this is an early or pilot project, then training on various aspects of warehousing will most likely be required. These training sessions should be factored into the implementation schedule as well and, ideally, should take place before the actual skills are required.

▶ Warehouse Planning Tips and Caveats

The actual data warehouse planning activity will rarely be a straightforward exercise. Before conducting your planning activity, read through this section for planning tips and caveats.

Follow the Data Trail

In the absence of true decision support systems, enterprises have, over the years, been forced to find stopgap or interim solutions for producing the managerial or decisional reports that decision-makers require. Some of these solutions require only simple extraction programs that are regularly run to produce the required reports. Other solutions require a complex series of steps that combine manual data manipulation, extraction programs, conversion formulas, and spreadsheet macros.

In the absence of a data warehouse, many of the managerial reporting requirements are classified as ad hoc reports. As a result, most of these report generation programs and processes are largely undocumented and are known only by the people who actually produce the reports. This naturally leads to a lack of standards (i.e., different people may apply different formulas and rules to the same data item), and possible inconsistencies each time the process is executed. Fortunately, the warehouse project team will be in a position to introduce standards and consistent ways of manipulating data.

Following the data trail (see Figure 8–2) from the current management reports, back to their respective data sources can prove to be a very enlightening exercise for Data Warehouse Planners.

Through this exercise, the data warehouse planner will find:

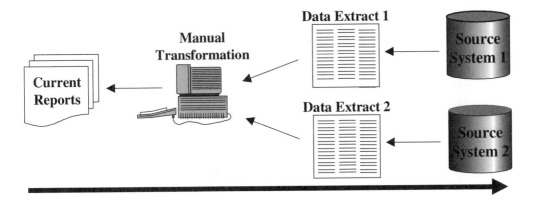

Figure 8–2   Follow the Data Trail

- **All data sources currently used for decisional reporting.** At the very least, these data sources should also be included in the decisional source system audit. The team has the added benefit of knowing beforehand which fields in these systems are considered important.
- **All current extraction programs.** The current extraction programs are a rich input for the source-to-target field mapping. Also, if these programs manipulate or transform or convert the data in any way, the transformation rules and formulas may also prove helpful to the warehousing effort.
- **All undocumented manual steps to transform the data.** After the raw data have been extracted from the operational systems, a number of manual steps may be performed to further transform the data into the reports that enterprise managers currently use. Interviews with the appropriate persons should provide the team with an understanding of these manual conversion and transformation steps (if any).

Aside from the above items, it is also likely that the data warehouse planner will find subtle flaws in the way reports are produced today. It is not unusual to find inconsistent use of business terms, formulas, and business rules, depending on the person who creates and reads the reports. This lack of standard terms and rules contributes directly to the existence of conflicting reports from different groups in the same enterprise, i.e., the existence of "different versions of the truth."

Limitations Imposed by Currently Available Data

Each data item that is required to produce the reports required by decision-makers comes from one or more of the source systems available to the enterprise. Understandably, there will be data items that are not readily supported by the source systems.

Data limitations generally fall into one of the following types.

Missing Data Items. A data item is considered missing, if no provisions were made to collect or store this data item any of the source systems. This omission particularly occurs with data items that may have no bearing on the day-to day operations of the enterprise but will have tactical or managerial implications.

For example, not all loan systems record the industry to which each loan customer belongs; from an operational level, such information may not necessarily be considered critical. Unfortunately, a bank that wishes to track its risk exposure for any given industry will not be able to produce an industry exposure report if customer industry data are not available at the source systems.

Incomplete (Optional) Data Items. A data item may be classified as "nice to have" in the operational systems, and so provisions are made to store the data, but no rules are put in place to enforce the collection of such data. These optional data items are available for some customers products, accounts, or orders but may be unavailable for others.

Returning to the above example, a loan system may have a field called Customer Industry, but the application developers may have made the field optional, in recognition of the fact that data about a customer's industry are not readily available. In cases such as this, only a partial industry exposure report can be produced, i.e., only customers with actual data can be classified meaningfully in the report.

Wrong Data. Errors occur when data are stored in one or more source systems but are not accurate. There are many potential reasons or causes for this, including the following ones:

- **Data entry error.** A genuine error is made during data entry. The wrong data are stored in the database.
- **Data item is mandatory but unavailable.** A data item may be defined as mandatory but it may not be readily available, and the random substitution of other information has no direct impact

on the day-to-day operations of the enterprise. This implies that any data can be entered without adversely affecting the operational processes.

Returning to the above example, if Customer Industry was a mandatory customer data item and the person creating the customer record does not know the industry to which the customer belongs, he is likely to select, at random, any of the industry codes that are recognized by the system. Only by so doing will he or she be able to create the customer record.

Another data item that can be randomly substituted is the social security number, especially if these numbers are stored for reference purposes only, and not for actual processing. Data entry personnel remain focused on the immediate task of creating the customer record—which the system refuses to do without all the mandatory data items. Data entry personnel are rarely in a position to see the consequences of recording the wrong data.

Improvements to Source Systems

From the above examples, it is easy to see how the scope of a data warehousing initiative can be severely compromised by data limitations in the source systems. Most pilot data warehouse projects are thus limited only to the data that are available. However, improvements can be made to the source systems in parallel with the warehousing projects. The team should therefore properly document any source system limitations that are encountered. These documents can be used as inputs to upcoming maintenance projects on the operational systems.

A decisional source system audit report may have a source system review section that covers the following topics:

- **Overview of operational systems.** This section lists all operational systems covered by the audit. A general description of the functionality and data of each operational system is provided. A list of major tables and fields may be included as an appendix. Current users of each of the operational systems are optionally documented.

- **Missing data items.** List all the data items that are required by the data warehouse but are currently not available in the source systems. Explain why each item is important (e.g., cite reports or queries where these data items are required). For each data item, identify the source system where the data item is best stored.
- **Data quality improvement areas.** For each operational system, list all areas where the data quality can be improved. Suggestions as to how the data quality improvement can be achieved can also be provided.
- **Resource and effort estimate.** For each operational system, it might be possible to provide an estimate or the cost and length of time required to either add the data item or improve the data quality for that data item.

▶ In Summary

Data warehouse planning is conducted to clearly define the scope of one data warehouse rollout. The combination of the top-down and

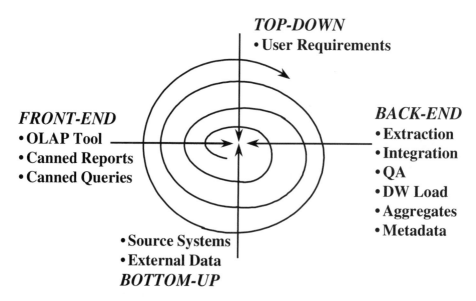

Figure 8–3   The Four Tracks in Warehouse Development

bottom-up tracks gives the planning process the best of both worlds—a requirements-driven approach that is grounded on available data.

The clear separation of the front-end and back-end tracks encourages the development of warehouse subsystems for extracting, transporting, cleaning, and loading warehouse data independently of the front-end tools that will be used to access the warehouse.

The four tracks converge when a prototype of the warehouse is created and when actual warehouse implementation takes place.

Each rollout repeatedly executes the four tracks (top-down, bottom-up, back-end and front-end), and the scope of the data warehouse is iteratively extended as a result. Figure 8–3 illustrates the concept.

Data Warehouse Implementation

The data warehouse implementation approach presented in this chapter describes the activities related to implementing one rollout of the data warehouse. The activities discussed here build on the results of the data warehouse planning described in the previous chapter.

The data warehouse implementation team builds or extends an existing warehouse schema based on the final logical schema design produced during planning. The team also builds the warehouse subsystems that ensure a steady, regular flow of clean data from the operational systems into the data warehouse. Other team members install and configure the selected front-end tools to provide users with access to warehouse data.

An implementation project should be scoped to last between three to six months. The progress of the team varies, depending (among other things) on the quality of the warehouse design, the quality of the implementation plan, the availability and participation of enterprise resource persons, and the rate at which project issues are resolved.

User training and warehouse testing activities take place toward the end of the implementation project, just prior to the deployment to users. Once the warehouse has been deployed, the day-to-day warehouse management, maintenance, and optimization tasks begin. Some members of the implementation team may be asked to stay on and assist with the maintenance activities to ensure continuity. The other members of the project team may be asked to start planning the next warehouse rollout or may be released to work on other projects.

▶ Acquire and Set Up Development Environment

Acquire and set up the development environment for the data warehouse implementation project. This activity includes the following tasks, among others: install the hardware, the operating system, the relational database engine; install all warehousing tools; create all necessary network connections; and create all required user IDs and user access definitions.

Note that most data warehouses reside on a machine that is physically separate from the operational systems. In addition, the relational database management system used for data warehousing need not be the same database management system used by the operational systems.

At the end of this task, the development environment is set up, the project team members are trained on the (new) development environment, and all technology components have been purchased and installed.

▶ Obtain Copies of Operational Tables

There may be instances where the team has no direct access to the operational source systems from the warehouse development environment. This is especially possible for pilot projects, where the network connection to the warehouse development environment may not yet be available.

Regardless of the reason for the lack of access, the warehousing team must establish and document a consistent, reliable, and easy-to-follow procedure for obtaining copies of the relevant tables from the operational systems. Copies of these tables are made available to the warehousing team on another medium (most likely tape) and are restored on the warehouse server. The creation of copies can also be automated through the use of replication technology.

The warehousing team must have a mechanism for verifying the correctness and completeness of the data that are loaded onto the warehouse server. One of the most effective completeness checks is meaningful business counts (e.g., number of customers, number of accounts, number of transactions) that are computed and compared to ensure data completeness. Data quality utilities can help assess the correctness of the data.

The use of copied tables as described above implies additional space requirements on the warehouse server. This should not be a problem during the pilot project.

Finalize Physical Warehouse Schema Design

Translate the detailed logical and physical warehouse design from the warehouse planning stage into a final physical warehouse design, taking into consideration the specific, selected database management system.

The key considerations are:

- **Schema design.** Finalize the physical design of the fact and dimension tables and their respective fields. The warehouse database administrator (DBA) may opt to divide one logical dimension (e.g., customer) into two or more separate ones (e.g., a customer dimension and a customer demographic dimension) to save on space and improve query performance.
- **Indexes.** Identify the appropriate indexing method to use on the warehouse tables and fields, based on the expected data volume and the anticipated nature of warehouse queries. Verify initial assumptions made about the space required by indexes to ensure that sufficient space has been allocated.
- **Partitioning.** The warehouse DBA may opt to partition fact and dimension tables, depending on their size and on the partitioning features that are supported by the database engine. The warehouse DBA who decides to implement partitioned views must consider the trade-offs between degradation in query per-

formance and improvements in warehouse manageability and space requirements.

▶ Build or Configure Extraction and Transformation Subsystems

Easily 60 percent to 80 percent of a warehouse implementation project is devoted to the back-end of the warehouse. The back-end subsystems must extract, transform, clean, and load the operational data into the data warehouse. Understandably, the back-end subsystems vary significantly from one enterprise to another due to differences in the computing environments, source systems, and business requirements. For this reason, much of the warehousing effort cannot simply be automated away by warehousing tools.

Extraction Subsystem

The first among the many subsystems on the back-end of the warehouse is the data extraction subsystem. The term *extraction* refers to the process of retrieving the required data from the operational system tables, which may be the actual tables or simply copies that have been loaded into the warehouse server.

Actual extraction can be achieved through a wide variety of mechanisms, ranging from sophisticated third-party tools to custom-written extraction scripts or programs developed by in-house IT staff. Third-party extraction tools are typically able to connect to mainframe, midrange and UNIX environments; thus freeing their users from the nightmare of handling heterogeneous data sources. These tools also allow users to document the extraction process (i.e., they have provisions for storing metadata about the extraction).

These tools, unfortunately, are quite expensive. For this reason, organizations may also turn to writing their own extraction programs. This is a particularly viable alternative if the source systems are on a uniform or homogenous computing environment (e.g., all data reside on the same RDBMS, and they make use of the same operating system). Custom-written extraction programs, however, may be difficult to maintain, especially if these programs are not well documented. Considering how quickly business requirements will change in the warehousing environment, ease of maintenance is an important factor to consider.

Transformation Subsystem

The transformation subsystem literally transforms the data in accordance with the business rules and standards that have been established for the data warehouse.

Several types of transformations are typically implemented in data warehousing.

- **Format changes.** Each of the data fields in the operational systems may store data in different formats and data types. These individual data items are modified during the transformation process to respect a standard set of formats. For example, all date formats may be changed to respect a standard format, or a standard data type is used for character fields such as names, addresses.
- **Deduplication.** Records from multiple sources are compared to identify duplicate records based on matching field values. Duplicates are merged to create a single record of a customer, a product, an employee, or a transaction. Potential duplicates are logged as exceptions that are manually resolved. Duplicate records with conflicting data values are also logged for manual correction if there is no system of record to provide the "master" or "correct" value.
- **Splitting up fields.** A data item in the source system may need to be split up into one or more fields in the warehouse. One of the most commonly encountered problems of this nature deals with customer addresses that have simply been stored as several lines of text. These textual values may be split up into distinct fields: street number, street name, building name, city, mail or zip code, country, etc.

- **Integrating fields.** The opposite of splitting up fields is integration. Two or more fields in the operational systems may be integrated to populate one warehouse field.

- **Replacement of values.** Values that are used in operational systems may not be comprehensible to warehouse users. For example, system codes that have specific meanings in operational systems are meaningless to decision-makers. The transformation subsystem replaces the original with new values that have a business meaning to warehouse users.

- **Derived values.** Balances, ratios, and other derived values can be computed using agreed formulas. By precomputing and loading these values into the warehouse, the possibility of miscomputation by individual users is reduced. A typical example of a precomputed value is the average daily balance of bank accounts. This figure is computed using the base data and is loaded as-is into the warehouse.

- **Aggregates.** Aggregates can also be precomputed for loading into the warehouse. This is an alternative to loading only atomic (base-level) data in the warehouse and creating in the warehouse the aggregates records based on the atomic warehouse data.

The extraction and transformation subsystems (see Figure 9–1) create load images, i.e., tables and fields populated with the data that are to be loaded into the warehouse. The load images are typically stored in tables that have the same schema as the warehouse itself. By so doing, the extraction and transformation subsystems greatly simplify the load process.

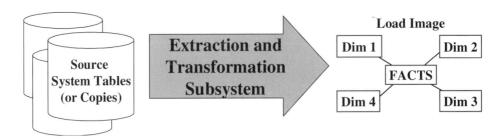

Figure 9–1   Extraction and Transformation Subsystems

▶ Build or Configure Data Quality Subsystem

Data quality problems are not always apparent at the start of the implementation project, when the team is concerned more about moving massive amounts of data rather than the actual individual data values that are being moved. However, data quality (or to be more precise, the lack of it) will quickly become a major, show-stopping problem if it is not addressed directly.

One of the quickest ways to inhibit user acceptance is to have poor data quality in the warehouse. Furthermore, the *perception* of data quality is in some ways just as important as the actual quality of the data warehouse. Data warehouse users will make use of the warehouse only if they believe that the information they will retrieve from it is correct. Without user confidence in the data quality, a warehouse initiative will soon lose support and eventually die off.

A data quality subsystem on the back-end of the warehouse therefore is a critical component of the overall warehouse architecture.

Causes of Data Errors

An understanding of the causes of data errors makes these errors easier to find. Since most data errors originate from the source systems, source system database administrators and system administrators, with their day-to-day experiences working with the source systems, are very critical to the data quality effort.

Data errors typically result from one or more of the following causes.

- **Missing values.** Values are missing in the source systems due either to incomplete records or optional data fields.
- **Lack of referential integrity.** Referential integrity in source systems may not be enforced because of inconsistent system codes or codes whose meanings have changed over time.
- **Errors in precomputed data.** Some of the data in the warehouse can be precomputed prior to warehouse loading as part of the transformation process. If the computations or formulas are wrong, then erroneous data will be loaded into the warehouse.
- **Different units of measure.** The use of different currencies and units of measure in different source systems may lead to data er-

rors in the warehouse if figures or amounts are not first converted to a uniform currency or unit of measure prior to further computations or data transformation.

- **Duplicates.** Deduplication is performed on source system data prior to the warehouse load. However, the deduplication process depends on comparisons of data values to find matches. If the data were not available to start with, the quality of the deduplication may be compromised. Duplicate records may therefore be loaded into the warehouse.

- **Fields to be split up.** As mentioned earlier, there are times when a single field in the source system has to be split up to populate multiple warehouse fields. Unfortunately, it is not possible to manually split up the fields one at a time because of the volume of the data. The team often resorts to some automated form of field-splitting, which may not be 100 percent correct.

- **Multiple hierarchies.** Many warehouse dimensions will have multiple hierarchies for analysis purposes. For example, the time dimension typically has a *day-month-quarter-year* hierarchy. This same time dimension may also have a *day-week* hierarchy and a *day-fiscal month-fiscal quarter-fiscal year* hierarchy. Lack of understanding of these multiple hierarchies in the different dimensions may result in erroneous warehouse loads.

- **Conflicting or inconsistent terms and rules.** The conflicting or inconsistent use of business terms and business rules may mislead warehouse planners into loading two distinctly different data items into the same warehouse field, or vice versa. Inconsistent business rules may also cause the misuse of formulas during data transformation.

Data Quality Improvement Approach

Below is an approach for improving the overall data quality of the enterprise.

- **Assess current level of data quality.** Determine the current data quality level of each of the warehouse source systems. While the enterprise may have a data quality initiative that is independent of the warehousing project, it is best to focus the data quality efforts on warehouse source systems—these systems obviously contain data that are of interest to enterprise decision-makers.

- **Identify key data items.** Set the priorities of the data quality team by identifying the key data items in each of the warehouse source systems. Key data items, by definition, are the data items that must achieve and maintain a high level of data quality. By prioritizing data items in this manner, the team can target its efforts on the more critical data areas and therefore provides greater value to the enterprise.

- **Define cleansing tactics for key data items.** For each key data item with poor data quality, define an approach or tactic for cleaning or raising the quality of that data item. Whenever possible, the cleansing approach should target the source systems first, so that errors are corrected at the source and not propagated to other systems.

- **Define error-prevention tactics for key data items.** The enterprise should not stop at error-correction activities. The best way to eliminate data errors is to prevent them from happening in the first place. If error-producing operational processes are not corrected, they will continue to populate enterprise databases with erroneous data. Operational and data-entry staff must be made aware of the cost of poor data quality. Reward mechanisms within the organization may have to be modified to create a working environment that focuses on preventing data errors at the source.

- **Implement quality improvement and error-prevention processes.** Obtain the resources and tools to execute the quality improvement and error-prevention processes. After some time, another assessment may be conducted, and a new set of key data items may be targeted for quality improvement.

Data Quality Assessment and Improvements

Data quality assessments can be conducted at any time at different points along the warehouse back-end. As shown in Figure 9–2, assessments can be conducted on the data while it is in the source systems, in warehouse load images or in the data warehouse itself.

Note that while data quality products assist in the assessment and improvement of data quality, it is unrealistic to expect any single pro-

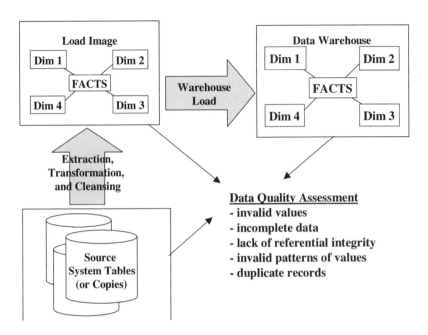

Figure 9–2   Data Quality Assessments at the Warehouse Back-End

gram or data quality product to find and correct all data quality errors in the operational systems or in the data warehouse. Nor is it realistic to expect data quality improvements to be completed in a matter of months. It is unlikely that an enterprise will ever bring its databases to a state that is 100 percent error free.

Despite the long-term nature of the effort, however, the absolute worst thing that any warehouse Project Manager can do is to ignore the data quality problem in the vain hope that it will disappear. The enterprise must be willing and prepared to devote time and effort to the tedious task of cleaning up data errors rather than sweeping the problem under the rug.

Correcting Data Errors at the Source

All data errors found are, under ideal circumstances, corrected at the source, i.e., the operational system database is updated with the correct values. This practice ensures that subsequent data users at both the operational and decisional levels will benefit from clean data.

Experience has shown, however, that correcting data at the source may prove difficult to implement for the following reasons:

- **Operational responsibility.** The responsibility for updating the source system data will naturally fall into the hands of operational staff, who may not be so inclined to accept the additional responsibility of tracking down and correcting past data-entry errors.
- **Correct data are unknown.** Even if the people in operations know that the data in a given record are wrong, there may be no easy way to determine the correct data. This is particularly true of customer data (e.g., a customer's social security number). The people in operations have no other recourse but to approach the customers one at a time to obtain the correct data. This is tedious, time-consuming, and potentially irritating to customers.

Other Considerations

Many of the available warehousing tools have features that automate different areas of the warehouse extraction, transformation, and data quality subsystems.

The more data sources there are, the higher the likelihood of data quality problems. Likewise, the larger the data volume, the higher the number of data errors to correct.

The inclusion of historical data in the warehouse will also present problems due to changes (over time) in system codes, data structures, and business rules.

▶ Build Warehouse Load Subsystem

The warehouse load subsystem takes the load images created by the extraction and transformation subsystems and loads these images directly into the data warehouse. As mentioned earlier, the data to be loaded are stored in tables that have the same schema design as the warehouse itself. The load process is therefore fairly straightforward from a data standpoint.

Basic Features of a Load Subsystem

The load subsystem should be able to perform the following:

- **Drop indexes on the warehouse.** When new records are inserted into an indexed table, the relational database management system immediately updates the index of the table in response. In the context of a data warehouse load, where up to hundreds of thousands of records are inserted in rapid succession into one single table, the immediate re-indexing of the table after each insert results in a significant processing overhead. As a consequence, the load process slows down dramatically. To avoid this problem, drop the indexes on the relevant warehouse tables prior to each load.

- **Load dimension records.** In the source systems, each record of a customer, product, or transaction is uniquely identified through a key. Likewise, the customers, products, and transactions in the warehouse must be identifiable through a key value. Source system keys are often inappropriate as warehouse keys, and a key generation approach is therefore used during the load process. Insert new dimension records, or update existing records based on the load images.

- **Load fact records.** The primary key of a Fact table is the concatenation of the keys of its related dimension records. Each fact record therefore makes use of the generated keys of the dimension records. Dimension records are loaded prior to the fact records to allow the enforcement of referential integrity checks. The load subsystem therefore inserts new fact records or updates old records based on the load images. Since the data warehouse is essentially a time series, most of the records in the Fact table will be new records.

- **Compute aggregate records, using base fact and dimension records.** After the successful load of atomic or base-level data into the warehouse, the load subsystem may now compute aggregate records by using the base-level fact and dimension records. This step is performed only if the aggregates are not precomputed for direct loading into the warehouse.

- **Rebuild or regenerate indexes.** Once all loads have been completed, the indexes on the relevant tables are rebuilt or regenerated to improve query performance.

- **Log load perceptions.** Log all referential integrity violations during the load process as load exceptions. There are two types of referential integrity violations: (a) missing key values—one of the key fields of the fact record does not have a value; and (b) wrong key values—the key fields have values, but one or more of them do not have a corresponding dimension record. In both cases, the warehousing team has the option of (a) not loading the record until the correct key values are found or (b) loading the record, but replacing the missing or wrong key values with hard-coded values that users can recognize as a load exception.

The load subsystem, as described above, assumes that the load images do not yet make use of warehouse keys; i.e., the load images contain only source system keys. The warehouse keys are therefore generated as part of the load process.

Warehousing teams may opt to separate the key generation routines from the load process. In this scenario, the key generation routine is applied on the initial load images (i.e., the load images created by the extraction and transformation subsystems). The final load images (with warehouse keys) are then loaded into the warehouse.

Loading Dirty Data

There are ongoing debates about loading dirty data (i.e., data that fail referential integrity checks) into the warehouse. Some teams prefer to load only clean data into the warehouse, arguing that dirty data can mislead and misinform. Others prefer to load all data, both clean and dirty, provided that the dirty data are clearly marked as dirty.

Depending on the extent of data errors, the use of only clean data in the warehouse can be equally or more dangerous than relying on a mix of clean and dirty data. If more than 20 percent of data are dirty and only 80 percent are loaded into the warehouse, the warehouse users will be making decisions based on an incomplete picture.

The use of hard-coded values to identify warehouse data with referential integrity violations on one dimension allows warehouse users to still make use of the warehouse data on clean dimensions.

Consider the example in Figure 9–3. If a Sales Fact record is dependent on Customer, Date (Time dimension) and Product and if the Customer

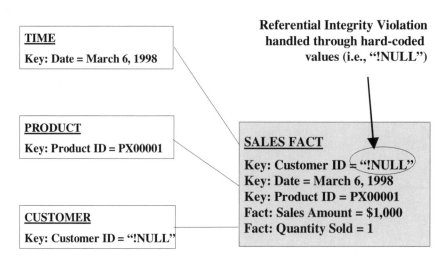

Figure 9–3   Loading Dirty Data

key is missing, then a "Sales per Product" report from the warehouse will still produce the correct information.

When a "Sales per Customer" report is produced (as shown in Figure 9–4), the hard-coded value that signifies a referential integrity violation will be listed as a Customer ID, and the user is aware that the corresponding sales amount cannot be attributed to a valid customer.

By handling referential integrity violations during warehouse loads in the manner described above, the users get a full picture of the facts on

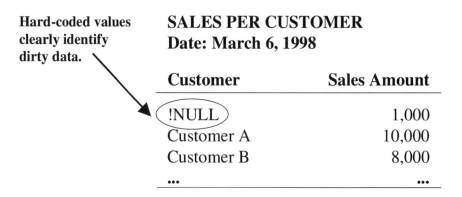

Figure 9–4   Sample Report with Dirty Data Identified Through Hard-coded Values

clean dimensions and are clearly aware when dirty dimensions are used.

The Need for Load Optimization

The time required for a regular warehouse load is often of great concern to warehouse designers and project managers. Unless the warehouse was designed and architected to be fully available 24 hours a day, the warehouse will be offline and unavailable to its users during the load period.

Much of the challenge in building the load subsystem therefore lies in optimizing the load process to reduce the total time required. For this reason, parallel load features in later releases of relational database management systems and parallel processing capabilities in SMP and MPP machines are especially welcome in data warehousing implementations.

Test Loads

The team may want to test the accuracy and performance of the warehouse load subsystem on dummy data before attempting a real load with actual load images. The team should know as early as possible how much load optimization work is still required.

Also, by using dummy data, the warehousing team does not have to wait for the completion of the extraction and transformation subsystems to start testing the warehouse load subsystem.

Warehouse load subsystem testing, of course, is possible only if the data warehouse schema is already up and available.

▶ Set Up Data Warehouse Schema

Create the data warehouse schema in the development environment while the team is constructing or configuring the warehouse back-end subsystems (i.e., the data extraction and transformation subsystems, the data quality subsystem, and the warehouse load subsystem).

As part of the schema setup, the warehouse DBA must do the following:

- **Create warehouse tables.** Implement the physical warehouse database design by creating all base-level fact and dimension tables, core and custom tables, and aggregate tables.
- **Build Indexes.** Build the required indexes on the tables according to the physical warehouse database design.
- **Populate special referential tables and records.** The data warehouse may require special referential tables or records that are not created through regular warehouse loads. For example, if the warehouse team will use hard-coded values to handle loads with referential integrity violations, the warehouse dimension tables must have records that use the appropriate hard-coded value to identify fact records that have referential integrity violations.

It is usually helpful to populate the data warehouse with test data as soon as possible. This provides the front-end team with the opportunity to test the data access and retrieval tools, even while actual warehouse data are not yet available.

Figure 9–5 presents a typical data warehouse schema.

▶ Set Up Data Warehouse Metadata

Metadata have traditionally been defined as "data about data." While such a statement does not seem very helpful, it is actually quite appropriate as a definition—metadata describe the contents of the data warehouse, indicate where the warehouse data originally came from, and document the business rules that govern the transformation of the data.

Warehousing tools also use metadata as the basis for automating certain aspects of the warehousing project.

Chapter 13 in the **Technology** section of this book discusses metadata in depth.

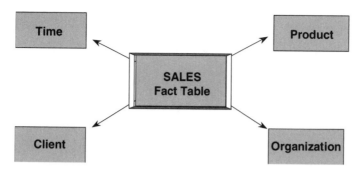

Figure 9–5   Sample Warehouse Schema

▶ Set Up Data Access and Retrieval Tools

The data access and retrieval tools are equivalent to the tip of the warehousing iceberg. While they may represent as little as 10 percent of the entire warehousing effort, they are all that users see of the warehouse. As a result, these tools are critical to the acceptance and usability of the warehouse.

Acquire and Install Data Access and Retrieval Tools

Acquire and install the selected data access tools in the appropriate environments and machines. The front-end team will find it prudent to first install the selected data access tools on a test machine that has access to the warehouse. The test machine should be loaded with the software typically used by the enterprise. Through this activity, the front-end team may identify unforeseen conflicts between the various software programs without inconveniencing anyone.

Verify that the data access and retrieval tools can establish and hold connections to the data warehouse over the corporate network.

In the absence of actual warehouse data, the team may opt to use test data in the data warehouse schema to test the installation of front-end tools.

Build Predefined Reports and Queries

The prototype initially developed during warehouse planning is refined by incorporating user feedback and by building all predefined reports and queries that have been agreed on with the end-users.

Different front-end tools have different requirements for the efficient distribution of predefined reports and queries to all users. The front-end team should therefore perform the appropriate administration tasks as required by the selected front-end tools.

By building these predefined reports and queries, the data warehouse implementation team is assured that the warehouse schema meets the decisional information requirements of the users.

Support staff who will eventually man the warehouse Help Desk should participate in this activity, since this participation provides excellent learning opportunities.

Set Up Role or Group Profiles

Define role or group profiles on the database management system. The major database management systems provide the use of a role or a group to define the access rights of multiple users through one role definition.

The warehousing team must determine the appropriate role definitions for the warehouse. The following roles are recommended as a minimum:

- **Warehouse user.** The typical warehouse user is granted *Select* rights on the production warehouse tables. Updates are not allowed.
- **Warehouse administrator.** This role is assigned to users strictly for the direct update of data warehouse dimension records. *Select* and *Update* rights are granted on the warehouse dimension records.
- **Warehouse developer.** This role applies to any warehouse implementation team member who works on the back-end of the warehouse. Users with this role can create development warehouse objects but cannot modify or update the structure and content of production warehouse tables.

Chapter **9** I Data Warehouse Implementation

Set Up User Profiles and Map These to Role Profiles

Define user profiles for each warehouse user and assign one or more roles to each user profile to grant the user access to the warehouse. While it is possible for multiple users to use the same user profile, this practice is greatly discouraged for the following reasons:

- **Collection of warehouse statistics.** Warehouse statistics are collected as part of the warehouse maintenance activities. The team will benefit from knowing (a) how many users have access to the warehouse, (b) which users are actually making use of the warehouse, and (c) how often a particular user makes use of the warehouse.
- **Warehouse security.** The warehousing team must be able to track the use of the warehouse to a specific individual, not just to a group of individuals. Users may also be less careful with IDs and passwords if they know these are shared. Unique user IDs are also required should the warehouse start restricting or granting access based on record values in warehouse tables (e.g., a branch manager can see only the records related to his or her branch).
- **Audit trail.** If one or more users have *Update* access to the warehouse, distinct user IDs will allow the warehouse team to track down the warehouse user responsible for each update.
- **Query performance complaints.** In cases where a query on the warehouse server is slow or has stalled, the warehouse administrator will be better able to identify the slow or stalled query when each user has a distinct user ID.

▶ Perform the Production Warehouse Load

The production data warehouse load can be performed only when the load images are ready and both the warehouse schema and metadata are set up.

Prior to the actual production warehouse load, it is good practice to conduct partial loads to get some indication of the total load time. Also, since the data warehouse schema design may require refinement, particularly when the front-end tools are first set up, it will be easier and quicker to make changes to the data warehouse schema when very little data have been loaded. Only when the end users have had a chance to provide positive feedback should large volumes of data be loaded into the warehouse.

Data warehouses are not refreshed more than once every 24 hours. If the user requirements call for up-to-the-minute information for operational monitoring purposes, then a data warehouse is not the solution; these requirements should be addressed through an Operational Data Store.

The warehouse is typically available to end users during the working day. For this reason, warehouse loads typically take place at night or over a weekend.

If the retention period of the warehouse is several years, the warehouse team should first load the data for the current time period and verify the correctness of the load. Only when the load is successful should the team start loading historical data into the warehouse. Due to potential changes to the schemas of the source systems over the past few years, it is natural for the warehouse team to start from the most current period and work in reverse chronological order when loading historical data.

▶ Conduct User Training

The IT organization is encouraged to fully take over the responsibility of conducting user training, contrary to the popular practice of having product vendors or warehouse consultants handle this activity. Instead, the IT organization should ask product vendors or consultants to assist in the preparation of the first warehousing classes. Doing so will enable the warehousing team to conduct future training courses independently.

Scope of User Training

Conduct training for all intended users of this rollout of the data warehouse. Prepare training materials if required. The training should cover the following topics:

- **What is a warehouse?** Different people have different expectations of what a data warehouse is. Start the training with a warehouse definition.
- **Warehouse scope.** All users must know the contents of the warehouse. The training should therefore clearly state what is not supported by the current warehouse rollout. Trainers might need to know what functionality has been deferred to later phases, and why.
- **Use of front-end tools.** The users should learn how to use the front-end tools. Highly usable front-ends should require fairly little training. Distribute all relevant user documentation to training participants.
- **Load timing and publication.** Users should be informed of the schedule for warehouse loads (e.g., "the warehouse is loaded with sales data on a weekly basis, and a special month-end load is performed for the GL expense data"). Users should also know how the warehouse team intends to publish the results of each warehouse load.
- **Warehouse support structure.** Users should know how to get additional help from the warehousing team. Distribute Help Desk phone numbers, etc.

Who Should Attend the Training?

Training should be conducted for all intended end users of the data warehouse. Some senior managers, particularly those who do not use computers every day, may ask their assistants or secretaries to attend the training in their place. In this scenario, the senior manager should be requested to attend at least the portion of the training that deals with the warehouse scope.

Different Users Have Different Training Needs

An understanding of the users' computing literacy provides insight to the type and pace of training required. If the user base is large enough, it may be helpful to divide the trainees into two groups—a basic class and an advanced class. Power users will otherwise quickly become bored in a basic class, and beginners will feel overwhelmed if they are in an advanced class. Attempting to meet the training needs of both types of users in one class may prove to be difficult and frustrating.

At the end of the training, it is good practice to identify training participants who will most likely require post-training followup and support from the warehouse implementation team. Also ask participants to evaluate the warehouse training; constructive criticism will allow the trainers to deliver better training in the future.

Training as a Prerequisite to Testing

A subset of the users will be requested to test the warehouse. This user subset may have to undergo user training earlier than others, since user training is a prerequisite to user testing. Users cannot adequately test the warehouse if they do not know what is in it or how to use it.

▶ Conduct User Testing and Acceptance

The data warehouse, like any system, must undergo user testing and acceptance. Some considerations are discussed below.

Conduct Warehouse Trials

Representatives of the end-user community are requested to test this warehouse rollout. In general, the following aspects should be tested:

- **Support of specified queries and reports.** Users test the correctness of the queries and reports of this warehouse rollout. In many cases, this is achieved by preparing the same report manually (or through existing mechanisms) and comparing this report to the one produced by the warehouse. All discrepancies are accounted for, and the appropriate corrections are made. The team should not discount the possibility that the errors are in the manually prepared report.

- **Performance/response time.** Under the most ideal circumstances, each warehouse query will be executed in less than one or two seconds. However, this may not be realistically achievable, depending on the warehouse size (number of rows and dimensions) and the selected tools. Warehouse optimization at the hardware and database levels can be used to improve response times. The use of stored aggregates will likewise improve warehouse performance.
- **Usability of client front-end.** Training on the front-end tools is required, but the tools must be usable for the majority of the users.
- **Ability to meet report frequency requirements.** The warehouse must be able to provide the specified queries and reports at the frequency (i.e., daily, weekly, monthly, quarterly, or yearly) required by the users.

Acceptance

The rollout is considered accepted when the testing for this rollout is completed to the satisfaction of the user community. A concrete set of acceptance criteria can be developed at the start of the warehouse rollout for use later as the basis for acceptance. The acceptance criteria are helpful to users because they know exactly what to test. It is likewise helpful to the warehousing team because they know what must be delivered.

▶ In Summary

Data warehouse implementation is without question the most challenging part of data warehousing. Not only will the team have to resolve the technical difficulties of moving, integrating, and cleaning data, they will also face the more difficult task of addressing policy issues, resolving organizational conflicts, and untangling logistical delays.

In general, the following areas present the most problems during warehouse implementation and bear the most watching:

- **Dirty data.** The identification and cleanup of dirty data can easily consume more resources than the project can afford.
- **Underestimated logistics.** The logistics involved in warehousing typically require more time than originally expected. Tasks such as installing the development environment, collecting source data, transporting data, and loading data are generally beleaguered by logistical problems. The time required to learn and configure warehousing tools likewise contributes to delays.
- **Policies and political issues.** The progress of the team can slow to a crawl if a key project issue remains unresolved too long.
- **Wrong warehouse design.** The wrong warehouse design results in unmet user requirements or inflexible implementations. It also creates rework for the schema as well as all the back-end subsystems: extraction and transformation, quality assurance, and loading.

At the end of the project, however, a successful team has the satisfaction of meeting the information needs of key decision-makers in a manner that is unprecedented in the enterprise.

Part 4

Technology

A quick browse through the **Process** section of this book makes it quite clear that a data warehouse project requires a wide array of technologies and tools. The data warehousing products market (particularly the software segment) is a rapidly growing one; new vendors continuously announce the availability of new products, while existing vendors add warehousing-specific features to their existing product lines.

Understandably, the gamut of tools makes tool selection quite confusing. This section of the book aims to lend order to the warehousing tools market by classifying these tools and technologies. The two main categories, understandably, are:

- **Hardware and operating systems.** These refer primarily to the warehouse servers and their related operating systems. Key issues include database size, storage options, and backup and recovery technology.
- **Software.** This refers primarily to the tools that are used to extract, clean, integrate, populate, store, access, distribute, and present warehouse data. Also included in this category are metadata repositories that document the data warehouse. The major database vendors have all jumped on the data warehousing bandwagon and have introduced, or are planning to introduce, features that allow their database products to better support data warehouse implementations.

In addition, this section of the book focuses on two key technology issues in data warehousing:

- **Warehouse schema design.** We present an overview of the dimensional modeling techniques, as popularized by Ralph Kimball, to produce database designs that are particularly suited for warehousing implementations.
- **Warehouse metadata.** We provide a quick look at warehouse metadata—what it is, what it should encompass, and why it is critical in data warehousing.

Hardware and Operating Systems

The term *hardware and operating systems* refers to the server platforms and operating systems that serve as the computing environment of the data warehouse. Warehousing environments are typically separate from the operational computing environments (i.e., a different machine is used) to avoid potential resource contentions between operational and decisional processing. Enterprises are correctly wary of computing solutions that may compromise the performance levels of mission-critical operational systems.

The major hardware vendors have all established data warehousing initiatives or partnership programs with other firms in a bid to provide comprehensive data warehousing solution frameworks to their customers. This is very consistent with the solution integrator role that major hardware vendors typically play on large computing projects.

▶ Parallel Hardware Technology

As we mentioned, the two primary categories of parallel hardware used for data warehousing are the symmetric multiprocessing (SMP) machines and massively parallel processing (MPP) machines. Figure 10–1 illustrates the architecture of these two machines.

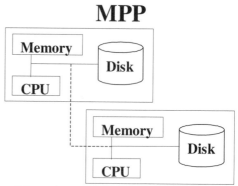

SMP

MPP

- One Node
- Many Processors per Node
- Scale Up by Adding CPUs
  or by Clustering

- Many Nodes
- One / More Processors per Node
- Each Node Has its Own Memory
- Scale Up by Adding A Node

Figure 10–1   SMP vs. MPP Hardware Configuration

SMPs have multiple CPUs that share a common memory and input/output. Known also as a "Shared Everything" architecture, this machine is limited by the scalability and performance limits of the bus that connects its various components. Such architectures scale up by adding more CPUs, upgrading existing ones, or by clustering together several SMP machines.

MPPs in contrast, allow multiple, independent CPUs, connected to each other by a high-speed network. Each CPU has its own copy of the operating system and can essentially function as an independent processor. MPP architectures scale up by adding nodes or CPUs. Unfortunately, not all applications can take advantage of the parallel architecture of MPPs; applications that have been designed to work on only one processor will fail to take advantage of parallel processing on multiple processors.

▶ Hardware Selection Criteria

The following selection criteria are recommended for hardware selection.

Chapter **10** | Hardware and Operating System

- **Scalability.** The warehouse solution is able to scale up in terms of space and processing power. This is particularly important if the warehouse is projected to grow at a rapid rate.
- **Financial stability.** The product vendor has proven to be a strong and visible player in the hardware segment, and its financial performance indicates growth or stability.
- **Price/performance.** The product performs well in a price/performance comparison with other vendors of similar products.
- **Delivery lead time.** The product vendor can deliver the hardware or an equivalent service unit within the required time frame. If the unit is not readily available within the same country, there may be delays due to importation logistics.
- **Reference sites.** The hardware vendor has a reference site that is using a similar unit for the same purpose. The warehousing team can either arrange a site visit or interview representatives from the site visit. Alternatively, an onsite test of the unit can be conducted, especially if no reference is available.
- **Availability of support.** Support for the hardware and its operating system is available, and support response times are within the acceptable down time for the warehouse.

Examples of hardware and operating system platforms are provided below for reference purposes only and are by no means an attempt to provide a complete list of companies with warehousing platforms.

The tools are listed in alphabetical order by company name; the sequence does not imply any form of ranking.

- **Digital.** 64-bit AlphaServers and Digital Unix or Open VMS. Both SMP and MPP configurations are available.
- **HP.** HP 9000 Enterprise Parallel Server.
- **IBM.** RS6000 and the AIX operating system have been positioned for data warehousing. The AS/400 has been used for data mart implementations.
- **Microsoft.** The Windows NT operating system has been positioned quite successfully for data mart deployments.
- **Sequent.** Sequent NUMA-Q and the DYNIX operating system.

▶ In Summary

Major hardware vendors have understandably established data warehousing initiatives or partnership programs with both software vendors and consulting firms in a bid to provide comprehensive data warehousing solutions to their customers.

Due to the potential size explosion of data warehouses, an enterprise is best served by a powerful hardware platform that is scalable both in terms of processing power and disk capacity. If the warehouse achieves a mission-critical status in the enterprise, then the reliability, availability, and security of the computing platform become key evaluation criteria.

The clear separation of operational and decisional computing platforms also gives enterprises the opportunity to use a different computing platform for the warehouse (i.e., different from the operational systems).

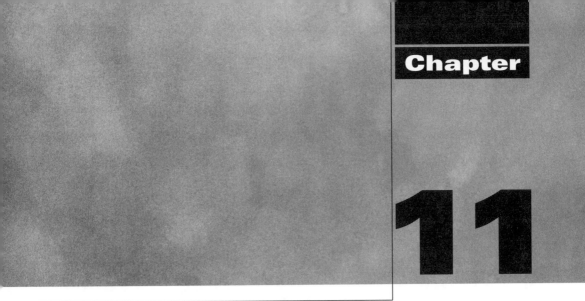

Warehousing Software

A warehousing team will require several different types of tools during the course of a warehousing project. These software products generally fall into one or more of the categories illustrated in Figure 11–1 and described below.

- **Extraction and transformation.** As part of the data extraction and transformation process, the warehouse team requires tools that can extract, transform, integrate, clean, and load data from source systems into one or more data warehouse databases. Middleware and gateway products may be required for warehouses that extract data from host-based source systems.
- **Warehouse storage.** Software products are also required to store warehouse data and their accompanying metadata. Relational database management systems in particular are well suited to large and growing warehouses.
- **Data access and retrieval.** Different types of software are required to access, retrieve, distribute, and present warehouse data to its end users.

Tool examples listed throughout this chapter are provided for reference purposes only and are by no means an attempt to provide a complete list of vendors and tools. The tools are listed in alphabetical

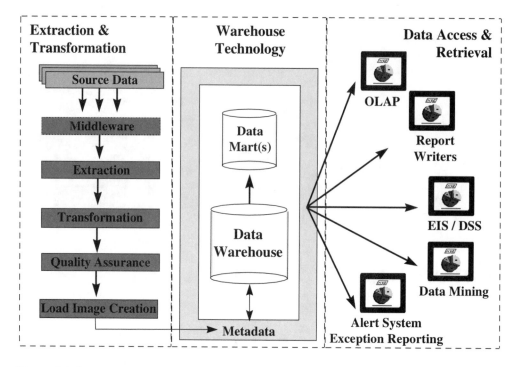

Figure 11–1   Data Warehouse Software Components

order by company name; the sequence does not imply any form of ranking.

Also, many of the sample tools listed automate more than one aspect of the warehouse back-end process. Thus, a tool listed in the extraction category may also have features that fit into the transformation or data quality categories.

▶ Middleware and Connectivity Tools

Connectivity tools provide transparent access to source systems in heterogeneous computing environments. Such tools are expensive but quite often prove to be invaluable because they provide transparent access to databases of different types, residing on different platforms.

Examples of commercial middleware and connectivity tools include:

- **IBM.** DataJoiner
- **Oracle.** Transparent Gateway
- **SAS.** SAS/Connect
- **Sybase.** Enterprise Connect

▶ Extraction Tools

There are now quite a number of extraction tools available, making tool selection a potentially complicated process.

Tool Selection

Warehouse teams have many options when it comes to extraction tools. In general, the choice of tool depends greatly on the following factors:

- **The source system platform and database.** Extraction and transformation tools cannot access all types of data sources on all types of computing platforms. Unless the team is willing to invest in middleware, the tool options are limited to those that can work with the enterprise's source systems.
- **Built-in extraction or duplication functionality.** The source systems may have built-in extraction or duplication features, either through application code or through database technology. The availability of these built-in tools may help reduce the technical difficulties inherent in the data extraction process.
- **The batch windows of the operational systems.** Some extraction mechanisms are faster or more efficient than others. The batch windows of the operational systems determine the available time frame for the extraction process and therefore may limit the team to a certain set of tools or extraction techniques.

The enterprise may opt to use simple custom-programmed extraction scripts for open, homogeneous computing environments; although without a disciplined approach to documentation, such an approach may create an extraction system that is difficult to maintain. Sophisticated extraction tools are a better choice for source systems in proprietary, heterogeneous environments, although these tools are quite expensive.

Extraction Methods

There are two primary methods for extracting data from source systems (see Figure 11–2):

- **Bulk extractions.** The entire data warehouse is refreshed periodically by extractions from the source systems. All applicable data are extracted from the source systems for loading into the warehouse. This approach heavily taxes the network connection between source and target databases, but such warehouses are easier to set up and maintain.
- **Change-based replication.** Only data that have been newly inserted or updated in the source systems are extracted and loaded into the warehouse. This approach places less stress on the network (due to the smaller volume of data to be transported) but

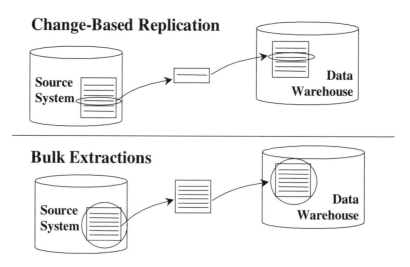

Figure 11–2   Extraction Options

requires more complex programming to determine when a new warehouse record must be inserted or when an existing warehouse record must be updated.

Examples of extraction tools include:

- **Apertus Carleton.** Passport
- **Evolutionary Technologies.** ETI Extract
- **Platinum.** InfoPump

▶ Transformation Tools

Transformation tools are aptly named; they transform extracted data into the appropriate format, data structure, and values that are required by the data warehouse.

Most transformation tools provide the features illustrated in Figure 11–3 and described below.

- **Field splitting and consolidation.** Several logical data items may be implemented as a single physical field in the source systems, resulting in the need to split up a single source field into more than one target warehouse field. At the same time, there will be many instances when several source system fields must be consolidated and stored in one single warehouse field. This is especially true when the same field can be found in more than one source system.
- **Standardization.** Standards and conventions for abbreviations, date formats, data types, character formats, etc., are applied to individual data items to improve uniformity in both format and content. Different naming conventions for different warehouse object types are also defined and implemented as part of the transformation process.
- **Deduplication.** Rules are defined to identify duplicate stores of customers or products. In many cases, the lack of data makes it difficult to determine whether two records actually refer to the same customer or product. When a duplicate is identified, two or more records are merged to form one warehouse record. Po-

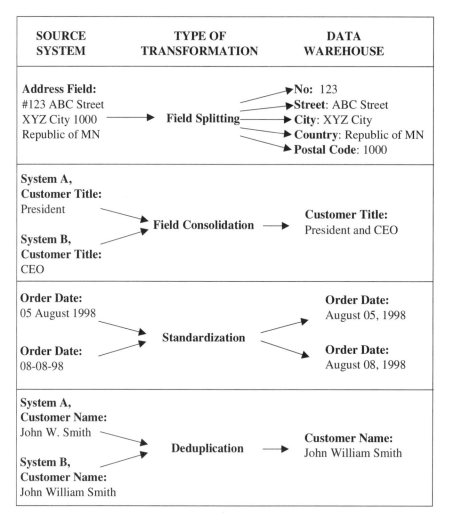

SOURCE SYSTEM	TYPE OF TRANSFORMATION	DATA WAREHOUSE
Address Field: #123 ABC Street XYZ City 1000 Republic of MN	**Field Splitting**	**No:** 123 **Street**: ABC Street **City**: XYZ City **Country**: Republic of MN **Postal Code**: 1000
System A, Customer Title: President **System B, Customer Title:** CEO	**Field Consolidation**	**Customer Title:** President and CEO
Order Date: 05 August 1998 **Order Date:** 08-08-98	**Standardization**	**Order Date:** August 05, 1998 **Order Date:** August 08, 1998
System A, Customer Name: John W. Smith **System B, Customer Name:** John William Smith	**Deduplication**	**Customer Name:** John William Smith

Figure 11–3   Data Transformations

tential duplicates can be identified and logged for further verification.

Warehouse load images (i.e., records to be loaded into the warehouse) are created toward the end of the transformation process. Depending on the team's key generation approach, these load images may or may not yet have warehouse keys.

Examples of transformation tools include the following:

- **Apertus Carleton.** Enterprise/Integrator
- **Data Mirror.** Transformation Server
- **Informatica.** PowerMart Designer

▶ Data Quality Tools

Data quality tools assist warehousing teams with the task of locating and correcting data errors that exist in the source system or in the data warehouse. Experience has shown that easily up to 15 percent of the raw data extracted from operational systems are inconsistent or incorrect. A higher percentage of data are likely to be in the wrong format.

Variations in naming conventions, abbreviations, and formats result in inconsistencies that increase the difficulty of locating duplicate records. For example, "14/F," "14th Floor," and "14th Flr." all mean the same thing to operational staff but may not be recognized as equivalent during the warehouse load.

Erroneous spelling of names, addresses, etc., due to homonyms likewise cause inconsistencies. Updates (e.g., change of address) in one system that are not propagated to other source systems also cause data quality problems.

Data quality tools can help identify and correct data errors, ideally at the source systems. If corrections at the source are not possible, data quality tools can also be used on the warehouse load images or on the warehouse data itself. However, this practice will introduce inconsistencies between the source systems and the warehouse data; the warehouse team may inadvertently create data synchronization problems.

It is interesting to note that while dirty data continue to be one of the biggest issues for data warehousing initiatives, research indicates that data quality investments consistently receive but a small percentage of total warehouse spending.

Examples of data quality tools include the following:

- **DataFlux.** Data Quality Workbench
- **Pine Cone Systems.** Content Tracker

- **Prism.** Quality Manager
- **Vality Technology.** Integrity Data Reengineering

▶ Data Loaders

Data loaders load transformed data (i.e., load images) into the data warehouse. If load images are available on the same RDBMS engine as the warehouse, then stored procedures can be used to handle the warehouse loading.

If the load images do not yet have warehouse keys, then data loaders must generate the appropriate warehouse keys as part of the load process.

▶ Database Management Systems

A database management system is required to store the cleansed and integrated data for easy retrieval by business users. Two flavors of database management systems are currently popular: relational databases and Multidimensional databases.

Relational Database Management Systems (RDBMS)

All major relational database vendors have already announced the availability or upcoming availability of data warehousing related features in their products. These features aim to make the respective RDBMSes particularly suitable to very large database (VLDB) implementations. Examples of such features are bit-mapped indexes and parallel query capabilities.

Examples of these products include

- **IBM.** DB2
- **Informix.** Informix RDBMS

- **Microsoft.** SQL Server
- **Oracle.** Oracle RDBMS
- **Red Brick Systems.** Red Brick Warehouse
- **Sybase.** RDBMS Engine—System 11

Multidimensional Databases (MDDBs)

Multidimensional database engines store data in hypercubes, i.e., pages of numbers that are paged in and out of memory on an as-needed basis, depending on the scope and type of query. This approach is in contrast to the use of tables and fields in relational databases.

Different MDDB engines have different limitations as to the number of dimensions and variables (facts) that can be stored. As a result, most MDDB engines have maximum database sizes below 100 gigabytes. New versions of these products, however, continuously push the limits further back by increasing the number of dimensions supported, as well as the corresponding storage capacity.

Examples of these products include:

- **Arbor.** Essbase
- **BrioQuery.** Enterprise
- **Dimensional Insight.** DI-Diver
- **Oracle.** Express Server

Convergence of RDBMSes and MDDBs

Many relational database vendors have announced plans to integrate multidimensional capabilities into their RDBMSes. This integration will be achieved by caching SQL query results on a multidimensional hypercube on the database. Such Database OLAP technology (sometimes referred to as DOLAP) aims to provide warehousing teams with the best of both OLAP worlds.

▶ Metadata Repository

Although there is a current lack of metadata repository standards, there is a consensus that the metadata repository should support the documentation of source system data structures, transformation business rules, the extraction and transformation programs that move the data, and data structure definitions of the warehouse or data marts. In addition, the metadata repository should also support aggregate navigation, query statistics collection, and end-user help for warehouse contents.

Metadata repository products are also referred to as information catalogs and business information directories. Examples of metadata repositories include:

- **Apertus Carleton.** Warehouse Control Center
- **Informatica.** PowerMart Repository
- **Intellidex.** Warehouse Control Center
- **Prism.** Prism Warehouse Directory

▶ Data Access and Retrieval Tools

Data warehouse users derive and obtain information through these types of tools. Data access and retrieval tools are currently classified into the subcategories below.

Online Analytical Processing (OLAP) Tools

OLAP tools allow users to make ad hoc queries or generate canned queries against the warehouse database. The OLAP category has since divided further into the multidimensional OLAP (MOLAP) and relational OLAP (ROLAP) markets.

MOLAP products run against a multidimensional database (MDDB). These products provide exceptional responses to queries and typically have additional functionality or features, such as budgeting and forecasting capabilities. Some of the tools also have built-in statistical functions. MOLAP tools are better suited to power users in the enterprise.

ROLAP products, in contrast, run directly against warehouses in relational databases (RDBMS). While the products provide slower response times than their MOLAP counterparts, ROLAP products are simpler and easier to use and are therefore suitable to the typical warehouse user. Also, since ROLAP products run directly against relational databases, they can be used directly with large enterprise warehouses.

Examples of OLAP tools include:

- **Arbor Software.** Essbase OLAP
- **Cognos.** Powerplay
- **Intranet Business Systems.** R/OLAPXL

Reporting Tools

These tools allow users to produce canned, graphic-intensive, sophisticated reports based on the warehouse data. There are two main classifications of reporting tools: report writers and report servers.

Report writers allow users to create parameterized reports that can be run by users on an as-needed basis. These typically require some initial programming to create the report template. Once the template has been defined, however, generating a report can be as easy as clicking a button or two.

Report servers are similar to report writers but have additional capabilities that allow their users to schedule when a report is to be run. This feature is particularly helpful if the warehouse team prefers to schedule report generation processing during the night, after a successful warehouse load. By scheduling the report run for the evening, the warehouse team effectively removes some of the processing from the daytime, leaving the warehouse free for ad hoc queries from online users. Some report servers also come with automated report distribution capabilities. For example, a report server can e-mail a newly generated report to a specified user or generate a web page that users can access on the enterprise intranet. Report servers can also store copies of reports for easy retrieval by users over a network on an as-needed basis.

Examples of reporting tools include:

- **IQ Software.** IQ/SmartServer
- **Seagate Software.** Crystal Reports

Executive Information Systems (EIS)

EIS systems and other Decision Support Systems (DSS) are packaged applications that run against warehouse data. These provide different executive reporting features, including "what if" or scenario-based analysis capabilities and support for the enterprise budgeting process.

Examples of these tools include:

- **Comshare.** Decision
- **Oracle.** Oracle Financial Analyzer

While there are packages that provide decisional reporting capabilities, there are EIS and DSS development tools that enable the rapid development and maintenance of custom-made decisional systems.

Examples include:

- **Microstrategy.** DSS Executive
- **Oracle.** Express Objects

Data Mining

Data mining tools search for inconspicuous patterns in transaction-grained data to shed new light on the operations of the enterprise. Different data mining products support different data mining algorithms or techniques (e.g., market basket analysis, clustering), and the selection of a data mining tool is often influenced by the number and type of algorithms supported.

Regardless of the mining techniques, however, the objectives of these tools remain the same: crunching through large volumes of data to identify actionable patterns that would otherwise have remained undetected.

Data mining tools work best with transaction-grained data. For this reason, the deployment of data mining tools may result in a dramatic increase in warehouse size. Due to disk costs, the warehousing team may find itself having to make the painful compromise of storing transaction-grained data for only a subset of its customers. Other teams may compromise by storing transaction-grained data for a short time on a first-in-first-out basis (e.g., transactions for all customers, but for the last six months only).

One last important note about data mining: Since these tools infer relationships and patterns in warehouse data, a clean data warehouse will always produce better results than a dirty warehouse. Dirty data may mislead both the data mining tools and their users by producing erroneous conclusions.

Examples of data mining products include:

- **ANGOSS.** KnowledgeSTUDIO
- **Data Distilleries.** Data Surveyor
- **HyperParallel.** //Discovery
- **IBM.** Intelligent Miner
- **Integral Solutions.** Clementine
- **Magnify.** PATTERN
- **NeoVista Software.** Decision Series
- **Syllogic.** Syllogic Data Mining Tool

Exception Reporting and Alert Systems

These systems highlight or call an end-user's attention to data or a set of conditions about data that are defined as exceptions. An enterprise typically implements three types of alerts:

- **Operational alerts from individual operational systems.** These have long been used in OLTP applications and are typically used to highlight exceptions relating to transactions in the operational system. However, these types of alerts are limited by the data scope of the OLTP application concerned.
- **Operational alerts from the Operational Data Store.** These alerts require integrated operational data and therefore are possible

only on the Operational Data Store. For example, a bank branch manager may wish to be alerted when a bank customer who has missed a loan payment has made a large withdrawal from his deposit account.

- **Decisional alerts from the data warehouse.** These alerts require comparisons with historical values and therefore are possible only on the data warehouse. For example, a sales manager may wish to be alerted when the sales for the current month are found to be at least 8 percent less than sales for the same month last year.

Products that can be used as exception reporting or alert systems include:

- **Compulogic.** Dynamic Query Messenger
- **Pine Cone Systems.** Activator Module (Content Tracker)

Web-Enabled Products

Front-end tools belonging to the above categories have gradually been adding web-publishing features. This development is spurred by the growing interest in intranet technology as a cost-effective alternative for sharing and delivering information within the enterprise.

▶ Data Modeling Tools

Data modeling tools allow users to prepare and maintain an information model of both the source database and the target database. Some of these tools also generate the data structures based on the models that are stored or are able to create models by reverse engineering existing databases. IT organizations that have enterprise data models will quite likely have documented these models using a data modeling tool. While these tools are nice to have, they are not a prerequisite for a successful data warehouse project.

As an aside, some enterprises make the mistake of adding the enterprise data model to the list of data warehouse planning deliverables.

While an enterprise data model is helpful to warehousing, particularly during the source system audit, it is definitely not a prerequisite of the warehousing project. Making the enterprise model a prerequisite or a deliverable of the project will only serve to divert the team's attention from building a warehouse to documenting what data currently exists.

Examples include:

- **Cayenne Software.** Terrain
- **Relational Matters.** Syntagma Designer
- **Sybase.** PowerDesigner WarehouseArchitect

▶ Warehouse Management Tools

These tools assist warehouse administrators in the day-to-day management and administration of the warehouse. Different warehouse management tools support or automate different aspects of the warehouse administration and management tasks.

For example, some tools focus on the load process and therefore track the load histories of the warehouse. Other tools track the types of queries that users direct to the warehouse and identify which data are not used and therefore are candidates for removal.

Examples include:

- **Pine Cone Systems.** Usage Tracker, Refreshment Tracker
- **Red Brick Systems.** Enterprise Control and Coordination

▶ Source Systems

Data warehouses would not be possible without source systems, i.e., the operational systems of the enterprise that serve as the primary source of warehouse data. Although strictly speaking, the source systems are *not* data warehousing software products, they do influence the selection of these tools or products.

The computing environments of the source systems generally determine the complexity of extracting operational data. As can be expected, heterogeneous computing environments increase the difficulties that a data warehouse team may encounter with data extraction and transformation.

Application packages (e.g., integrated banking or integrated manufacturing and distribution systems) with proprietary database structures will also pose data access problems.

External data sources may also be used. Examples include Bloomberg News, Lundberg, A.C. Nielsen, Dun and Bradstreet, Mailcode or Zipcode Data, Dow Jones News Service, Lexis, New York Times Services, and Nexis.

▶ In Summary

Quite a number of technology vendors are supplying warehousing products in more than one category, and a clear trend toward the integration of different warehousing products is evidenced by efforts to share metadata across different products and by the many partnerships and alliances formed between warehousing vendors.

Despite this, there is still no clear market leader for an integrated suite of data warehousing products. Warehousing teams are still forced to take on the responsibility of integrating disparate products, tools, and environments or to rely on the services of a solution integrator. Until this situation changes, enterprises should carefully evaluate the fit of the tools they eventually select for different aspects of their warehousing initiative. The integration problems posed by the source system data are difficult enough without adding tool integration problems to the project.

12

Warehouse Schema Design

Dimensional modeling is a term used to refer to a set of data modeling techniques that have gained popularity and acceptance for data warehouse implementations. The acknowledged guru of dimensional modeling is Ralph Kimball, and the most thorough literature currently available on dimensional modeling is his book entitled *The Data Warehouse Toolkit: Practical Techniques for Building Dimensional Data Warehouses,* published by John Wiley & Sons (ISBN: 0-471-15337-0).

This chapter introduces dimensional modeling as one of the key techniques in data warehousing and is not intended as a replacement for Ralph Kimball's book.

▶ OLTP Systems Use Normalized Data Structures

Most IT professionals are quite familiar with normalized database structures, since normalization is the standard database design technique for the relational databases of Online Transactional Processing (OLTP) systems. Normalized database structures make it possible for

211

operational systems to consistently record hundreds of thousands of discrete, individual transactions, with minimal risk of data loss or data error.

Although normalized databases are appropriate for OLTP systems, they quickly create problems when used with decisional systems.

Users Find Normalized Data Structures Difficult to Understand

Any IT professional who has asked a business user to review a fully normalized entity relationship diagram has first-hand experience of this problem. Normalized data structures simply do not map to the natural thinking processes of business users. It is unrealistic to expect business users to navigate through such data structures.

If business users are expected to perform queries against the warehouse database on an ad hoc basis and if IT professionals want to remove themselves from the report-creation loop, then users must be provided with data structures that are simple and easy to understand. Normalized data structures do not provide the required level of simplicity and friendliness.

Normalized Data Structures Require Knowledge of SQL

To create even the most basic of queries and reports against a normalized data structure requires knowledge of SQL (Structured Query Language)—something that should not be expected of business users, especially decision-makers. Senior executives should not have to learn how to write programming code, and even if they knew how, their time is better spent on nonprogramming activities.

Unsurprisingly, the use of normalized data structures results in many hours of IT resources devoted to writing reports for operational and decisional managers.

Normalized Data Structures Are Not Optimized to Support Decisional Queries

By their very nature, decisional queries require the summation of hundreds to tens of thousands of figures stored in perhaps as many rows in the database. Such processing on a fully normalized data structure is slow and cumbersome.

Consider the sample data structure in Figure 12–1.

If a business manager requires a Product Sales per Customer report (see Figure 12–2), the program code must access the Customer, Account, Account Type, Order, Order Line Item, and Product tables to compute the totals. The WHERE clause of the SQL statement will be straightforward but long; records of the different tables have to be related to one another to produce the correct result.

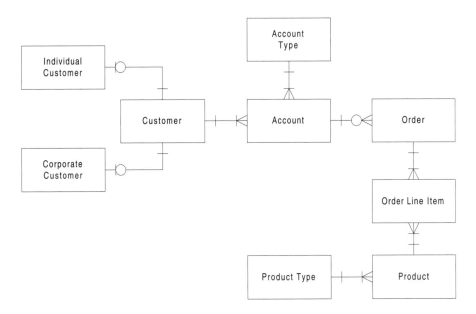

Figure 12–1   Example of a Normalized Data Structure

PRODUCT SALES PER CUSTOMER
Date: March 6, 1998

Customer	Product Name	Sales Amount
Customer A	Product X	1,000
	Product Y	10,000
Customer B	Product X	8,000
...	...	...

Figure 12–2   Product Sales per Customer Sample Report

▶ Dimensional Modeling for Decisional Systems

Dimensional modeling provides a number of techniques or principles for denormalizing the database structure to create schemas that are suitable for supporting decisional processing. These modeling principles are discussed in the following sections.

▶ Two Types of Tables: Facts and Dimensions

Two types of tables are used in dimensional modeling: Fact tables and Dimensional tables.

Fact Tables

Fact tables are used to record actual facts or measures in the business. Facts are the numeric data items that are of interest to the business.

Below are examples of facts for different industries:

- **Retail.** Number of units sold, sales amount
- **Telecommunications.** Length of call in minutes, average number of calls

- **Banking.** Average daily balance, transaction amount
- **Insurance.** Claims amounts
- **Airline.** Ticket cost, baggage weight

Facts are the numbers that users analyze and summarize to gain a better understanding of the business.

Dimension Tables

Dimension tables, on the other hand, establish the context of the facts. Dimensional tables store fields that describe the facts.

Below are examples of dimensions for the same industries:

- **Retail.** Store name, store zip code, product name, product category, day of week
- **Telecommunications.** Call origin, call destination
- **Banking.** Customer name, account number, data, branch, account officer
- **Insurance.** Policy type, insured party
- **Airline.** Flight number, flight destination, airfare class

Facts and Dimensions in Reports

When a manager requires a report showing the revenue for Store X, at Month Y, for Product Z, the manager is using the Store dimension, the Time dimension, and the Product dimension to describe the context of the revenue (fact).

Thus, for the sample report in Figure 12–3, sales region and country are dimensional attributes; "2Q, 1997" is a dimensional value. These data items establish the context and lend meaning to the facts in the report—sales targets and sales actuals.

FOR 2Q, 1997 Sales Region	Country	Targets (in '000s)	Actuals (in '000s)	
Asia	Philippines	14,000	15,050	
	Hong Kong	10,000	10,500	
Europe	France	4,000	4,050	
	Italy	6,000	8,150	
North America	United States	1,000	1,500	
	Canada	**7,000**	**500**	◄
Africa	Egypt	5,600	6,200	

Figure 12–3   Second Quarter Sales Sample Report

▶ A Schema Is a Fact Table Plus Its Related Dimension Tables

Visually, a dimensional schema looks very much like a star, hence the use of the term *star schema* to describe dimensional models. Fact tables reside at the center of the schema, and their dimensions are typically drawn around it, as shown in Figure 12–4.

In Figure 12–4, the dimensions are Client, Time, Product and Organization. The fields in these tables are used to describe the facts in the Sales Fact table.

▶ Facts Are Fully Normalized, Dimensions Are Denormalized

One of the key principles of dimensional modeling is the use of fully normalized Fact tables together with fully denormalized Dimension tables. Unlike dimensional schemas, a fully normalized database schema no doubt would implement some of these dimensions as many logical (and physical) tables.

In Figure 12–4, note that because the Dimension tables are denormalized, the schema shows no outlying tables beyond the four dimensional

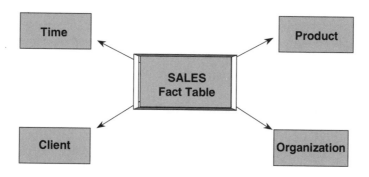

Figure 12–4 Dimensional Star Schema Example

tables. A fully normalized Product dimension, in contrast, may have the additional tables shown in Figure 12–5.

It is the use of these additional normalized tables that decreases the friendliness and navigability of the schema. By denormalizing the dimensions, one makes available to the user all relevant attributes in one table.

▶ Dimensional Hierarchies and Hierarchical Drilling

As a result of denormalization of the dimensions, each dimension will quite likely have hierarchies that imply the grouping and structure.

The easiest example can be found in the Time dimension. As shown in Figure 12–6, the Time dimension has a Day-Month-Quarter-Year hierarchy. Similarly, the Store dimension may have a City-Country-Region-All Stores hierarchy. The Product dimension may have a Product-Product Category-Product Department-All Products hierarchy.

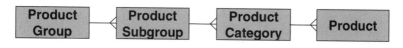

Figure 12–5 Normalized Product Tables

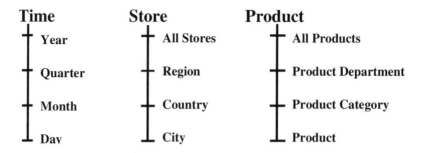

Figure 12–6 Dimensional Hierarchies

When warehouse users drill up and down for detail, they typically drill up and down these dimensional hierarchies to obtain more or less detail about the business.

For example, a user may initially have a sales report showing the total sales for all regions for the year. Figure 12–7 relates the hierarchies to the sales report.

For such a report, the business user is at (1) the Year level of the Time hierarchy; (2) the Region level of the Store hierarchy; and (3) the All Products level of the Product hierarchy.

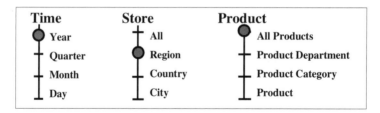

Product Sales

Year	Region	Sales
1996	Asia	1,000
	Europe	50,000
	Americas	20,000
1997	Asia	1,500
...	...	...

Figure 12–7 Dimensional Hierarchies and the Corresponding Report Sample

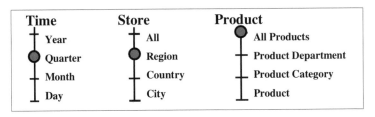

Product Sales

Year	Quarter	Region	Sales
1996	Q1	Asia	200
	Q2	Asia	200
	Q3	Asia	250
	Q4	Asia	350
	Q1	Europe	10,000
...	...	...	...

Figure 12–8   Drilling Down Dimensional Hierarchies

A drill-down along any of the dimensions can be achieved either by adding a new column or by replacing an existing column in the report. For example, drilling down the Time dimension can be achieved by adding Quarter as a second column in the report, as shown in Figure 12–8.

▶ The Time Dimension

One of the goals of the data warehouse is to offload historical data from the operational systems. Each fact in the data warehouse must therefore be time-stamped. This requirement is met through the Time dimension, which is always present in any warehouse schema.

Each record in the Time dimension represents a meaningful chunk of time for the enterprise. Time dimensions where each time record represents one day are fairly common, although there are data warehouses with Time dimensions where each record represents time intervals as small as one hour, or even a minute.

The level of detail for the Time dimension depends entirely on the business requirements. For example, if a telephone company needs to know which hours of the day contribute the most to revenue, then the Time dimension must be hourly (i.e., each Time dimension record represents one hour).

The Granularity of the Fact Table

The term *granularity* is used to indicate the level of detail stored in the fact table. The granularity of the Fact table follows naturally from the level of detail of its related dimensions.

For example, if each Time record represents a day, each Product record represents a product, and each Organization record represents one branch, then the grain of a sales Fact table with these dimensions would likely be: sales per product per day per branch.

Proper identification of the granularity of each schema is crucial to the usefulness and cost of the warehouse. Granularity at too high a level severely limits the ability of users to obtain additional detail. For example, if each time record represented an entire year, there will be one sales fact record for each year, and it would not be possible to obtain sales figures on a monthly or daily basis.

In contrast, granularity at too low a level results in an exponential increase in the size requirements of the warehouse. For example, if each time record represented an hour, there will be one sales fact record for each hour of the day (or 8,760 sales fact records for a year with 365 days for each combination of Product, Client, and Organization). If daily sales facts are all that are required, the number of records in the database can be reduced dramatically.

The Fact Table Key Concatenates Dimension Keys

Since the granularity of the fact table determines the level of detail of the dimensions that surround it, it follows that the key of the Fact table is actually a concatenation of the keys of each of its dimensions.

Table 12-1 Properties of Fact and Dimension Tables

Property	Client Table	Product Table	Time Table	Sales Table
Table Type	Dimension	Dimension	Dimension	Fact
One Record Is	One Client	One Product	One Day	Sales per Client per Product per Day
Key	Client Key	Product Key	Time Key	Client Key + Product Key + Time Key
Sample Fields or Attributes	First Name Last Name Gender City Weight Country	Product Name Color Size Product Class Product Group	Date Month Year Day of Month Day of Week Week Number Quarter Number Weekday Flag Holiday Flag	Amount Sold Quantity Sold

Thus, if the granularity of the sales schema is sales per client per product per day, the Sales Fact table key is actually the concatenation of the Client key, the Product key and the Time key (Day), as presented in Table 12-1.

▶ Aggregates or Summaries

Aggregates or Summaries are one of the most powerful concepts in data warehousing. The proper use of aggregates dramatically improves the performance of the data warehouse in terms of query response times, and therefore improves the overall performance and usability of the warehouse.

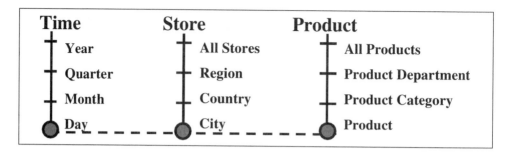

Figure 12-9   Base-Level Schemas Use the Bottom Level of Dimensional
Hierarchies

Computation of Aggregates is Based on Base-Level Schemas

An aggregate is a precalculated summary stored within the warehouse, usually in a separate schema. Aggregates are typically computed based on records at the most detailed (or base) level (see Figure 12–9). They are used to improve the performance of the warehouse for those queries that require only high-level or summarized data.

Aggregates are merely summaries of the base-level data at higher points along the dimensional hierarchies, as illustrated in Figure 12–10.

Rather than running a high-level query against base-level or detailed data, can users run the query against aggregated data. Aggregates provide dramatic improvements in performance because of significantly smaller number of records.

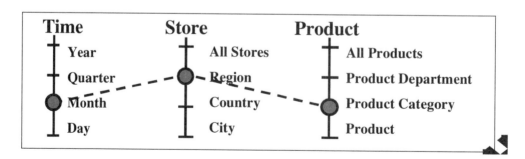

Figure 12-10   Aggregate Schemas Are Higher Along the Dimensional
Hierarchies

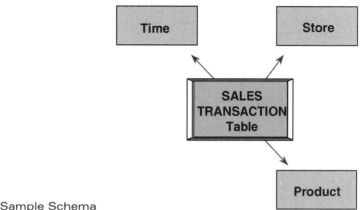

Figure 12–11   Sample Schema

Aggregates Have Fewer Records than Do Base-Level Schemas

Consider the schema in Figure 12–11 with the following characteristics:

- the grain of the base-level Fact table is Product by Store by Week,
- there are 10 Stores in the organization,
- there are 100 Products per Brand, and
- there is at least one Sale per Product per Store per Week.

With the assumptions outlined above, it is possible to compute the number of fact records required for different types of queries:

If a Query Involves . . .	Then it Must Retrieve or Summarize
1 Product, 1 Store, and 1 Week	only 1 record from the Schema
1 Product, All Stores, 1 Week	10 records from the Schema
1 Brand, 1 Store, 1 Week	100 records from the Schema
1 Brand, All Stores, 1 Year	52,000 records from the Schema

If aggregates had been precalculated and stored so that each aggregate record provides facts for a brand per store per week, the third query above (1 Brand, 1 Store, 1 Week) would require only 1 record, instead of 100 records. Similarly, the fourth query above (1 Brand, All Stores, 1 Year) would require only 520 records instead of 52,000. The resulting improvements in query response times are obvious.

▶ Dimensional Attributes

Dimensional attributes play a very critical role in dimensional star schemas. The attribute values are used to establish the context of the facts.

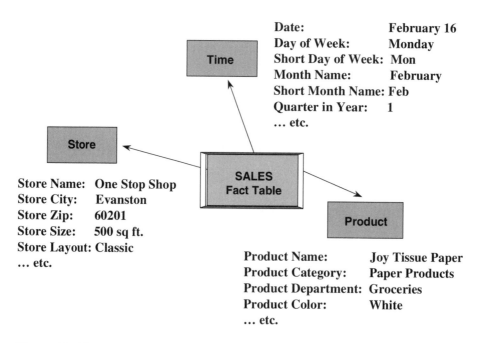

Figure 12–12   Sample Schema with Attributes

For example, a fact table record may have the following keys: Date, Store ID, Product ID (with the corresponding Time, Store, and Product dimensions). If the key fields have the values "February 16, 1998," "101," and "ABC" respectively, then the dimensional attributes in the Time, Store, and Product dimensions can be used to establish the context of the facts in the Fact Record; see Figure 12–12 for an example.

From Figure 12–12, it can be quickly understood that one of the sales records in the Fact table refers to the sale of Joy Tissue Paper at the One Stop Shop on the day of February 16.

▶ Multiple Star Schemas

A data warehouse will most likely have multiple star schemas, i.e., many Fact tables. Each schema is designed to meet a specific set of information needs. Multiple schemas, each focusing on a different aspect of the business, are natural in a dimensional warehouse.

Equally normal is the use of the same Dimension table in more than one schema. The classic example of this is the Time dimension. The enterprise can reuse the Time dimension in all warehouse schemas, provided that the level of detail is appropriate.

For example, a retail company that has one star schema to track profitability per store may make use of the same Time dimension table in the star schema that tracks profitability by product.

▶ Core and Custom Tables

There will many instances when distinct products within the enterprise are similar enough that these can share the same data structure in the warehouse. For example, banks that offer both current accounts and savings accounts will treat these two types of products differently, but the facts that are stored are fairly similar and can share the same data structure.

Unfortunately, there are also many instances when different products will have different characteristics and different interesting facts. Still within the banking example, a credit card product will have facts that are quite different from the current account or savings account. In this scenario, the bank has heterogeneous products that require the use of Core and Custom tables in the warehouse schema design.

Core Fact and Dimension tables store facts that are common to all types of products, and Custom Fact and Dimension tables store facts that are specific to each distinct heterogeneous product.

Thus, if warehouse users wish to analyze data across all products, they will make use of the Core Fact and Dimension tables. If users wish to analyze data specific to one type of product, they will make use of the appropriate Custom Fact and Dimension tables.

Note that the keys in the Custom tables are identical to those in the Core tables. Each Custom Dimension table is a subset of the Core Dimension table, with the Custom tables containing additional attributes specific to each heterogeneous product.

▶ In Summary

Dimensional modeling presents warehousing teams with simple but powerful concepts for designing large-scale data warehouses using relational database technology.

- **Dimensional modeling is simple.** Dimensional modeling techniques make it possible for warehouse designers to create database schemas that business users can easily grasp and comprehend. There is no need for extensive training on how to read diagrams, and there are no confusing relationships between different data items. The dimensions mimic perfectly the multidimensional view that users have of the business.

- **Dimensional modeling promotes data quality.** By its very nature, the star schema allows warehouse administrators to enforce referential integrity checks on the warehouse. Since the fact record key is a concatenation of the keys of its related dimensions, a fact record is successfully loaded only if the corresponding dimensions records are duly defined and also exist in the database.

By enforcing foreign key constraints as a form of referential integrity check, warehouse DBAs add a line of defense against corrupted warehouse data.

- **Performance optimization is possible through aggregates.** As the size of the warehouse increases, performance optimization becomes a pressing concern. Users who have to wait hours to get a response to a query will quickly become discouraged with the warehouse. Aggregates are one of the most manageable ways by which query performance can be optimized.

- **Dimensional modeling makes use of relational database technology.** With dimensional modeling, business users are able to work with multidimensional views without having to use multidimensional database (MDDB) structures: Although MDDBs are useful and have their place in the warehousing architecture, they have severe size limitations.

  Dimensional modeling allows IT professionals to rely on highly scalable relational database technology for their large-scale warehousing implementations, without compromising on the usability of the warehouse schema.

Warehouse Metadata

Metadata have traditionally been defined as *data about data*. While such a catchy statement may not seem very helpful, it is actually quite appropriate as a definition—metadata are a form of abstraction that describes the structure and contents of the data warehouse.

▶ Metadata Are a Form of Abstraction

It is fairly easy to apply abstraction on concrete, tangible items. Information technology professionals do this all the time when they design operational systems. A concrete product is abstracted and described by its properties (i.e., data attributes)—for example, name, color, weight, size, price. A person can also be abstracted and described through his name, age, gender, occupation, etc.

Abstraction complexity increases when the item that is abstracted is not as concrete; however, such abstraction is still routinely performed in operational systems. For example, a banking transaction can be described by the transaction amount, transaction currency, transaction type (e.g., withdrawal), and the date and time when the transaction took place.

Figure 13–1 and Figure 13–2 present two metadata examples for data warehouses; the first example provides sample metadata for warehouse fields. The second provides sample metadata for warehouse dimensions. These metadata are supported by the WAREHOUSE DESIGNER software product that accompanies this book.

In data warehousing, abstraction is applied to the data sources, extraction and transformation rules and programs, data structure, and contents of the data warehouse itself. Since the data warehouse is a repository of data, the results of such an abstraction—the metadata—can be described as "data about data."

▶ Why Are Metadata Important?

Metadata are important to a data warehouse for several reasons. To explain why, we examine the different uses of metadata.

Metadata Example for Warehouse Fields

- **Field Name.** The name of the field, as it will be used in the physical table.
- **Caption.** The name of the field, as it should appear to users.
- **Data Type.** The appropriate data type for the field, as supported by the target RDBMS.
- **Index Type.** The type of index to be used on this attribute.
- **Key?.** Whether this is a Key field in the Dimension table.
- **Format.** The format of this field.
- **Description.** A description or definition of this field.

Figure 13–1   Metadata Example for Warehouse Fields

> ## Metadata Example for Warehouse Dimension Table
>
> - **Name.** The physical table name to be used in the database.
> - **Caption.** The business or logical name of the dimension; used by warehouse users to refer to the dimension.
> - **Description.** The standard definition of the dimension.
> - **Usage Type.** Indicates if a warehouse object is used as a fact or as a dimension.
> - **Key Option.** Indicates how keys are to be managed for this dimension. Valid values are Overwrite, Generate New, and Create Version.
> - **Source.** Indicates the primary data source for this dimension. This field is provided for documentation purposes only.
> - **Online?.** Indicates whether the physical table is actually populated correctly and is available for use by the users of the data warehouse.

Figure 13–2   Metadata Example for Warehouse Dimensions

Metadata Establish the Context of the Warehouse Data

Metadata help warehouse administrators and users locate and understand data items, both in the source systems and in the warehouse data structures. For example, the date value 02/05/1998 may mean different dates depending on the date convention used. The same set of numbers can be interpreted as February 5, 1998 or as May 2, 1998. If metadata describing the format of this date field were available, the definite and unambiguous meaning of the data item could be easily determined.

In operational systems, software developers and database administrators deal with metadata every day. All technical documentation of source systems are metadata in one form or another. Metadata, however, remain for the most part transparent to the end users of operational systems. They perceive the operational system as a black box and interact only with the user interface.

This practice is in direct contrast to data warehousing, where the users of decisional systems actively browse through the contents of the data warehouse and must first understand the warehouse contents before they can make effective use of the data.

Metadata Facilitate the Analysis Process

Consider the typical process that business analysts follow as part of their work. Enterprise analysts must go through the process of locating data, retrieving data, interpreting and analyzing data to yield information, presenting the information, and then recommending courses of action.

To make the data warehouse useful to enterprise analysts, the metadata must provide warehouse end users with the information they need to easily perform the analysis steps. Thus, metadata should allow users to quickly locate data that are in the warehouse. The metadata should also allow analysts to interpret data correctly by providing information about data formats (as in the above data example) and data definitions.

As a concrete example, when a data items in the warehouse Fact table is labeled "Profit," the user should be able to consult the warehouse metadata to learn how the Profit data item is computed.

Metadata Are a Form of Audit Trail for Data Transformation

Metadata document the transformation of source data into warehouse data. Warehouse metadata must be able to explain how a particular piece of warehouse data was derived from the operational systems. All business rules that govern the transformation of data to new values or new formats are also documented as metadata.

This form of audit trail is required if users are to gain confidence in the veracity and quality of warehouse data. It is also essential to the user's understanding of warehouse data to know where they came from.

In addition, some warehousing products use this type of metadata to generate extraction and transformation scripts for use on the warehouse back-end.

Metadata Improve or Maintain Data Quality

Metadata can improve or maintain warehouse data quality through the definition of valid values for individual warehouse data items. Prior to actual loading into the warehouse, the warehouse load images can be reviewed by a data quality tool to check for compliance with valid values for key data items. Data errors are quickly highlighted for correction.

Metadata can even be used as the basis for any error-correction processing that should be done if a data error is found. Error-correction rules are documented in the metadata repository and executed by program code on an as needed basis.

▶ Metadata Types

Although there are still ongoing discussions and debates regarding standards for metadata repositories, it is generally agreed that metadata repository must consider the metadata types described in the next subsections.

Administrative Metadata

Administrative metadata contain descriptions of the source databases and their contents, the data warehouse objects, and the business rules used to transform data from the sources into the data warehouse.

- **Data sources.** These are descriptions of all data sources used by the warehouse, including information about the data ownership. Each record and each data item is defined to ensure a uniform understanding by all warehousing team members and warehouse users. Any relationships between different data sources (e.g., one provides data to another) are also documented.
- **Source-to-target field mapping.** The mapping of source fields (in operational systems) to target fields (in the data warehouse) explains what fields are used to populate the data warehouse. It

also documents the transformations and formatting changes that were applied to the original, raw data to derive the warehouse data.

- **Warehouse schema design.** This model of the data warehouse describes the warehouse servers, databases, database tables, fields, and any hierarchies that may exist in the data. All referential tables, system codes, etc., are also documented.
- **Warehouse back-end data structure.** This is a model of the back-end of the warehouse, including staging tables, load image tables, and any other temporary data structures that are used during the data transformation process.
- **Warehouse back-end tools or programs.** A definition of each extraction, transformation, and quality assurance program or tool that is used to build or refresh the data warehouse. This definition includes how often the programs are run, in what sequence, what parameters are expected, and the actual source code of the programs (if applicable). If these programs are generated, the name of the tool and the date and time when the programs were generated should also be included.
- **Warehouse architecture.** If the warehouse architecture is one where an enterprise warehouse feeds many departmental or vertical data marts, the warehouse architecture should be documented as well. If the data mart contains a logical subset of the warehouse contents, this subset should also be defined.
- **Business rules and policies.** All applicable business rules and policies are documented. Examples include business formulas for computing costs or profits.
- **Access and security rules.** Rules governing the security and access rights of users should likewise be defined.
- **Units of measure.** All units of measurement and conversion rates used between different units should also be documented, especially if conversion formulas and rates change over time.

End-User Metadata

End-user metadata help users create their queries and interpret the results. Users may also need to know the definitions of the warehouse data, their descriptions, and any hierarchies that may exist within the various dimensions.

- **Warehouse contents.** Metadata must describe the data structure and contents of the data warehouse in user-friendly terms. The volume of data in various schemas should likewise be presented. Any aliases that are used for data items are documented as well. Rules used to create summaries and other precomputed totals are also documented.
- **Predefined queries and reports.** Queries and reports that have been predefined and that are readily available to users should be documented to avoid duplication of effort. If a report server is used, the schedule for generating new reports should be made known.
- **Business rules and policies.** All business rules applicable to the warehouse data should be documented in business terms. Any changes to business rules over time should also be documented in the same manner.
- **Hierarchy definitions.** Descriptions of the hierarchies in warehouse dimensions are also documented in end-user metadata. Hierarchy definitions are particularly important to support drilling up and down warehouse dimensions.
- **Status information.** Different rollouts of the data warehouse will be in different stages of development. Status information is required to inform warehouse users of the warehouse status at any point in time. Status information may also vary at the table level. For example, the base-level schemas of the warehouse may already be available and online to users while the aggregates are being computed.
- **Data quality.** Any known data quality problems in the warehouse should be clearly documented for the users. This will prompt users to make careful use of warehouse data.
- **Warehouse load history.** A history of all warehouse loads, including data volume, data errors encountered, and load time frame. This should be synchronized with the warehouse status information. The load schedule should also be available—users need to know when new data will be available.
- **Warehouse purging rules.** The rules that determine when data is removed from the warehouse should also be published for the

benefit of warehouse end-users. Users need this information to understand when data will become unavailable.

Optimization Metadata

Metadata are maintained to aid in the optimization of the data warehouse design and performance. Examples of such metadata include:

- **Aggregate definitions.** All warehouse aggregates should also be documented in the metadata repository. Warehouse front-end tools with aggregate navigation capabilities rely on this type of metadata to work properly.
- **Collection of query statistics.** It is helpful to track the types of queries that are made against the warehouse. This information serves as an input to the warehouse administrator for database optimization and tuning. It also helps to identify warehouse data that are largely unused.

▶ Versioning

Given the fact that a data warehouse contains data over different time periods, it is important to consider the effect that time may have on the business rules, source-to-target mappings, aggregate definitions, and other types of metadata in the warehouse.

Users must have access to the correct metadata for the time period they are currently studying. Without the appropriate user metadata for all time periods in the warehouse, the business users cannot be blamed for jumping to wrong conclusions and making decisions based on misinterpreted data.

Similarly, IT staff require this information for warehouse maintenance purposes. What at first glance seems to be an error in data transformation or processing may in reality be simply a change in policy or business rules.

Metadata versions, therefore, must be carefully tracked and made available to both users and the warehouse team.

Metadata as the Basis for Automating Warehousing Tasks

Although metadata have traditionally been used as a form of after-the-fact documentation, there is a clear trend in data warehousing toward metadata taking on a more active role. Almost all the major data warehouse products or tools allow their users to record and maintain metadata about the warehouse, and make use of the metadata as a basis for automating one or more aspects of the back-end warehouse process.

For example:

- **Extraction and transformation.** Users of extraction and transformation tools can specify source-to-target field mappings and enter all business rules that govern the transformation of data from the source to the target. The mapping (which is a form of metadata) serves as the basis for generating scripts that automate the extraction and transformation process.
- **Data quality.** Users of data quality tools can specify valid values for different data items in either the source system, load image, or the warehouse itself. These data quality tools use such metadata as the basis for identifying and correcting data errors.
- **Schema generation.** Similarly, users of WAREHOUSE DESIGNER (one of the tools provided with this book) use the tool to record metadata relating to the data structure of a dimensional data warehouse or data mart into the tool. WAREHOUSE DESIGNER then uses the metadata as the basis for generating the SQL Data Definition Language (DDL) statements that create data warehouse tables, fields, indexes, aggregates, etc.
- **Front-end tools.** Front-end tools also make use of metadata to gain access to the warehouse database. R/OLAPXL (the ROLAP front-end tool that accompanies this book) makes use of metadata to display warehouse tables and fields and to redirect queries to summary tables (i.e., aggregate navigation).

In Summary

Although quite a lot has been written or said about the importance of metadata, there is yet to be a consistent and reliable implementation of warehouse metadata and metadata repositories on an industry-wide scale.

To address this industry-wide issue, an organization called the Meta Data Coalition was formed to define and support the ongoing evolution of a metadata interchange format. The coalition has released a metadata interchange specification that aims to be the standard for sharing metadata among different types of products. At least 30 warehousing vendors are currently members of this organization.

Until a clear metadata standard is established, enterprises have no choice but to identify the type of metadata required by their respective warehouse initiatives, then acquire the necessary tools to support their metadata requirements.

Warehousing Applications

The successful implementation of data warehousing technologies creates new possibilities for enterprises. Applications that previously were not feasible due to the lack of integrated data are now possible. In this chapter, we take a quick look at the different types of enterprises that implement data warehouses and the types of applications that they have deployed.

▶ The Early Adopters

Among the early adopters of warehousing technologies were the telecommunications, banking, and retail sectors.

Thus, most early warehousing applications can be found in these industries. For example:

- **Telecommunication** companies were interested in analyzing (among other things) network utilization, the calling patterns of their clients, and the profitability of their product offerings. Such information was and still is required for formulating, mod-

239

ifying, and offering different subscription packages with special rates and incentives to different customers.

- **Banks** were and still are interested in effectively managing the bank's asset and liability portfolios, analyzing product and customer profitability, and profiling customers and households as a means of identifying target marketing and cross-selling opportunities.

- The **retail** sector was interested in sales trends, particularly buying patterns that are influenced by changing seasons, sales promotions, holidays, and competitor activities. With the introduction of customer discount cards, the retail sector was able to attribute previously anonymous purchases to individual customers. Individual buying habits and likes are now used as inputs to formulating sales promotions and guiding direct marketing activities.

▶ Types of Warehousing Applications

Although warehousing found its early use in different industries with different information requirements, it is still possible to categorize the different warehousing applications into the following types and tasks.

Sales and Marketing

- **Performance trend analysis.** Since a data warehouse is designed to store historical data, it is an ideal technology for analyzing performance trends within an organization. Warehouse users can produce reports that compare current performance to historical figures. Their analysis may highlight trends that reveal a major opportunity or confirm a suspected problem. Such performance trend analysis capabilities are crucial to the success of planning activities (e.g., sales forecasting).

- **Cross-selling.** A data warehouse provides an integrated view of the enterprise's many relationships with its customers. By obtaining a clearer picture of customers and the services that they avail themselves of, the enterprise can identify opportunities for cross-selling additional products and services to existing customers.

- **Customer profiling and target marketing.** Internal enterprise data can be integrated with census and demographic data to analyze and derive customer profiles. These profiles consider factors such as age, gender, marital status, income brackets, purchasing history, and number of dependents. Through these profiles, the enterprise can, with some accuracy, estimate how appealing customers will find a particular product or product mix. By modeling customers in this manner, the enterprise has better inputs to target marketing efforts.

- **Promotions and product bundling.** The data warehouse allows enterprises to analyze their customers' purchasing histories as an input to promotions and product bundling. This is particularly helpful in the retail sector, where related products from different vendors can be bundled together and offered at a more attractive price. The success of different promotions can be evaluated through the warehouse data as well.

- **Sales tracking and reporting.** Although enterprises have long been able to track and report on their sales performance, the ready availability of data in the warehouse dramatically simplifies this task.

Financial Analysis and Management

- **Risk analysis and management.** Integrated warehouse data allow enterprises to analyze their risk exposure. For example, banks want to effectively manage their mix of assets and liabilities. Loan departments want to manage their risk exposure to sectors or industries that are not performing well. Insurance companies want to identify customer profiles and individual customers who have consistently proven to be unprofitable and to adjust their pricing and product offerings accordingly.

- **Profitability analysis.** If operating costs and revenues are tracked or allocated at a sufficiently detailed level in operational systems, a data warehouse can be used for profitability analysis. Users can slice and dice through warehouse data to produce reports that analyze the enterprise's profitability by customer, agent or salesman, product, time period, geography, organizational unit, and any other business dimension that the user requires.

General Reporting

- **Exception reporting.** Through the use of exception reporting or alert systems, enterprise managers are made aware of important or significant events (e.g., more than x% drop in sales for the current month, current year vs. same month, last year). Managers can define the exceptions that are of interest to them. Through exceptions or alerts, enterprise managers learn about business situations before they escalate into major problems. Similarly, managers learn about situations that can be exploited while the window of opportunity is still open.

Customer Care and Service

- **Customer relationship management.** Warehouse data can also be used as the basis for managing the enterprise's relationships with its many customers. Customers will be far from pleased if different groups in the same enterprise ask them for the same information more than once. Customers appreciate enterprises that never forget special instructions, preferences, or requests. Integrated customer data can serve as the basis for improving and growing the enterprise's relationships with each of its customers and are therefore critical to effective customer relationship management.

▶ Specialized Applications of Warehousing Technology

Data warehousing technology can be used to develop highly specialized applications, as discussed below.

Call Center Integration

Many organizations, particularly those in the banking, financial services, and telecommunications industries, are looking into Call Center applications to better improve their customer relationships. As with any Operational Data Store or data warehouse implementation, Call Center applications face the daunting task of integrating data from many disparate sources to form an integrated picture of the customer's relationship with the enterprise.

What has not readily been apparent to implementors of call centers is that Operational Data Store and data warehouse technologies are the appropriate IT architecture components to support Call Center applications. Consider Figure 14–1.

- Data from multiple sources are integrated into an Operational Data Store to provide a current, integrated view of the enterprise operations.
- The Call Center application uses the Operational Data Store as its primary source of customer information. The Call Center

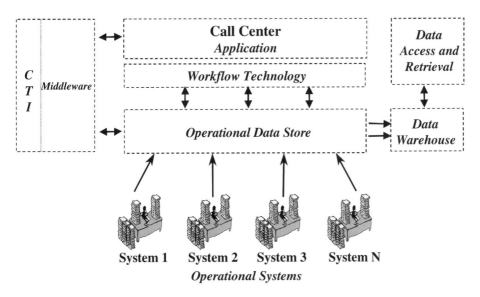

Figure 14–1 Call Center Architecture Using Operational Data Store and Data Warehouse Technologies

also extends the contents of the Operational Data Store by directly updating the ODS.

- Workflow technologies facilitate the routing of data from Call Center workstations to the Operational Data Store.
- Computer telephony used in conjunction with the appropriate middleware are integrated with both the Operational Data Store and the Call Center applications.
- At regular intervals, the Operational Data Store feeds the enterprise data warehouse. The data warehouse has its own set of data access and retrieval technologies to provide decisional information and reports.

Credit Bureau Systems

Credit bureaus for the banking, telecommunications, and utility companies can benefit from the use of warehousing technologies for integrating negative customer data from many different enterprises. Data are integrated, then stored in a repository that can be accessed by all authorized users, either directly or through a network connection.

For this process to work smoothly, the credit bureau must set standard formats and definitions for all the data items it will receive. Data providers extract data from their respective operational systems and submit these data, using standard data storage media.

The credit bureau transforms, integrates, deduplicates, cleans, and loads the data into a warehouse that is designed specifically to meet the querying requirements of both the credit bureau and its customers.

The credit bureau can also use data warehousing technologies to mine and analyze the credit data to produce industry-specific and cross-industry reports. Patterns within the customer database can be identified through statistical analysis (e.g., typical profile of a blacklisted customer) and can be made available to credit bureau customers.

Warehouse management and administration modules, such as those that track and analyze queries, can be used as the basis for billing credit bureau customers.

▶ In Summary

The bottom line of any data warehousing investment rests on its ability to provide enterprises with genuine business value. Data warehousing technology is merely an enabler; the true value comes from the improvements that enterprises make to decisional and operational business processes—improvements that translate to better customer service, higher-quality products, reduced costs, or faster delivery times.

Data warehousing applications, as described in this chapter, enable enterprises to capitalize on the availability of clean, integrated data. Warehouse users are able to transform data into information and to use that information to contribute to the enterprise's bottom line.

Part 5

Where to Now?

After the initial data warehouse project is completed, it may seem that the bulk of the work is done. In reality, however, the warehousing team has taken just the first step of a long journey.

This section of the book explores the next steps by considering the following:

- **Warehouse maintenance and evolution.** This chapter presents the major considerations for maintaining and evolving the warehouse.
- **Warehousing trends.** This chapter looks at trends in data warehousing and their possible implications on future warehousing projects.

Warehouse Maintenance and Evolution

With the data warehouse in production, the warehousing team will face a new set of challenges—the maintenance and evolution of the warehouse.

▶ Regular Warehouse Loads

New or updated data must be loaded regularly from the source systems into the data warehouse to ensure that the latest data are available to warehouse users. This loading is typically conducted during the evenings, when the operational systems can be taken offline. Each step in the back-end process—extract, transform, quality assure, and load—must be performed for each warehouse load.

New warehouse loads imply the need to calculate and populate aggregate tables with new records. In cases where the data warehouse feeds one or more data marts, the warehouse loading is not complete until the data marts have likewise been loaded with the latest data.

▶ Warehouse Statistics Collection

Warehouse usage statistics should be collected on a regular basis to monitor the performance and utilization of the warehouse. The following types of statistics will prove to be insightful.

- **Queries per day.** The number of queries that the warehouse responds to on any given day, categorized into levels of complexity whenever possible. Queries against summary tables also indicate the usefulness of these stored aggregates.
- **Query response times.** The time it takes for each query to execute.
- **Alerts per day.** The number of alerts or exceptions that are triggered by the warehouse on any given day, if an alert system is in place.
- **Valid users.** The number of users who have access to the warehouse.
- **Users per day.** The number of users who actually make use of the warehouse on any given day. This number can be compared to the number of valid users.
- **Frequency of use.** The number of times a user actually logs on to the data warehouse within a given time frame. This statistic indicates how much the warehouse supports the user's day-to-day activities.
- **Session length.** The length of time a user stays online each time he logs on to the data warehouse.
- **Time of day, day of week, day of month.** The time of day, day of week, and day of month when each query is executed. This statistic may highlight periods where there is constant, heavy usage of warehouse data.
- **Subject areas.** Identifies which of the subject areas in the warehouse are more frequently used. This information also serves as a guide for subject areas that are candidates for removal.
- **Warehouse size.** The number of records of data for each warehouse table after each warehouse load. This statistic is a useful indicator of the growth rate of the warehouse.
- **Warehouse contents profile.** Statistics about the warehouse contents (e.g., total number of customers or accounts, number of employees, number of unique products, etc.). This information provides interesting metrics about the business growth.

▶ Warehouse User Profiles

As more users access the warehouse, the usability of the data access and retrieval tools becomes critical. The majority of users will not have the patience to learn a whole new set of tools and will simply continue the current and convenient practice of submitting requests to the IT department.

The warehouse team must therefore evaluate the profiles of each of the intended warehouse users. This user evaluation can also be used as input to tool selection and to determine the number of licenses required for each data access and retrieval tool.

In general, there are three types of warehouse end users, and their preferred method for interacting with the data warehouse varies accordingly. These users are:

- **Senior and executive management.** These end users generally prefer to view information through predefined reports with built-in hierarchical drilling capabilities. They prefer reports that use graphical presentation media, such as charts and models, to quickly convey information.
- **Middle management and senior analysts.** These individuals prefer to create their own queries and reports, using the available tools. They create information in an ad hoc style, based on the information needs of senior and executive management. However, their interest is often limited to a specific product group, a specific geographical area, or a specific aspect of the enterprise's performance. The preferred interfaces for users of this type is spreadsheets and front-ends that provide budgeting and forecasting capabilities.
- **Business analyst and IT support.** These individuals are among the heaviest users of warehouse data and are the ones who perform actual data collection and analysis. They create the charts and reports that are required to present their findings to senior management. They also prefer to work with tools that allow them to create their own queries and reports.

The above categories describe the typical user profiles. The actual preference of individual users may vary, depending on individual IT literacy and working style.

▶ Security and Access Profiles

A data warehouse contains critical information in a readily accessible format. It is therefore important to keep secure not only the warehouse data but also the information that is distilled from the warehouse.

OLTP approaches to security, such as the restriction of access to critical tables, will not work with a data warehouse because of the exploratory fashion by which warehouse data are used. Most analysts will use the warehouse in an ad hoc manner and will not necessarily know at the outset what subject areas they will be exploring or even what range of queries they will be creating. By restricting user access to certain tables, the warehouse security may inadvertently inhibit analysts and other warehouse users from discovering critical and meaningful information.

Initial warehouse rollouts typically require fairly low security because of the small and targeted set of users intended for the initial rollouts. There will therefore be a need to revisit the security and access profiles of users as each rollout is deployed.

When users leave an organization, their corresponding user profiles should be removed to prevent the unauthorized retrieval and use of warehouse data.

Also, if the warehouse data are made available to users over the public Internet infrastructure, the appropriate security measures should be put in place.

▶ Data Quality

Data quality (or the lack thereof) will continue to plague warehousing efforts in the years to come. The enterprise will need to determine how data errors will be handled in the warehouse. There are two general approaches to data quality problems.

- **Only clean data gets in.** Only data that are certified 100 percent correct are loaded into the warehouse. Users are confident that the warehouse contains correct data and can take decisive action based on the information it provides. Unfortunately, since data errors may take a long time to identify, and even more to fix, it may be a while before a full warehouse load is completed. Also, a vast majority of queries (e.g., who are our top-10 customers? how many product combinations are we selling?) will not be meaningful if a warehouse load is incomplete.

- **Clean as we go.** All data are loaded into the warehouse, but mechanisms are defined and implemented to identify and correct data errors. Although such an approach allows warehouse loads to take place, the quality of the data is suspect and may result in misleading information and ill-informed decisions. The questionable data quality may also cause problems with user acceptance—users will be less inclined to use the warehouse if they do not believe the information it provides.

It is unrealistic to expect that all data quality errors will be corrected during the course of one warehouse rollout. However, acceptance of this reality does not mean that data quality efforts are for naught and can be abandoned.

Whenever possible, correct the data in the source systems so that cleaner data are provided in the next warehouse load. Provide mechanisms for clearly identifying dirty warehouse data. If users know which parts of the warehouse are suspect, they will still be able to find value in the data that are correct.

It is an unfortunate fact of life that older enterprises have larger data volumes and, consequently, a larger volume of data errors.

▶ Data Growth

Initial warehouse deployments may not face space or capacity problems, but as time passes and the warehouse size grows with each new data load, the proper management of data growth expansion proliferation grows in importance.

There are several ways to handle data growth, including:

- **Use of aggregates.** The use of stored aggregates significantly reduces the space required by the data, especially if the data are required only at a highly summarized level. The detailed data can be deleted or archived after aggregates have been created. Note however, that the removal of detailed data implies the loss of the ability to drill down for more detail. Also, new summaries at other levels may not be derivable from the current portfolio of aggregate schemas.

- **Limiting the time frame.** Although users will want the warehouse to store as much data for as long as possible, there may be a need to compromise by limiting the length of historical data in the warehouse.

- **Removing unused data.** Using query statistics gathered over time, it is possible for warehouse administrators to identify rarely used data in the warehouse. These records are ideal candidates for removal since their storage results in costs with very little business value.

▶ Updates to Warehouse Subsystems

As time passes, a number of conditions will necessitate changes to the data structure of the warehouse, its staging areas, its back-end subsystems, and, consequently, its metadata. We describe some of these conditions in the following subsections.

Source System Evolution

As the source systems evolve, so by necessity does the data warehouse. It is therefore critical that any plans to change the scope, functionality, and availability of the source systems also consider any possible impact on the data warehouse. The CIO is in the best position to ensure that the project efforts are coordinated across multiple projects.

- **Changes in scope.** Scope changes in operational systems typically imply one or more of the following: the availability of new data in an existing system, the removal of previously available data in an existing system, or the migration of currently available data to a new or different computing environment. An example of the latter is the deployment of a new system to replace an existing one.

- **Change in functionality.** There are times when the data structure already existing in the operational systems remains the same but the processing logic and business rules governing the input of future data is changed. Such changes require updates to data integrity rules and metadata used for quality assurance. All quality assurance programs should likewise be updated.

- **Change in availability.** Additional demands on the operational system may affect the availability of the source system (e.g., smaller batch windows). The batch windows may affect the schedule of regular warehouse extractions and may place new efficiency and performance demands on the warehouse extraction and transformation subsystems.

Use of New or Additional External Data

Some data are commercially available for purchase and can be integrated into the data warehouse as the business needs evolve. Not that the use of external data presents its own set of difficulties due to the likelihood of incompatible formats or level of detail.

The use of new or additional external data has the same impact on the warehouse back-end subsystems as do changes to internal data sources.

▶ Database Optimization and Tuning

As query statistics are collected and user base increases, there will be a need to perform database optimization and tuning tasks to maintain an acceptable level of warehouse performance.

To avoid or control the impact of nasty surprises, inform users when changes are made to the production database. Keep in mind that any changes to the database should first be tested in a safe environment.

Databases can be tuned through a number of approaches, including but not limited to the following:

- **Use of parallel query options.** Some of the major database management systems offer options that will split up a large query into several smaller queries that can be run in parallel. The results of the smaller queries are then combined and presented to users as a single result set. While such options have costs, their implementation is transparent to users, who notice only the improvements in response time.
- **Indexing strategies.** As very large database (VLDB) implementations are becoming more popular, database vendors are offering indexing options or strategies to improve the response times to queries against very large tables.
- **Dropping of referential integrity checking.** While debates still exist as to whether or not referential integrity checking should be left on during warehouse loading, it is an undeniable fact that when referential integrity is turned off, the loading of warehouse data becomes faster. Some parties reason that since data are checked prior to warehouse loading, there will be no need to enforce referential integrity constraints.

▶ Data Warehouse Staffing

Not all organizations with a data warehouse choose to create a permanent unit to administer and maintain it. Each organization will have to decide if a permanent unit is required to maintain the data warehouse.

A permanent unit has the advantage of focusing the warehouse staff formally on the care and feeding of the data warehouse. A permanent unit also increases the continuity in staff assignments by decreasing the possibility of losing staff to other IT projects or systems in the enterprise.

The use of matrix organizations in place of permanent units has also proven to be effective, provided that roles and responsibilities are clearly defined and that the IT division is not undermanned.

If the warehouse development was partially or completely outsourced to third parties because of a shortage of internal IT resources, the enterprise may find it necessary to staff up at the end of the warehouse rollout. As the project draws to a close, the consultants or contractors will be turning over the day-to-day operations of the warehouse to internal IT staff. The lack of internal IT resources may result in haphazard turnovers. Alternatively, the enterprise may have to outsource the maintenance of the warehouse.

Warehouse Staff and User Training

The enterprise may find it helpful to establish a training program for both technology staff and end users.

User Training

Warehousing overview. Half-day overviews can be prepared for executive or senior management to manage expectations.

User roles. User training should also cover general data warehousing concepts and explain how users are involved during data warehouse planning, design, and construction activities.

Warehouse contents and metadata. Once a data warehouse has been deployed, the user training should focus strongly on the contents of the warehouse. Users must understand the data that are now available to them and must understand also the limitations imposed by the scope of the warehouse. The contents and usage of business metadata should also be explained.

Data access and retrieval tools. User training should also focus on the selected end-user tools. If users find the tools difficult to use, the IT staff will quickly find themselves saddled with the unwelcome task of creating reports and queries for end users.

Warehouse Staff Training

Warehouse staff require training on a number of topics covering the planning, design, implementation, management, and maintenance of data warehouses. Depending on their project roles, the staff will need to specialize or focus on different areas or different aspects of the warehousing life cycle. For example, the metadata administrator needs specialized courses on metadata repository management. Whereas the warehouse DBA needs dimensional modeling training.

Readers may find it helpful to refer to the training program recommended by the Committee for Data Warehousing Education at the Data Warehousing Institute (www.dw-insitute.com).

▶ Subsequent Warehouse Rollouts

The data warehouse is extended continuously. Data warehouse design and construction skills will always be needed as long as end-user requirements and business situations continue to evolve. Each subsequent rollout is designed to extend the functionality and scope of the warehouse.

As new user requirements are studied and subsequent warehouse rollouts get underway, the overall data warehouse architecture is revisited and modified as needed.

Data marts are deployed as needed within the integrating framework of the warehouse. Avoid multiple, unrelated data marts because these will merely create unnecessary data management and administration problems.

▶ Chargeback Schemes

It may be necessary at some point for the IT Department to start charging user groups for warehouse usage, as a way of obtaining continuous funding for the data warehouse initiative.

Note that chargeback schemes will work only if there are reliable mechanisms to track and monitor usage of the warehouse per user. They also put the warehouse to the test—users will have to feel that they are getting their money's worth each time they use the warehouse. Warehouse usage will drop if users feel that the warehouse has no value.

Disaster Recovery

The challenges of deploying new technology may cause warehouse administrators to place a lower priority on disaster recovery. As time passes and more users come to depend on the data warehouse, however, the warehouse achieves mission-critical status. The appropriate disaster recovery procedures are therefore required to safeguard the continuous availability and reliability of the warehouse.

Ideally, the warehouse team conducts a dry run of the disaster recovery procedure at least once prior to the deployment of the warehouse. Disaster recovery drills on a regular basis will also prove helpful.

Some disasters may require the reinstallation of operating systems and database management systems aside from the reloading of warehouse data and population of aggregate tables. The recovery procedures should consider this possibility.

A final note: Review the disaster recovery plan at the end of each rollout. The plan may have to be updated in light of changes to the architecture, scope, and size of the warehouse.

In Summary

A data warehouse initiative does not stop with one successful warehouse deployment. The warehousing team must sustain the initial momentum by maintaining and evolving the data warehouse.

Unfortunately, maintenance activities remain very much in the background—often unseen and unappreciated until something goes wrong. Many people do not realize that evolving a warehouse can be trickier than the initial deployment. The warehousing team has to meet a new set of information requirements without compromising the performance of the initial deployment and without limiting the warehouse's ability to meet future requirements.

16

Warehousing Trends

This chapter takes a look at trends in the data warehousing industry and their possible implications on future warehousing projects.

▶ Continued Growth of the Data Warehouse Industry

The data warehousing industry continues to grow in terms of spending, product availability and projects. Our research efforts indicate that up to 90 percent of multi-national companies will have data warehouses or are planning to build one by 1999. The size of the market is expected to grow rapidly, doubling in spending roughly once every two years until the year 2000.

The number of data warehouse vendors continues to increase, as does the number of available warehousing products. Such a trend, however, may abate in the face of market consolidation, which began in the mid-1990s and continues to this day.

Small companies with compatible products can be seen merging (e.g., the November 1997 merger of Apertus Technologies and Carleton Corporation) to create larger, more competitive warehouse players. Larger, established corporations have set objectives of becoming end-to-end warehouse solutions providers and are acquiring technologies from niche players to fulfill these goals (e.g., the February 1998 acquisition of Intellidex Systems by Sybase and the March 1998 acquisition of Logic Works by Platinum Technologies).

Partnerships and alliances between vendors continue to be popular. The increasing maturity of the warehousing software market is inevitably turning warehouse software into off-the-shelf packages that can be pieced together. Already companies are positioning groups of products (their own or a combination of products from multiple vendors) as integrated warehousing solutions.

▶ Increased Adoption of Warehousing Technology by More Industries

The industries to first adopt data warehousing technologies have been the telecommunications, banking, and retail vertical markets. The impetus for their early adoption of warehousing technologies has been attributed largely to government deregulation, and increased competition between industry players—conditions that heightened the need for integrated information.

Over the past few years, however, other industries have begun investing strongly in data warehousing technologies. These include, but are not limited to, companies in financial services, healthcare, insurance, manufacturing, petrochemical, pharmaceutical, transportation and distribution, as well as utilities.

Despite the increasing adoption of warehousing technologies by other industries, however, our research indicates that the telecommunications and banking industries continue to lead in warehouse-related spending, with as much as 15 percent of their technology budgets allocated to warehouse-related purchases and projects.

Increased Maturity
of Data Mining Technologies

Data mining tools will continue to mature, and more organizations will adopt this type of warehousing technology. Learning from data mining applications will become more widely available in the trade press and other commercial publications, thereby increasing the chances of data mining success of late adopters.

Data mining initiatives are typically driven by marketing and sales departments and are understandably more popular in large companies with very large databases. Since these tools work best with detailed data at the transaction grain, the popularity of data mining tools will naturally coincide with a boom in very large (terabyte-size) data warehouses. Data mining projects will also underscore further the importance of data quality in warehouse implementations.

Emergence and Use of Metadata
Interchange Standards

There is currently no metadata repository that is a clear industry leader for warehouse implementations. Each product vendor has defined its own set of metadata repository standards as required by its respective products or product suite.

Efforts have long been underway to define an industry-wide set of metadata interchange standards, and a Metadata Interchange Specification is available from the Meta Data Coalition, which has at least 30 vendor companies as members.

Increased Availability
of Web-Enabled Solutions

Data warehousing technologies continue to be affected by the increased popularity of intranets and intranet-based solutions. As a result, more and more data access and retrieval tools are becoming web enabled, while more organizations are requiring web-enabled features as a warehousing requirement for their data access and retrieval tools.

Some organizations have started using the Internet as a cost-effective mechanism for providing remote users with access to warehouse data. Understandably, organizations are concerned about the security requirements of such a setup. The warehouse no doubt contains the most integrated, and cleanest data in the entire enterprise. Such highly critical and sensitive data may fall into the wrong hands if the appropriate security measures are not implemented.

▶ Popularity of Windows NT for Data Mart Projects

The Windows NT operating system will continue to gain popularity as a data mart operating system. The operating system is frequently bundled with hardware features that are candidates for base-level or low-end warehousing platforms.

▶ Availability of Warehousing Modules for Application Packages

Companies that develop and market major operational application packages will soon be offering warehousing modules as part of their suite of applications. These application packages include SAP, Baan, and PeopleSoft. Companies that offer these application packages are in a position to capitalize on the popularity of data warehousing by creating warehousing modules that make use of data in their applications.

These companies are familiar with the data structures of their respective applications and they can therefore offer configurable warehouse back-ends to extract, transform, quality assure, and load operational data into a separate decisional data structure designed to meet the basic decisional reporting requirements of their customers.

Understandably, each enterprise will want the ability to customize these basic warehousing modules to meet their specific requirements; customization is definitely possible with the right people using the right development tools.

▶ More Mergers and Acquisitions Among Warehouse Players

Mergers and acquisitions will continue in the data warehouse market, driven by large corporations acquiring niche specialties, and small companies merging to create a larger warehouse player.

Examples include:

- The 1995 acquisition of Stanford Technological Group by Informix
- The 1995 acquisition of IRI Software's OLAP technologies by Oracle Corporation
- The 1996 acquisition of Panorama Software Systems (and their OLAP technology) by Microsoft Corporation
- The 1997 merger of Carleton Corporation and Apertus Technologies
- The 1998 announcement by Platinum Technologies of its intent to purchase HP Intelligent Warehouse
- The 1998 announced acquisition of Intellidex Systems by Sybase Inc., for the former's metadata repository product
- The 1998 announced acquisition of Logic Works, Inc., by Platinum Technologies

▶ In Summary

In all respects, the data warehousing industry shows all signs of continued growth at an impressive rate. Enterprises can expect more mature products in almost all software segments, especially with the availability of second- or third-generation products. Improvements in price/performance ratios will continue in the hardware market.

Some vendor consolidation can be expected, although new companies and products will continue to appear. More partnerships and alliances between different vendors can also be expected.

Part 6

Appendices

The following appendices are provided with this book:

A. R/olapXL User's Manual
B. Warehouse Designer User's Manual
C. Online Data Warehousing Resources
D. Tool and Vendor Inventory
E. Software License Agreement

R/olapXL® User's Manual

▶ Welcome to R/olapXL!

R/olapXL is a Relational Online Analytical Processing tool that runs on top of Microsoft® Excel® for Windows95™, the popular spreadsheet software from Microsoft Corporation. It is a powerful analysis and report writing tool for dimensional data warehouses and data marts.

The **Client Installation** that accompanies this book is provided freely, and you may copy it to as many computers as you wish, provided that the following disclaimer accompanies each installation:

 Intranet Business Systems, Inc., and its distributors and resellers disclaim all liability for any use you make of this software and for anything this software may do to your data or to your computing environment.

R/olapXL users can easily access and load data into MS Excel worksheets from any data warehouse or data mart that uses a star schema or a dimensional schema. Once data are in MS Excel, users can manipulate the data by using the spreadsheet's standard features.

R/olapXL does not require any knowledge or familiarity with SQL, database design, or programming. R/olapXL does, however, assume that:

- Users are familiar with MS Excel and with the data in their warehouse or data mart
- Standard MS Excel functionality will be used to manipulate the data once they have been retrieved
- The data warehouse or data mart resides on an ODBC-compliant database

Sample Database and Reports

The R/OLAPXL Client Installation comes with an MS Access database containing a sample *schema* populated with sample data, and a set of MS Excel spreadsheets containing sample reports.

You can create and save your own reports at any time using the data provided in the accompanying MS Access database. You can also overwrite the examples provided. The reports are stored in the `Samples` folder under the R/OLAPXL directory.

ODBC Drivers Required

R/OLAPXL uses ODBC Drivers to locate data sources. You will need the MS Access ODBC Driver to use the sample database. The Access ODBC Driver is typically provided with MS Excel.

The R/OLAPXL Server

The R/OLAPXL Client cannot be used with your own databases without the R/OLAPXL Server. The R/OLAPXL Server comes with an Administrators Guide that describes the server configuration that is required before R/OLAPXL can access your own databases.

Manual Contents

This *R/OLAPXL User's Guide* for the R/OLAPXL Client software is intended for the end user or report author who will be running reports from a desktop PC.

The *R/olapXL User's Guide* contains the following sections:

- The *Preface* contains information about R/olapXL and this manual.
- The *Installation* section contains guidelines for installing the software.
- The *Tutorial* quickly describes the steps for modifying and running an existing R/olapXL report.
- The *User's Guide* section contains detailed how-to instructions for R/olapXL features and provides a brief discussion of the two R/olapXL toolbars.
- The *Macro Programming* section describes R/olapXL functions that allow users to create macros that increase the usability of reports.
- The R/olapXL messages section . . .

Conventions Used in This Manual

The following icons are used throughout this manual:

 A Warning Message

 Step-by-Step, How-to Instructions

 A Note

The typefaces shown in the following table are used throughout this manual.

Typeface	Description	Sample
Garamond	Normal text	. . . a pop-up window . . .
Italicized Garamond	R/olapXL terms	Your *schema* can be . . .
BOLD COURIER UPPER CASE	File, directory names	Copy the **CTL3D.DLL** file . . .
Courier	Text to type in	. . . enter a Set Name . . .
Bold Arial	Buttons, dialog box	Select **OK** when done.

Other Documentation

Three files are also provided in the **DOCS** subdirectory of the R/ᴏʟᴀᴘXL installation as additional documentation.

The **README.TXT** file provides an overview of the R/ᴏʟᴀᴘXL software and enumerates the steps required to install the program. The file can be viewed and printed by any word processor that recognizes text files.

A file called **HISTORY.TXT** also accompanies this installation. The file contains late-breaking news and developments that have not been documented in this *User's Guide*.

A copy of the R/ᴏʟᴀᴘXL Frequently Asked Questions Guide is also included in this installation package. The document is in Hypertext Markup Language (HTML) and contains the answers to many common questions asked about R/ᴏʟᴀᴘXL. The file is named **RXL-FAQ.HTML** and can be viewed with any World Wide Web browser. The latest version of the Guide can be downloaded from Intranet's website: http://www.intranetsys.com.

System Requirements

The R/ᴏʟᴀᴘXL Client software requires:

- An Intel 80486-DX/100 or compatible processor (or faster)
- The MS Windows 95 operating system already installed
- A copy of the MS Excel for Windows 95 version 7.0 or the MS Excel 97 software already installed
- ODBC Drivers to locate data sources. You will need the MS Access ODBC Driver to access data in the sample database provided. You will also need the ODBC Driver for the database management system used by your data warehouse or data mart. (Note: the driver must be ODBC Level 2 compliant).
- Approximately eight (i.e., 7.7) Mbytes of hard-disk space
- Any World Wide Web browser (for viewing the FAQ Guide)

The R/ᴏʟᴀᴘXL Client runs independently on each PC. Please note that a connection to your own databases is possible only with the R/ᴏʟᴀᴘXL Server.

▶ Installation

Installation Procedure

➡ **To install the R/ᴏʟᴀᴘXL Client Software:**

1. If you're installing from diskettes, Insert Disk 1 of the R/ᴏʟᴀᴘXL Client Software in drive A. Run `setup.exe` from drive A. This file launches an installation wizard that will guide you through the initial steps of installing R/ᴏʟᴀᴘXL.

2. If you're installing from a CD-ROM, go to the R/ᴏʟᴀᴘXL sub-directory. Run `setup.exe`.

3. After completing the installation steps with the wizard, add the R/ᴏʟᴀᴘXL Sample Retail Database to the list of Data Sources on your PC.
   a. Open the PC's "Control Panel" by clicking on START Settings Control Panel.
   b. Double-click on the 32Bit ODBC icon.
   c. Click on the **Add** command button.
   d. Select the MS Access Driver (`*.mdb`) and click **OK**.
   e. In the new window, enter `ROLAPXL_DEMO` as the Data Source name.
   f. Enter `RolapXL Demonstration Database` as the description. You may also choose to leave this blank.
   g. In the Database group, click on the **Select** button.
   h. Change the drive and directory to the R/ᴏʟᴀᴘXL **Samples** folder. Click on the **RetailDB.mdb** file.
   i. Click **OK** to confirm your selection.
   j. Click **OK** to save the data source definition.

4. Now that the sample retail database is a recognized data source, you need to install R/ᴏʟᴀᴘXL as an MS Excel Add-in:
   a. Launch an instance of MS Excel. Leave a workbook open.
   b. From the Tools menu, choose Add-ins.
   c. Click on the **Browse** command button.
   d. Change the drive and directory to the R/ᴏʟᴀᴘXL folder. Click on the file called **RolapXL.xla.**
   e. Enable the Add-in, then click **OK**.

Successful Installation

You will know that R/olapXL has been successfully installed by checking the following:

- **Intalled Files.** A new directory is created. If you used the default directory name and path during the installation process, the new directory will be called **Rolapxl** and can be found in the **Program Files** subdirectory. The **Rolapxl** directory contains two other folders:
  - **Samples.** This folder contains the sample *schema* and R/olapXL reports.
  - **DOCS.** This folder contains documentation about the program.
- **Changes in Excel.** If R/olapXL has been successfully installed, a new menu option called R/olapXL will appear in MS Excel, and two new toolbars will also become visible.

Uninstalling R/olapXL

R/olapXL updates the Windows Registry on your PC whenever you install R/olapXL. We therefore strongly recommend *against* directly deleting the contents of the R/olapXL subdirectory.

R/olapXL comes with its own uninstaller, which you should use if you wish to uninstall the product.

To uninstall the R/olapXL Client Software:

1. Remove R/olapXL as an Excel Add-in (Optional).
   Launch an instance of MS Excel. Leave a workbook open. From the Tools menu, choose Add-ins. Disable the Add-in, then click **OK**. Close MS Excel.

If you do not disable the R/olapXL add-in before uninstalling, you will receive an error message stating that the add-in cannot be found when you start your next MS Excel session.

This message indicates that R/olapXL features are no longer available to you. It does not, however, affect any other aspect of MS Excel usage.

2. Click on the START menu of Windows 95. Choose Settings, then Control Panel.
3. From the Control Panel window, double-click on **Add/Remove Programs**.
4. In the dialog box that appears, select R/olapXL.
5. Click on the **Add/Remove** button. The R/olapXL uninstaller executes and guides you through the steps to uninstall R/olapXL.

 The R/olapXL Uninstaller removes all R/olapXL files that were copied into your machine. It also tries to remove any subdirectories that were created during the installation of R/olapXL.

If you have placed files of your own in any of the R/olapXL subdirectories, the uninstaller does not delete the subdirectory (and its parent directories) where your files can be found. In this scenario, although R/olapXL was successfully uninstalled, you will receive messages similar to the following: "Unable to remove the directory C:\Program Files\RolapXL" and "Some components cannot be removed from your computer."

▶ Tutorial

This tutorial describes the steps to open, modify, save, and close an existing R/olapXL report. The tutorial assumes the use of sample data and reports provided with R/olapXL Client Software.

Starting Up R/oLAPXL

To start R/oLAPXL, launch the MS Excel software. Once MS Excel is running, R/oLAPXL functionality will now be available to you, provided that the software has been properly installed. You should see R/oLAPXL as one of the menu options in the MS Excel toolbar.

The R/olapXL Menu

Selecting a Data Source

After MS Excel and R/oLAPXL have loaded properly, you may now select a data source for your R/oLAPXL reports.

> R/oLAPXL will prompt you for the appropriate data source each time you start using the software.

To make use of the sample retail schema provided with the R/oLAPXL client software, you must select it as a data source.

 To use the Retail Sample Schema as a Data Source:

1. After MS Excel and R/oLAPXL have both loaded, choose Select Schema from the R/oLAPXL menu,
   -or-
   Click on the Select Schema toolbar button on the R/oLAPXL toolbar.
2. If you have just opened R/oLAPXL or are using R/oLAPXL functionality for the first time in this session of MS Excel, you will be prompted to select a data source.
3. In the dialog box that appears, click on the Machine Data Source tab.
   If R/oLAPXL was installed and the data source name has been defined, you will see a data source entry named **Access_ Retail**.

4. Click on **Access_Retail,** then click on the **OK** button.
   Another dialog box will appear, prompting you for a log-in name and password. Leave the log-in name and password blank, then click on the **OK** button.

Opening a R/ᴏʟᴀᴘXL Report

After an appropriate data source has been selected, you may open an existing R/ᴏʟᴀᴘXL Report.

 To open an existing R/ᴏʟᴀᴘXL Report:

1. From the File menu, choose Open.
   -or-
   Click on the standard Open button on the MS Excel toolbar.
2. Use the dialog box to select the existing R/ᴏʟᴀᴘXL file.
   -or-
   Type the appropriate path and file name.

Use any of the MS Excel files (`* .xls`) provided in the **Samples** folder under the **RolapXL** subdirectory.

3. Click on the **OK** button when done.

 The R/ᴏʟᴀᴘXL Client software saves all R/ᴏʟᴀᴘXL-specific data in MS Excel workbook files. All R/ᴏʟᴀᴘXL report files are therefore MS Excel workbook files.

Running the R/ᴏʟᴀᴘXL Report

When the report (MS Excel file) has opened successfully, you will find the report as it was last saved.

If the report had been run in the past, the retrieved data should still be visible on the worksheet.

Running the report causes R/ᴏʟᴀᴘXL to retrieve the requested data from the database. Any previously retrieved data are overwritten automatically with "fresh" data from the database.

To Run a R/ᴏʟᴀᴘXL Report:

1. From the R/ᴏʟᴀᴘXL menu, choose Run Report.
   -or-
   Click on the Run Report button on the R/ᴏʟᴀᴘXL toolbar.

> 📄 Depending on its size and complexity, a R/ᴏʟᴀᴘXL report may take anywhere between a few seconds to several minutes to complete.

Printing a R/ᴏʟᴀᴘXL Report

Printing a R/ᴏʟᴀᴘXL Report is no different from printing a MS Excel worksheet.

 To Print a R/ᴏʟᴀᴘXL Report:

1. From the MS Excel File menu, choose Print.
2. Use the dialog box to select desired print settings.
3. Click on the **OK** button when done.

> 📄 Please refer to MS Excel user's manual for a comprehensive discussion of its printing features.

Modifying a R/ᴏʟᴀᴘXL Report

A R/ᴏʟᴀᴘXL report can be modified through any of the following actions:

- Adding a new (R/ᴏʟᴀᴘXL or Derived) column
- Moving or deleting an existing (R/ᴏʟᴀᴘXL or Derived) column
- Assigning a new constraint
- Editing an existing constraint
- Rerunning a report against new data

These topics are covered in more detail in the following sections.

▶ User's Guide

This section guides you through the common tasks associated with using the R/OLAPXL Client software.

Basic Concepts

R/OLAPXL works with dimensional data warehouses and data marts. An understanding of dimensional modeling concepts is therefore helpful to the proper usage of this software. For further reading on dimensional modeling, please refer to Chapter 12.

Creating a R/OLAPXL Report

R/OLAPXL saves data in MS Excel files. MS Excel for Windows 95 saves a set of worksheets together as an MS Excel workbook. The files are saved with the file name extension *** .xls.**

Each workbook contains all retrieved data, charts, formulas, and formats that you have defined. The workbook is also used to store the parameters of the R/OLAPXL reports you have created.

You will find that opening and saving a R/OLAPXL report is no different from opening and saving an MS Excel workbook.

When you open a new MS Excel workbook, the workbook file is a standard MS Excel file with blank sheets. None of the worksheets have been initialized as R/OLAPXL worksheets.

Turn the active MS Excel spreadsheet into a R/OLAPXL worksheet by selecting a *Schema* with which to work. By selecting the *Schema,* you select the database tables from which you will retrieve data.

Once a Schema has been selected, R/OLAPXL loads the appropriate data and transforms the MS Excel worksheet into a R/OLAPXL worksheet.

➲ **To create a new R/OLAPXL Report:**

1. Open a new MS Excel workbook, or open any existing MS Excel workbook.

2. Select a *Schema* with which to work.

   From the R/OLAPXL menu, choose Select Schema.
   -or-
   On the R/OLAPXL toolbar, click the Select Schema button.

3. On the pop-up window that appears, click on the desired *Schema*, then click on the **Select** command button to confirm your selection.

 Do not select a new *Schema* while you are in the process of defining a R/OLAPXL report. Doing so will make R/OLAPXL discard any changes made to the currently active sheet.

Saving R/OLAPXL Reports

When you close a file, MS Excel checks to see whether you've made changes to it. If you haven't made any changes, the file closes. If you have made changes, MS Excel asks you whether you want to save them.

 To save a R/OLAPXL Report for the first time:

1. From the File menu, choose Save As.
2. Type the name of the R/OLAPXL report. Because this is the first time you are saving the R/OLAPXL report, you should give it a unique name.
3. When you've typed the name of the R/OLAPXL report and selected the desired directory, choose **OK**.

   Note that this procedure is no different from saving an MS Excel workbook for the first time.

 To save an existing R/OLAPXL Report:

1. From the File menu, choose Save.
   -or-
   Click on the Save toolbar button.

   Note that this procedure is no different from saving an MS Excel workbook.

Do not attempt to save a R/olapXL workbook in an earlier version of MS Excel. This tool is not downward compatible.

Closing a R/olapXL Report

Closing a R/olapXL Report is no different from closing any MS Excel workbook.

 To close a R/olapXL Report:

1. From the File menu, choose Close.
   -or-
   Double-click the workbook's Close box.

   If you've made changes to the workbook since you last saved it, MS Excel will ask whether you want to save your changes before closing.

2. Choose **Yes** to save your changes and close the workbook.

   If you don't want to save your changes, Choose **No**; MS Excel will close the file without saving your changes.

▶ Working with R/olapXL Columns

Specify the data items to be retrieved from the data warehouse or data mart by adding R/olapXL Columns to your worksheet.

You can only include data items that are available from the *Schema* you had selected earlier.

A R/olapXL column is the most basic unit of data that appears on a R/olapXL report. Each column corresponds to a field from either the *Fact table* or the *Dimension tables*.

You can have as many R/olapXL columns in your report as you wish, provided that these data elements are available from the selected schema or are derivable from fields in the selected schema.

Adding a R/olapXL Column

Add as many R/OLAPXL Columns to the MS Excel spreadsheet as are necessary to produce the report you need.

 To Add a R/olapXL Column to a Report:

1. Position the cursor on the MS Excel column you wish to use.
2. From the R/olapXL menu, choose Assign R/olapXL Column
   -or-
   On the R/olapXL toolbar, click on the Assign R/olapXL Column button.
3. On the pop-up window, select the appropriate *Fact* or *Dimension Table* you wish to use.
4. On the same pop-up window, select the appropriate *Fact* or *Dimensional Attribute* you wish to use.
5. Click on the **Place** command button to place the selected *Fact* or *Dimensional Attribute* on the column.
   -or-
   If your cursor is not positioned on the appropriate column, use the **Left** and **Right** command buttons to position the cursor on the correct column before clicking on **Place**.
   -or-
   Click on the **Insert** command button to insert a column. This will also place the selected attribute on the newly inserted column.
6. Use the **Delete** command button to delete the current column if desired.
7. Use the **Close** command button to close the pop-up window when you have finished adding columns to your report.

 On the right-hand side of the pop-up window are two checkboxes labeled Fact and Additive.

"Fact" becomes enabled when the selected table is a *Fact* table. "Additive" becomes enabled when the selected attribute is an *Additive Fact*.

Moving a R/olapXL Column

You can easily change the sequence of R/olapXL Columns in your report by using the R/olapXL toolbar.

 To Move a R/olapXL Column:

1. Select the column you wish to move by clicking on the column heading or on any cell in that column.
2. On the R/olapXL toolbar, click on the Move Column to Left or Move Column to Right button, as appropriate.

> Moving a column on a R/olapXL worksheet does not in any way affect the structure or sequence of data in the data warehouse or the data mart.

Deleting R/olapXL Columns

Deleting a R/olapXL Column is no different from deleting any MS Excel column. Several options are available, each supported by the standard MS Excel software.

 To Delete a R/olapXL Column, Option 1:

1. Select the column to delete by clicking on the column heading.
2. From the Edit Menu, Choose Delete.

 To Delete a R/olapXL Column, Option 2:

1. Select any cell on the column you wish to delete.
2. From the Edit Menu, Choose Delete.
3. On the pop-up window, Choose Entire Column.
4. Click on **OK**.

 To Delete a R/olapXL Column, Option 3:

1. Use the right mouse button to click on any cell on the column you wish to delete.

2. On the pop-up menu, choose Delete.
3. On the pop-up window that appears, Choose Entire Column.
4. Click on **OK**.

 Deleting a column from a R/olapXL worksheet does not delete data from the data warehouse or the data mart.

Using Derived Columns

R/olapXL allows you to enter formulas to derive new values based on data retrieved from the data warehouse or data mart. These derived columns can be inserted anywhere in the R/olapXL report.

The cells with these formulas automatically recompute when new data are retrieved from the data warehouse or data mart.

Using Functions

A function can be applied to a fact or dimensional attribute in any R/olapXL report.

 By default, no functions are applied to non-numeric attributes, and the SUM function is the default for all numeric attributes.

R/olapXL supports the following functions:

- **SUM.** Applicable to numeric attributes, this function causes R/olapXL to add up the values of the factual attribute for all records that meet the constraints of the report. This is the default setting for any numeric fact.
- **COUNT.** Applicable to all attributes, this function causes R/olapXL to count the number of records that meet the constraints of the report.

- **MIN.** Applicable to dates and numeric attributes, this function causes R/olapXL to return the smallest distinct value of the factual attribute for all records that meet the constraints of the report.

- **MAX.** Applicable to dates and numeric attributes, this function causes R/olapXL to return the largest distinct value of the factual attribute for all records that meet the constraints of the report.

- **NONE.** Applicable only to dimensional attributes, this function causes R/olapXL to return one row for each record that meets the constraints of the report. This is the default setting for all dimensional attributes.

 You can enable the **DISTINCT** option when using R/olapXL functions. It instructs the database server to retrieve relevant rows and apply the used function only on unique instances of a particular record.

Drilling Up and Down Using R/olapXL Columns

R/olapXL supports two types of drills: *ad hoc* drills and *hierarchical* drills.

Ad Hoc Drills

Each time you add a *Dimensional Attribute* to your report, you are performing an *ad hoc* drill. For example, if your report currently has three columns—Country, Region, and Sales—you can drill further down by adding another dimensional attribute (e.g., Branch) before the Sales Fact column.

In general, as the dimensional attributes in your report increase, so will the level of detail of the facts in the report.

Hierarchical Drills

A *hierarchical* drill, on the other hand, is a drill-up or drill-down the hierarchy of a particular dimension. R/OLAPXL recognizes hierarchies within the data warehouse and automatically drills up or down the hierarchy when directed by the user.

Consider the following hierarchy in the Product Dimension:

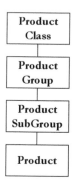

If the report currently displays Product SubGroup and you wish to drill up, R/OLAPXL will drill up to Product Group. If you wish to drill down, R/OLAPXL will drill down to Product.

Drilling Up Hierarchically

➲ To Drill Up Hierarchically:

1. From the R/OLAPXL menu, click on Drill-Up.
   -or-
   On the R/OLAPXL toolbar, click on the Drill-Up button.
   If more than one dimensional attribute is at a higher level in the hierarchy, R/OLAPXL presents you with a list of fields.
2. Choose one of the dimensional attributes, then click on the OK command button. R/OLAPXL will drill up the hierarchy to the selected attribute.

Drilling Down Hierarchically

Drilling down hierarchically follows the same principle.

➲ **To Drill Down Hierarchically:**

1. From the R/olapXL menu, click on Drill-Down.
    -or-
    On the R/olapXL toolbar, click on the Drill-Down button.
    If more than one dimensional attribute is at a lower level in
    the hierarchy, R/olapXL will present you with a list of fields.
2. Choose one of the dimensional attributes, then click on the
    OK command button. R/olapXL will drill down the hierarchy
    to the selected attribute.

Drilling To Hierarchically

R/olapXL also comes with a Drill-To option. While Drill-Up and Drill-
Down drill only one level higher or lower in the dimensional hierarchy, Drill-To allows the user to skip hierarchical levels.

Constraining Your R/olapXL Worksheet

Limit the data that R/olapXL retrieves from the data warehouse or
data mart by using *constraints*. A *constraint* is a conditional statement
with which any data item must comply before R/olapXL will retrieve
it. For example, if a business user wishes to see "sales figures for product X, at branch Y, for day Z," the user has actually specified the following constraints:

*   Product = "X"
*   Branch = "Y"
*   Day (or Date) = "Z"

R/olapXL recognizes *constraints* and limits the data that it retrieves so
that users get only the data they need.

Constraint Sets in R/olapXL

Each R/olapXL report starts with no constraints. To limit the data retrieved by R/olapXL, you must define one or more *Constraint Sets* and apply these *Constraint Sets* to the *Facts* in the report.

A *Constraint Set* is any combination of conditions that can be applied to a field in the report. You may choose to define these three conditions as one *Constraint Set*:

- Product = "X"
- Branch = "Y"
- Day (or Date) = "Z"

Each R/olapXL fact column can be assigned only one *constraint set*; however, each *constraint set* can have as many conditions as desired.

 To Create a Constraint Set:

1. From the R/olapXL menu, choose Manage Constraint Sets.
   -or-
   On the R/olapXL toolbar, click on the Manage Constraint Sets button.
2. On the pop-up window, click on the **New** command button. Another window will open.
3. On the new pop-up window, you will see the tables of the currently selected schema on a tree view. Name the Constraint Set you wish to create.

 Be careful when you choose a name for your Constraint Set. When the Constraint Set is applied to a column in your report, the Constraint Set name is added to the Column Title.

4. Click on the plus (+) and minus (−) symbols to expand or collapse a branch on the tree view until the attribute you wish to constrain becomes visible.
5. Select the attribute you wish to constrain, then click on the **New** command button.
   -or-
   Double-click on the attribute you wish to constrain.

6. On the small pop-up window, select a Function to Apply on the constraint value. Note that this is optional, and the function field can be left blank. Valid functions are SUM, MIN, MAX, and COUNT. The SUM function can be used only for numeric fields.

7. On the same pop-up window, select the appropriate operator value. Valid values are Equal (=), Less Than (<), Greater Than (>), Less Than or Equal (<=), Greater Than or Equal (>=) and Not Equal (<>), Like, Between, Not Between, In, and Not In. The Like operator can be used only on character fields.

The Between operator is typically used on numeric or date attributes (e.g., between 10 and 20, or between year 1997 and year 1998). However, this operator can also be used on character attributes. For example, you may have a constraint for Customer First Name with value BETWEEN A% and B%.

Note that the Between operator will *not* return the maximum value that meets the constraint. For example, if the last customer name that met the constraint value was "Byron Smith," this value will not be returned. To obtain a complete list of customers whose first names start with A or B, use the constraint value between A% and C%.

8. Enter the value that will be used to constrain the attribute.
   -or-
   Click on the List . . . command button to obtain a list of possible values. Select one of the values on the list, then click on the Select command button.

A List . . . command will take a very long time if there are many valid values in the database. A classic example is obtaining a list of customers when you have tens or hundreds of thousands of customers in your database.

Under such circumstances, you should constrain the list by using the like, between or in operators.

9. Repeat Steps 4 through 7 until all constraints have been defined for the appropriate attributes. Click on the **OK** command button to define the *Constraint Set.*

10. Click on the **New** command button to define another *Constraint Set,* or click on **Close** to end.

 To Assign a Constraint Set:

1. Click on any cell in the column you wish to constrain.
   -or-
   Click on the column heading of the column you wish to constrain.

2. From the R/olapXL menu, choose Assign Constraint Sets.
   -or-
   On the R/olapXL toolbar, click on the Assign Constraints Sets button. A pop-up window with all defined *Constraint Sets* will appear.

3. Click on the *Constraint Set* you wish to use.

4. Click on the **Assign** command button. The column title will be modified to include the name of the *Constraint Set* that was applied.

5. You can use the left and right arrows to change the selected column.

6. You can also remove a *Constraint Set* assignment by moving to the appropriate column, then clicking on the **Unassign** command button.

7. You can change *Constraint Sets* by selecting a new *Constraint Set* and assigning it to the appropriate column. The old *Constraint Set* assignment is overwritten.

8. Click on the **Close** button to end.

Only *Facts* can be assigned *Constraint Sets.* R/olapXL will not allow you to assign a *Constraint* Set to *Dimensional Attributes.*

➡ **To Edit a Constraint Set:**

1. From the R/olapXL menu, choose Manage Constraint Sets.
   -or-
   On the R/olapXL toolbar, click on the Manage Constraint Sets button.

2. On the pop-up window, select the Constraint Set you wish to modify, then click on the **Edit** command button. Another window should open.

3. On the new pop-up window, you will see the tables of the currently selected schema on a tree view. Click on the plus (+) and minus (−) symbols to expand or collapse a branch on the tree view. You can see the currently defined constraints. Expand or collapse the branches until the constraint you wish to modify becomes visible.

4. Select the constraint you wish to modify. Delete the constraint by clicking on the **Delete** command button, then create a new constraint.
   -or-
   Select the constraint you wish to modify. Click on the **Edit** command button.
   -or-
   Double-click on the constraint you wish to edit.

5. On the small pop-up window, modify the operator value as required. Valid values are Equal (=), Less Than (<), Greater Than (>), Less Than or Equal (<=), Greater Than or Equal (>=) and Not Equal (<>).

6. Modify the value that will be used to constrain the attribute.
   -or-
   Click on the **Browse** command button to obtain a list of possible values. Select one of the values on the list, then click on the **Select** command button.

7. Repeat Steps 3 through 6 until all constraints have been modified for the appropriate attributes. Click on the **OK** command button to save the new definition of this *Constraint Set*.

8. Select another *Constraint Set* and click on the **Edit** command button to modify another *Constraint Set,* or click on **Close** to end.

▶ Setting R/olapXL Options

The following R/olapXL options can be turned on or off depending on your requirements.

Rerun Report After Drilling

When you use R/olapXL's Hierarchical Drill feature, the report columns are modified to present you with greater or less detail. If this option (Re-run Report After Drilling) is enabled, R/olapXL will automatically rerun the report after the columns have been changed by a drill-up or drill-down.

If this option is disabled, you will need to explicitly run the report for R/olapXL to retrieve data from the data warehouse or data mart.

➲ **To Enable or Disable Automatic Rerun of Reports:**

1. From the R/olapXL menu, choose Options to bring up the R/olapXL Options dialog box.
   -or-
   On the R/olapXL toolbar, click on the **Options** button.
2. Enable or disable the option accordingly.
3. Click on the **OK** command button to save the new setting.

Start Cell

Each report in R/olapXL has its own Start Cell—the first cell from which the results of your queries are displayed. All retrieved data will be displayed below and to the right of this Start Cell.

Depending on the number of data items you wish to include in the header of your report or query, you may wish to change the starting cell of a query or report. By default, the starting cell of a R/olapXL worksheet is B3 (i.e., second column, third row).

To Change the Start Cell of a Report:

1. From the R/oLAPXL menu, choose Options to bring up the R/oLAPXL Options dialog box.
   -or-
   On the R/oLAPXL toolbar, click on the **Options** button.
2. Change the Start Cell by specifying the row letter(s) and column number of the new cell. The current Start Cell setting is displayed.
3. Click on the **OK** command button to save the new Start Cell.
4. R/oLAPXL will ask for confirmation to change the Start Cell. Click on the **Yes** button to immediately update the report. Clicking on the **No** button is equivalent to Cancel.

Suppress Repeating Values

R/oLAPXL allows you to suppress repeating values within report columns. A repeating value exists when two or more succeeding rows in one column contain the same value.

When this option is enabled, only the first row will have a displayed value; subsequent rows will be blank until another value is encountered.

 To Suppress Repeating Values in a Report:

1. From the R/oLAPXL menu, choose Options to bring up the R/oLAPXL Options dialog box.
   -or-
   On the R/oLAPXL toolbar, click on the **Options** button.
2. Enable or disable the option accordingly.
3. Click on the **OK** button to save the new setting. The new settings can be applied either immediately or when the report is rerun.

> If you intend to sort your query results, disable the option to suppress repeating values.

Cascading User Formulas in the Report Body

R/olapXL now allows you to specify whether user-defined formulas in a R/olapXL report should be cascaded down all cells of the report body.

 To Enable or Disable the Cascading Feature:

1. From the R/olapXL menu, choose Options.
   -or-
   On the R/olapXL toolbar, click on the **Options** button.
2. Enable or disable the option accordingly.
3. Click on the **OK** command button to save the new setting.

Running a R/olapXL Report

When you have finished adding the columns and (optionally) constraints to your R/olapXL worksheet, you are ready to run your report.

Running the report causes R/olapXL to retrieve the specified data from the data warehouse or data mart.

 To Run a R/olapXL Report:

1. From the R/olapXL menu, choose Run Report.
   -or-
   On the R/olapXL toolbar, click on the **Run Report** button.

 Depending on its size and complexity, a R/olapXL report may take anywhere between a few seconds to several minutes to run.

Using Subtotals

MS Excel can calculate and insert subtotals in a worksheet. You will need to specify three things: (1) the items for which you want to create subtotals; (2) the values to be summarized; and (3) the function to use on the values.

MS Excel outlines the worksheet so that you can show or hide as much detail as you need.

 The Subtotal features described here are applicable only to Excel 97. Unfortunately, Excel 95 does not provide the same level of support for subtotals. This feature is therefore disabled on Excel 95 installations.

R/olapXL makes use of standard Excel subtotal functionality but provides its own user interface to ease the management of subtotals in your R/olapXL reports.

Subtotals and Column Suppressing

R/olapXL will allow you to define Subtotal definitions for your report at any point in time. However, if you have applied column suppressing, R/olapXL will not allow you to apply the Subtotal definitions.

We strongly suggest that you disable column suppressing before applying subtotals to avoid subtotal computation errors.

Subtotals and Sorting

Subtotals will work best if your report is properly sorted by dimensional attributes. If you have changed the natural order of the report by using Excel's sort function, you may want to rerun the report to restore the original sort order.

 To Create Subtotals:

1. Select a cell in your R/olapXL report.

   Excel uses the active (current) cell to identify the report for which subtotals will be created.

2. From the R/OLAPXL menu, choose Subtotals.

   The Manage Subtotals dialog box will appear. This dialog box lists all the fields in your R/OLAPXL report.

3. Click on the checkbox corresponding to the field for which you want subtotals. A new dialog box (Subtotals For . . .) will appear.

4. In the new dialog box:
   a. Select the function that should be used with this subtotal by clicking on the drop-down list box and selecting the appropriate function.
   b. Indicate which fields should be computed. By default, R/OLAPXL selects all Fact fields.
   c. Click on the Page Break Between Groups checkbox if you wish to enforce page breaks for each new subtotal grouping.
   d. Click on the Summary Below Data checkbox if you wish to display grand totals at the bottom of the report.
   e. Click on **OK** to save the Subtotal definitions for this field.

 MS Excel will always compute for grand totals when subtotals are used on a report. You can display the totals either at the top of the report or at the bottom.

5. Repeat Step 3 for each field for which a subtotal is required.

6. When you have completed defining subtotals for all relevant fields, click on the **OK** button to immediately apply the new subtotal definitions

   -or-

7. Click on Close to close the dialog box. The new subtotal definitions will be applied the next time the report is rerun.

 Totals placed at the bottom of the report must have at least a single row interval from the last report row.

 To Remove Subtotals:

1. Select a cell in your R/OLAPXL report to indicate that you wish to work on this report.

2. From the R/olapXL menu, choose Subtotals.

   The main R/olapXL subtotal dialog box will appear. This dialog box lists all the fields in your R/olapXL and indicates which fields have subtotals defined.

3. Click on the corresponding checkbox to disable subtotals for one or more fields.

   -or-

   Click on the **Remove All** command button to remove all subtotals in your report.

4. R/olapXL will ask if you wish to remove subtotal definitions. Click on **Yes** if you wish to completely remove all subtotal definitions. Click on **No** if you wish to keep subtotal definitions but remove all subtotals from the report.

 The Subtotal feature works by identifying Report Regions. Excel will interpret an empty column between two report columns or any empty row as the end point of the report.

To make full use of the Subtotal feature, you must make use of contiguous rows and columns in your report.

Sorting R/olapXL Reports

MS Excel has a built-in sort feature that is limited to a maximum of three sort keys. R/olapXL builds on the standard Excel sort feature and extends it further by now allowing users to sort a data set, using an unlimited number of sort keys. Both R/olapXL columns and user-defined columns can be sorted, and the sort definition is preserved on every report rerun.

R/olapXL provides its own user interface to ease management of sorting in your R/olapXL reports.

Sorting and Column Suppressing

R/olapXL will allow you to define sort definitions for your report at any point in time. However, if you have applied column suppressing, the suppression of repeating values may lead to a confusing report.

R/olapXL will determine if suppression has been applied and will warn you if you try to sort data with suppressed repeating values.

We strongly suggest that you disable column suppressing before sorting any data set.

Sorting and Subtotals

Changing the sort order of a report while there are subtotals applied could lead to erroneous calculation. R/olapXL will prompt you to remove any subtotals whenever you try to apply a different sort order.

 To Create Sort Definitions:

1. Select a cell in your R/olapXL report. Excel uses the active (current) cell to identify the report for which sort definitions will be created.

2. From the R/olapXL menu, choose Sort. The Manage Sort dialog box will appear. This dialog box lists all the fields in your R/olapXL report.

3. Select the fields you wish to add to the sort definition from the left list box and transfer these to the right list box.

4. In the right list box, change the sort order if required. Select either Ascending or Descending order.

5. Click on **OK** to save the new sort definition and immediately apply the new sort order to your pre-existing data, if available.

 The Sort feature works by identifying Report Regions. Excel will interpret an empty column between two report columns or any empty row as the end point of the report.

To make full use of the Sort feature, you must make use of contiguous rows and columns in your report.

 To Remove Sort Definitions:

1. Select a cell in your R/olapXL report to indicate that you wish to work on this report.

2. From the R/olapXL menu, choose Sort. The main R/olapXL sort dialog box will appear. This dialog box lists all the fields in your R/olapXL report and indicates which fields are included in the sort definition.

3. Remove fields from the Sort Definition by selecting fields from the right list box and transferring these to the left list box.

Using Pivot Tables with your R/olapXL Reports

A Pivot table is a multidimensional view of data that provides improved readability. MS Excel provides standard Pivot table functionality; R/olapXL builds on top of these existing features to increase their usability.

For example, a typical spreadsheet will present data in the following format.

Country	Product	Sales
USA	Shoes	1,000
USA	Shirts	2,000
UK	Shoes	4,000
UK	Shirts	3,500
UK	Shorts	2,000
Australia	Shorts	1,500
Australia	Shirts	2,500

A Pivot table has four basic parts:

- **Page.** Shows data for one item at a time in the table
- **Column.** Shows items in the field as column labels (Products, in the above example)
- **Row.** Shows items in the field as row labels (Country, in the above example)
- **Data.** Summarized values in the body of the table

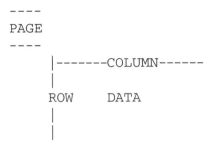

```
----
PAGE
----
        |-------COLUMN------
        |
        ROW      DATA
        |
        |
```

With Pivot tables, R/olapXL users can now obtain a summarized multidimensional view of the same data, where actual item or field values from a table are converted to either row values, column values, page values or data.

	Product		
	Shoes	Shirts	Shorts
Country			
USA	1,000	2,000	
UK	4,000	3,500	2,000
Australia		2,500	1,500

Pivot Table Data Sources

In order to create a R/olapXL Pivot table report, a R/olapXL table report is needed to serve as the source report for the Pivot table.

A R/olapXL Pivot report uses an existing table report as the source for its data. In contrast, a table report is fed by data fetched directly from the database. This difference in data sources allows users to do offline or mobile analysis. Since a Pivot report fetches its data from just another Excel worksheet, the results of drills and other functions applied on the Pivot report are almost instantaneous.

R/olapXL Pivot tables behave and function like standard Excel Pivot tables. Please refer to Excel's User's Guide to Pivot Tables for a detailed explanation.

With the exception of the **RUN** command, R/olapXL standard commands (toolbars and menus) are not available if the current report is a Pivot report.

 Ensure that the Source report of any R/olapXL Pivot table does not have column suppressing or subtotals defined. The source report must be bare—it should only contain plain data.

Manipulation of a R/olapXL Pivot report should be done by invoking the functions provided in the R/olapXL Pivot toolbar or through R/olapXL Pivot menu.

Commands for R/olapXL Pivot Table Reports

There are three main commands for R/olapXL Pivot table reports:

- New or View R/olapXL Pivot report
- View R/olapXL Pivot report source
- Refresh R/olapXL Pivot report

New or View R/olapXL Pivot Report

To create a R/olapXL Pivot report, click on the New or View R/olapXL Pivot Report via the R/olapXL toolbar or menu, making sure the current sheet is a R/olapXL table report and has data. This command will invoke the Pivot Table wizard. Simply follow the steps described by the wizard. Creating the Pivot report on a new sheet is recommended. Multiple Pivot table reports on a single sheet is allowed but discouraged.

 There can only be one Pivot table report assigned to a table report, and vice versa.

If a Pivot report has already been defined based on the current R/olapXL table report, this function will bring up the corresponding Pivot report.

Invoking this command while a R/olapXL Pivot report is active will launch the Excel Pivot table wizard; this is usually done when a Pivot report needs redefining or manipulation.

View R/olapXL Pivot Report Source

Invoke this command while a R/olapXL Pivot report is active to bring up the report's source data. This command will fail if the source is hidden or if the source was deleted.

Refresh R/olapXL Pivot Report

Invoke this command while a R/olapXL Pivot report is active to update the Pivot report based on the data in the Pivot Source report. This command will fail if the source was deleted.

You may also refresh a R/olapXL Pivot report by clicking on the **RUN** command. This command will refresh the Source report by retrieving data directly from the database; consequently, the Pivot report is refreshed, based on the newly acquired data. This method is ideal if the Pivot report is used as a Parameterized report.

Other Pivot Table Commands

Other commands included in the R/olapXL Pivot toolbar, namely, **Pivot Table Field, Hide Detail, Show Detail,** and **Show Pages,** are standard Pivot table commands available in the Excel Pivot Table toolbar. These were included in the R/olapXL Pivot toolbar to eliminate the need for switching between the standard Excel Pivot toolbar and R/olapXL Pivot toolbar. Please refer to Excel's online documentation for these commands.

Viewing R/olapXL SQL Statements

Technically inclined users may wish to view the SQL statements generated by R/olapXL for a given report.

 To View R/olapXL SQL Statements:

1. From the R/olapXL menu, choose SQL.

    R/olapXL will create a text file containing the SQL statements it
    generates to produce the report in the currently active worksheet.
    The text file will be stored in the R/olapXL application path.

 R/olapXL uses the following naming convention for the text
files it produces: **WorkbookName!SheetName.SQL**

For example, viewing the SQL statements of the first report in
our Retail sample reports workbook will create a file called
Retail.xls!Report 1.SQL in the R/olapXL directory.

---

2. If a file of the same name already exists, you will be prompted
    either to overwrite or to append to it.
3. Once the SQL statements have been saved, you will be given
    the option to view the SQL statements. R/olapXL uses
    NotePad to display the contents of the .SQL file.

▶ The R/olapXL Toolbars

Two toolbars are provided to increase the usability of R/olapXL.

-   The **Standard** toolbar contains shortcuts to standard R/olapXL
    functionality.
-   The **Pivot** toolbar contains shortcuts to the R/olapXL features
    related to the use of Pivot tables.

R/olapXL takes note of the positions of both these toolbars each time
R/olapXL is closed. When Excel is opened at a later time, R/olapXL
will place the toolbars at their last location.

The Standard Toolbar

The following table describes the tools on the Standard R/olapXL toolbar. The Standard R/olapXL toolbar is automatically displayed when R/olapXL has been successfully installed. Launch any of the main features of this software by clicking on one of the buttons on this toolbar.

Tool	Name	Description
	Select Schema	Provides a list of all available schemas for the user to select.
	Manage R/olapXL Columns	Allows users to insert, replace, or delete columns from their report.
	Manage Constraint Sets	Allows users to define Constraint Sets that can be applied to R/olapXL column.
	Assign Constraint Sets	Applies the constraint definition to the specified R/olapXL column.
	Drill Up	Drills one level up a dimensional hierarchy.
	Drill Down	Drills one level down a dimensional hierarchy.
	Drill To	Drills up or down a dimensional hierarchy by one or more levels.
	Sort	Allows users to sort the report data in a R/olapXL report.
	Subtotal	Allows users to create subtotals for the report.
	Function	Allows users to specify the function to apply on a report field.
	View SQL	Allows users to view the SQL statements generated by R/olapXL for a given report.
	Options	Allows users to set R/olapXL options.
	Run Report	Retrieves data from the data warehouse, based on user-specified columns and constraints.
	Move Column to Left	Moves the currently highlighted column to the right by one column.
	Move Column to Right	Moves the currently highlighted column to the left by one column.

The Pivot Toolbar

The following table describes the tools on the R/olapXL Pivot toolbar. The Pivot toolbar is automatically displayed when R/olapXL has been successfully installed. Launch any of the Pivot features by clicking on one of the buttons on this toolbar.

Tool	Name	Description
	New or View Pivot Report	Creates a new Pivot report or opens an existing Pivot report, using the active sheet as the data source.
	View R/olapXL Pivot Report Source	Displays the data source for the currently active Pivot report.
	Refresh R/olapXL Pivot Report	Refreshes the Pivot report, based on the data in the related data source.
	Pivot Table Field	Standard Excel Pivot command. Allows users to define Pivot field properties.
	Hide Detail	Standard Excel Pivot command. Hides source data detail for a Pivot field.
	Show Detail	Standard Excel Pivot command. Shows source data detail for a Pivot field.
	Show Pages	Standard Excel Pivot command. Displays Pivot report pages as separate worksheets.

▶ Macro Programming

MS Excel has an extensive macro programming environment and language that allows technical users to automate Excel tasks. These macros can improve the usability and sophistication of R/olapXL reports. Note, however, that the use of such features requires technical expertise and is suitable only to power users or Information Technology staff.

Simple Parameterized Reports

Parameterized reports can be created with Excel macros. Below is an example of a parameterized report that uses **Month** and **Year** as parameters.

SALES BY PRODUCT

Month: ⎡April⎤

Year: ⎡1997⎤

		Sales				
Department	Brand	Week 1	Week 2	Week 3	Week 4	Week 5

Below is a template of the Excel macro we will use. `"Macro_Name,"` `"Table,"` and `"Field"` will be different for each parameter in our report.

```
Sub MACRO_NAME()
On Error Resume Next
Dim loVar$
loVar$=API_SetConstraint ("!DEFAULT", "TABLE,"
 "FIELD")
If Len(Trim(loVar$))>0 Then
 ActiveSheet.Buttons(Application.Caller).
 Caption=loVar$
End If
End Sub
```

This macro allows a user to change the constraint currently applied on a *Constraint Set,* then displays the new constraint value on a button form.

Warehouse Schema Knowledge Is Required

To create a parameterized report, you must know the physical table and field names of the data items you intend to use as parameters. For example, if you intend to use **Month** and **Year** as parameters in your report, you must know the table names and field names for these two parameters.

In our sample retail schema, these two fields are:

Parameter	Table Name	Field Name
Month	Time_Dimension	Month_Name
Year	Time_Dimension	Year_No

Creating Parameterized Reports

The steps required to create an Excel macro vary slightly between MS Excel 95 and MS Excel 97 because of differences in the macro programming environments of these two versions. The step-by-step instructions below indicate the differences between the two.

 To Create a Parameterized R/olapXL Report:

1. Create and save your basic R/olapXL report.
2. Enter the macro programming environment of MS Excel.
   - **Excel 95:** From the Insert menu, choose Macro, then Module. An Excel Module will be inserted as a new sheet in the same workbook.
   - **Excel 97:** From the Tools menu, choose Macro, then Visual Basic Editor.
     -or-
     Press Alt-F11.
3. Create a macro reference to the R/olapXL add-in. This reference is required for the **API_SetConstraint** function to work properly.
   - From the Tools menu of the macro programming environment, choose References.
   - In the dialog box that appears, look for **R/olapXL.xls** and turn on the corresponding checkbox.
   - Click on the **OK** command button to close the dialog box.
4. Create a subroutine or macro for each field that will be used as a parameter.
   - **Excel 97:** From the Insert menu of the Visual Basic Editor, choose Module.
   - **Excel 95:** Click on the tab of the newly inserted Module.

5. In the window or sheet that appears, type in the sample Excel macro provided on the previous page.
   - In the macro text you just typed, change MACRO_NAME to a meaningful name. For example, if the macro is intended to specify the correct month, you could call it SetMonth.
   - Change FIELD to the name of the data warehouse field that will be used as a parameter. For example, you may be using the field called Month_Name.
   - Change TABLE to the name of the data warehouse table to which the field belongs. For example, you may be using the table called Time_Dimension.
   - Create a macro for each of the parameters in your report. You may choose to copy and paste your first macro within the same module, then modify the macro name, table name, and field name accordingly.
6. From the File menu, choose Save to save the new macro(s). If you have never saved the Excel file before, you will be prompted to provide a new file name. The macros will be saved as part of the same MS Excel file.
7. Return to MS Excel.
   - **Excel 95:** Click on your Report tab to return to your report.
   - **Excel 97:** Close the Visual Basic editor to return to Excel.
8. In Excel, create a *Constraint Set* called !DEFAULT. Create a constraint on any one of the parameterized fields. You may use any constraint value you wish.
9. Assign the !DEFAULT *Constraint Set* to the *Fact* fields of the report.
10. Add one button to your report for each of the parameters.
    a. From the View menu, choose Toolbars, then Forms. A new set of toolbars called Forms should appear.
    b. Click on the Button toolbar option, then create a button by dragging your mouse anywhere over your worksheet.
    c. MS Excel will prompt you for the appropriate macro to assign to this button. Select one of the macros you created earlier, then click on OK.
    d. Resize the button, using the handles on the corners of the button. Position the button properly on your worksheet by first clicking, then dragging on any part of the button border *except* the handles.
    e. You may wish to set the sizing and position properties of the button by right-clicking on button icon, and selecting

the Format Control option. Select the Properties tab, and choose the appropriate Object Positioning setting.

11. When all buttons have been created, click on each button, one at a time, to open the Define Constraint window in R/OLAPXL. Choose the appropriate constraint values for your report.

12. Run the report again to view the data now constrained by your parameters.

 Use the R/OLAPXL Options command to lower the Start Cell of your report. This should provide sufficient space for placing the parameter fields at the top of your report.

API_SetConstraint Function

The `API_SetConstraint` function is one of the key functions defined specifically for R/OLAPXL. The function will return either the name of a *Constraint Set* or a 0-length string if cancelled.

The valid parameters for this function are enumerated below. Only the first three are mandatory.

Optional	Name	Description
No	pConstraintSet	Constraint Set name
No	pTable	Table name in database
No	pField	Field name in database
Yes	pPublic	Valid values: true or false. True will make the constraint Public.
Yes	pConsFunction	Returns the chosen constraint function
Yes	pConsOperator	Returns the chosen constraint operator
Yes	pConsArgument	Returns the chosen constraint argument with delimiter (single quotes if character data)
Yes	pLastTimeConstraint	Returns the last time constraint argument without delimiter (e.g., between 6/30/97 and 8/31/97 returns 8/31/97)
Yes	pWsIdx	Returns the R/OLAPXL data structure index of a R/OLAPXL report sheet

If the pPublic parameter is set to true, R/OLAPXL will ignore the first parameter (Constraint Set Name), and instead will make the constraint Public for all Constraint Sets.

API_SetConstraintDirect Function

The `API_SetConstraintDirect` function directly sets a private constraint to a specified constraint set without showing the Constraints dialog box. This function will return true if it succeeds and false otherwise.

The valid parameters for this function are enumerated below. All parameters are mandatory.

Name	Description
pWsIdx	The R/OLAPXL data structure index of a R/OLAPXL report sheet; can be obtained by use of the API_SetConstraint (pWsIdx) function
pConstraintSet	The Constraint Set to be modified
pTable	Name of the table with the constraint to be modified
pField	Name of the field with the constraint to be modified
pFunction	The function to apply on the new constraint value
pOperator	The operator to be used on the new constraint value
pArgument	The argument to be used on the new constraint value

API_Value Function

There are times when a R/OLAPXL report will require one specific value from the database as a parameter or a constant. For these type of requirements, you can use the R/OLAPXL function called `API_VALUE`.

This function will accept any SELECT statement that returns a single value. The syntax for this function is:

```
API_VALUE (pSQL)
```

where `pSQL` can either be:

a. any String variable that contains the actual SELECT statement; or

b. the actual SELECT statement enclosed in double quotes(" ").

R/OLAPXL Sample Retail Database

The sample Retail database contains data for the months of February to May for the years 1996 and 1997.

Sales Fact

Field Name	Null?	Data Type	Remarks
UNITS_SOLD	NOT NULL	NUMBER	Number of units sold in a given period of time.
SALES AMOUNT	NOT NULL	NUMBER	Total sales amount.

Product Dimension

Field Name	Null?	Data Type	Remarks
SKU_NUMBER	NOT NULL	NUMBER(8)	Code assigned to the product.
SKU_DESCRIPTION	NOT NULL	CHAR(50)	Description of the product.
BRAND	NOT NULL	CHAR(30)	Brand of the product.
SUBCATEGORY	NOT NULL	CHAR(30)	Low-level classification of the product indicating its product type (Chocolate Cakes or Pound Cakes for Cakes, Rolls or Baguettes for Breads).

DEPARTMENT	NOT NULL	CHAR(30)	Department handling the sales of the product.
CATEGORY	NOT NULL	CHAR(30)	High-level classification of the product indicating its product type (Cakes or Breads).
PACKAGE_TYPE	NOT NULL	CHAR(30)	Type of packaging (plastic bag or box) used for the product.

Time Dimension

Field Name	Null?	Data Type	Remarks
CALENDAR_DATE	NOT NULL	DATE	All dates that are needed to support warehouse queries.
DAY_OF_WEEK_NAME	NOT NULL	CHAR(9)	Day corresponding to the calendar date.
DAY_OF_WEEK_SHORT_NAME	NOT NULL	CHAR(3)	Three-letter short name for the day of the week.
DAY_NO_OVERALL	NOT NULL	NUMBER(8)	Represents the calendar date as the number of days elapsed since the company started doing business.
HOLIDAY_FLAG	NOT NULL	NUMBER(1)	Flag indicating whether the calendar date is a holiday or not.
WEEKDAY_FLAG	NOT NULL	NUMBER(1)	Flag indicating if the calendar date falls on a weekday or a weekend.
WEEK_NO_IN_MONTH	NOT NULL	NUMBER(3)	Number corresponding to the week in month of the calendar date.
WEEK_NO_IN_QUARTER	NOT NULL	NUMBER(3)	Number corresponding to the week in quarter of the calendar date.
WEEK_NO_IN_YEAR	NOT NULL	NUMBER(3)	Number corresponding to the week in year of the calendar date.
WEEK_NO_OVERALL	NOT NULL	NUMBER(8)	Represents the calendar date as the number of weeks elapsed since the company started doing business.

MONTH_NAME	NOT NULL	CHAR(9)	Month name component of the calendar date.
MONTH_SHORT_NAME	NOT NULL	CHAR(3)	Three-letter short name for the month component of the calendar date.
MONTH_NO_IN_QUARTER	NOT NULL	NUMBER(3)	Number corresponding to the month in quarter of the calendar date.
MONTH_NO_IN_YEAR	NOT NULL	NUMBER(3)	Month number component of the calendar date.
MONTH_NO_OVERALL	NOT NULL	NUMBER(8)	Represents the calendar date as the number of months elapsed since the company started doing business.
QUARTER_NO_IN_YEAR	NOT NULL	NUMBER(3)	Number corresponding to the quarter in year of the calendar date.
QUARTER_NO_OVERALL	NOT NULL	NUMBER(8)	Represents the calendar date as the number of quarters elapsed since the company started doing business.
YEAR_NO	NOT NULL	NUMBER(8)	Year component of the calendar date.
YEAR_NO_OVERALL	NOT NULL	NUMBER(8)	Represents the calendar date as the number of years elapsed since the company started doing business.

Promotion Dimension

Field Name	Null?	Data Type	Remarks
PROMOTION_NAME	NOT NULL	CHAR(30)	Descriptive name of the promotion. Note that a special entry called NO_PROMOTION is added to handle all dates for which a promotion is not defined.
PROMOTION_TYPE	NOT NULL	CHAR(30)	Indicates what products are included in the promotion.

Field Name	Null?	Data Type	Remarks
START_DATE	NULL	DATE	Start date of the promotion period. Null is specified for the special entry NO_PROMOTION.
END_DATE	NULL	DATE	End date of the promotion period. Null is specified for the special entry NO_PROMOTION.

Store Dimension

Field Name	Null?	Data Type	Remarks
STORE_NAME	NOT NULL	CHAR(30)	Descriptive name of the store.
STORE_CODE	NOT NULL	NUMBER(3)	Code assigned to the store.
STORE_ADDRESS	NOT NULL	CHAR(30)	Location address of the store.
STORE_CITY	NOT NULL	CHAR(20)	City where the store is located.
STORE_COUNTRY	NOT NULL	CHAR(30)	Country where the store is located.
STORE_POSTAL_CODE	NOT NULL	NUMBER(8)	Postal code of the store.
SALES_DISTRICT	NOT NULL	CHAR(30)	Sales District where the store belongs.
SALES_REGION	NOT NULL	CHAR(30)	Sales Region where the store belongs.
STORE_MANAGER	NOT NULL	CHAR(30)	Name of the manager of the store.
STORE_LAYOUT_TYPE	NOT NULL	CHAR(30)	Type of layout of the store (1 floor, 2 floor, or 2-story)
STORE_OPENING_DATE	NOT NULL	DATE	Date when the store first opened for business.

▶ R/olapXL Messages

R/olapXL raises four types of messages:

- **Error Messages.** Error messages are raised when there are errors in the way R/olapXL is used. R/olapXL error messages are also used to raise server and database errors.
- **Informational Messages.** These messages provide users with additional information regarding R/olapXL usage.
- **Warning Messages.** Warning messages forewarn users of irreversible or potentially erroneous actions.
- **Prompts.** These messages prompt users for a response and are typically phrased in the form of a question.

Error Messages

This section enumerates and explains the error messages raised by R/olapXL. Please refer to MS Excel documentation for Excel error messages.

- **Error in Saving R/OLAPXL definition.** This message is raised when the R/olapXL file cannot be saved properly due to a system error.
- **Error in Loading R/OLAPXL definition.** This message is raised when the R/OLAPXL file cannot be loaded properly due to a system error.
- **An error occurred while connecting to database. Call your IT Department for assistance.** This message is raised when the connection to the database fails due to a system error.
- **Cannot proceed, please fill in the VALUES edit box.** This error occurs when you attempt to define a constraint without specifying a constraining value.
- **Cannot do this to a nonadjacent multi-area selection.** This error occurs when users attempt to move two or more nonadjacent columns.
- **Please include at least one Fact Table Column in report.** R/OLAPXL requires at least one fact in each R/OLAPXL report.

- **At least one PRIVATE CONSTRAINT is required to define a Constraint Set.** Each *Constraint Set* must have at least one private constraint defined.

- **A Constraint Set NAME is required.** Each *Constraint Set* must be given a unique name.

- **Constraint Set NAME already exists.** Each *Constraint Set* must be given a unique name.

- **No Relation Keys found in Metadata. Call your IT Department for assistance.** The metadata required to access the data warehouse are incomplete.

- **Error in managing R/OLAPXL columns.** This message is raised when an error occurs while users are managing R/OLAPXL columns.

- **Error encountered in selecting Schema.** This message is raised when a system error occurs while the user is selecting a *Schema*.

- **Error in creating OLE Instance.** This message is raised when a system error occurs while the R/OLAPXL is loading an OLE instance.

- **Error encountered in opening R/OLAPXL.** This message is raised when a system error occurs while R/OLAPXL is starting up.

- **Error encountered while executing a query.** This error occurs when the query execution fails.

- **Fact columns must always be placed after Dimension columns.** R/OLAPXL requires all Dimension columns to be placed to the left of Fact columns.

- **The number of rows returned from a query exceeded Excel's limit. Please constrain this report further.** MS Excel has a maximum number of rows. This error occurs when the number of rows returned by a query exceeds Excel's maximum. You may want to try constraining the report to return a smaller result set.

- **Error in assigning Constraint Set.** This message is raised when a system error occurs while a user is assigning a *Constraint Set*.

- **Error in drilling dimension columns. Active column is not a R/OLAPXL column.** R/OLAPXL's drilling functionality is applicable only to R/OLAPXL columns.

- **Error encountered in loading Metadata. There are no defined schemas; or no defined tables; or defined tables have no defined fields.** R/OLAPXL searches for schema, table, and field definitions in R/OLAPXL metadata. If one or more of these definitions are absent, this error occurs.

- **Maximum number of concurrent users (#) exceeded!** This message is raised when the number of concurrent users accessing the data warehouse or data mart exceeds the number of licensed users.
- **Unlicensed server environment!** This message is raised when the license key provided for R/OLAPXL server is invalid for the specified database.
- **Expired License!-License expired last `<date>`.** The R/OLAPXL server license has expired.
- **License version is `<ver no>`.** Current version is `<ver no>`. This error occurs when the client and server versions are incompatible.
- **The R/OLAPXL Sample Retail database has been corrupted. Please reinstall.** The **R/OLAPXL Client** software has been configured to work with only one MS Access database—the sample retail database. This message is raised when the sample retail database has been modified or when other Access databases are used.
- **Browse results contain more than 30,000 rows. Please specify another browse criterion.** This error message is raised when an attempt to browse for values returns more than 30,000 distinct values. Specify a browse criterion to limit the number of browse values.
- **Error in expression.** This error message is raised when the AND, BETWEEN, or NOT BETWEEN browse operator is used but the two required values are not provided. Specify the required values, or choose another operator.
- **Invalid date.** This error message is raised when the constraint that is applied on a date field is not convertible to a valid date. Specify a valid date.
- **The value before the "AND" expression operator must be greater than the value after it.** This error message is self-explanatory.
- **Numeric data required.** This error message is raised when the constraint that is applied on a numeric field is not convertible to a valid number. Specify a valid number.
- **A function is required to define a subtotal.** An Excel subtotal definition is incomplete without a function. Specify the function that is applicable for the subtotal you are defining.

- **At least one column must be selected to define a subtotal.** An Excel subtotal definition requires at least one selected column. Select the column(s) applicable to your subtotal definition.
- **Group By column in subtotals not found in current region. Make sure your report columns are contiguous.** The Report Region does not contain the column you intend to use to compute subtotals. Eliminate any empty columns between report columns to make your report contiguous.
- **Subtotaled column/s not found in current region. Make sure your report columns are contiguous.** The columns to be subtotaled are not in the current Report Region. Eliminate any empty columns between report columns to make your report contiguous.
- **Cannot apply subtotals. No rows detected in report.** The report does not contain any data and therefore cannot be subtotaled.
- **Multiple pivot reports detected on the current worksheet. Click on a pivot table cell and repeat this operation.** Excel does not know which Pivot report you wish to work on. Select the appropriate Pivot table by clicking on any cell within that table. This will activate the Pivot report.
- **Sort column/s not found in current region. Make sure your report columns are contiguous.** The columns to be sorted are not in the current Report Region. Eliminate any empty columns between report columns to make your report contiguous.

Informational Messages

This section enumerates and explains the informational messages raised by R/OLAPXL. Please refer to MS Excel documentation for Excel informational messages.

- **There are no Hierarchies defined for this column.** This message is raised when a user attempts to drill up or down on a R/OLAPXL column that has no hierarchies.
- **<field name> is already part of this report.** This message is raised when the user attempts to drill up or down to an attribute that is already part of the report.

- **`<sheet name>` is not a R/OLAPXL Worksheet.** This message is raised when the user attempts to use R/OLAPXL functionality on a non-R/OLAPXL worksheet.

- **`<sheet name>` is not an Excel Worksheet.** This message is raised when the active sheet is either a macro sheet, a chart, a module, or a dialog box.

- **Constraint already existing as Public.** This message is raised when the user attempts to define a constraint that already exists as a public constraint.

- **Constraint already existing as Private.** This message is raised when the user attempts to define a constraint that already exists as a private constraint.

- **No records were retrieved.** This message is raised when the query returns no records.

- **Please choose a Constraint Set for this column.** This message is raised when the user tries to assign a *Constraint Set* to a R/OLAPXL column when no *Constraint Set* has been selected.

- **Suppression of Repeating Values will be applied after the report is re-run.** R/OLAPXL allows you to suppress repeating values in a report. A repeating value exists when two or more succeeding rows in one column contain the same value. When this option is enabled, only the first row will have a displayed value; subsequent rows will be blank until another value is encountered.

- **Changes will be applied after re-running the report.** New settings will be applied only after the report has been rerun.

- **Cannot continue operation. Suppressed columns have been detected. Please remove all column suppressing and repeat this operation.** Column suppressing distorts the results of sort and subtotal operations. Disable column suppressing before trying again.

- **The R/OLAPXL table report being referenced does not have enough rows. A pivot table needs at least 2 rows of data.** This message is self-explanatory.

- **The report being referenced by this pivot report was already deleted or this is not a R/OLAPXL pivot report.** This message is self-explanatory.

- **You must first define report columns before sorting columns.** This message is self-explanatory.

Warning Messages

This section enumerates and explains the warning message(s) raised by R/OLAPXL. Please refer to MS Excel documentation for Excel warning messages.

- **Changing schemas will discard changes in the currently active worksheet.** Each R/olapXL worksheet works only with one schema. If you have started defining a R/olapXL report on the active worksheet, changing to another schema will cause R/olapXL to discard all changes to the report.
- **This will terminate the current connection and establish a new one. Continue?** This warning message appears when the Reconnect command is selected. Use the reconnection command only when you wish to connect to another data source.
- **The result of this query contains many rows and may take some time to display. You may wish to apply a tighter constraint. Continue displaying query results?** Some queries return very large result sets that may take a long time to display. This warning provides you with the opportunity to cancel your original query and apply tighter constraints before rerunning the report.
- **Suppressed columns have been detected. Proceeding further may lead to a confusing display. You may choose to Cancel, then Disable Column Suppressing before repeating this operation.** This message is self-explanatory.

Prompts

This section enumerates and explains the prompts raised by R/olapXL. Please refer to MS Excel documentation for Excel prompts.

- **Cancel plotting of result set?** Users may interrupt the plotting of query results on an Excel worksheet by pressing the escape (ESC) key. R/olapXL prompts users to confirm cancellation.
- **Delete PUBLIC Constraint?** Users are prompted to confirm the deleting of any public constraints.
- **Any columns that use this Constraint Set will also be deleted. Continue?** When users delete a Constraint Set, R/olapXL also deletes any columns that use that Constraint Set.

- **Do you also wish to remove all subtotal definitions?** When you choose to remove all subtotals, you will be asked if you also wish to remove all subtotal definitions. Note that subtotals can be removed from the active report without removing subtotal definitions.

- **Remove subtotal definition?** Confirmation is requested each time you remove a subtotal definition from any field in the report.

Warehouse Designer® User's Manual

▶ Welcome to Warehouse Designer!

WAREHOUSE DESIGNER is a dimensional data warehouse modeling tool that enables users to define data warehouse objects through a graphical user interface. It generates the necessary Structured Query Language Data Definition Language (SQL DDL) scripts for creating a data warehouse or data mart based on definitions specified by the user.

WAREHOUSE DESIGNER is fully compatible with R/OLAPXL®, a Relational Online Analytical Processing tool (also provided with this book) which runs on top of Microsoft Excel for Windows 95. WAREHOUSE DESIGNER automatically creates the warehouse metadata that R/OLAPXL needs to access the data warehouse or data mart.

This **Demo Installation** is provided freely, and you may copy it to as many computers as you wish, provided that the following disclaimer accompanies each installation.

 Intranet Business systems, Inc., and its distributors and re-sellers disclaim all liability for any use you make of this software and for anything this software may do to your data or to your computing environment.

The SQL DDL generation and WAREHOUSE DESIGNER metadata creation features are disabled in this **Demo Installation.** However, users can still define and save warehouse objects such as schemas, dimensions, facts, aggregate schemas, custom schemas, and drill hierarchies.

Manual Contents

This *Installation and User's Guide* for the WAREHOUSE DESIGNER is intended for the data warehouse database administrator (DBA) who will be creating the necessary database objects for the data warehouse.

This *Installation and User's Guide* contains the following sections:

- The *Preface* contains information about WAREHOUSE DESIGNER, and this manual.
- The *Installation* section contains guidelines for installing (and uninstalling) the software.
- The *User's Guide* section contains detailed how-to instructions for WAREHOUSE DESIGNER features.

Conventions Used in this Manual

The following icons are used throughout this manual:

 A Warning Message

 Step-by-Step, How-to Instructions

 A Note

The following typefaces are used throughout this manual:

Typeface	Description	Sample
Garamond	Normal text	. . . a pop-up window . . .
Italicized Garamond	WAREHOUSE DESIGNER terms	Your *Schema* can be . . .

BOLD COURIER UPPER CASE	File, directory names	Copy the CTL3D.DLL file . . .
Courier	Text to type in	. . . enter a Set Name . . .
Bold Arial	Buttons, dialog box	Select OK when done.

System Requirements

WAREHOUSE DESIGNER requires:

- An Intel 80486-DX/100 or compatible processor (or faster)
- A monitor capable of a resolution of 800 x 600 pixels
- The Microsoft Windows 95 operating system already installed
- Approximately 17 Mbytes of hard-disk space for the Microsoft Access Runtime, if it is not yet available, and approximately 1 Mbyte of hard-disk space for the WAREHOUSE DESIGNER (MDB).
- ODBC Drivers to locate data sources. These are not necessary for this demo installation but are a must for a full-featured copy of the product. You will also need the ODBC Driver for the database management system used by your data warehouse or data mart. (Note: the driver must be ODBC Level 2 compliant).
- Any World Wide Web browser (for viewing the FAQ Guide)

WAREHOUSE DESIGNER runs independently on each PC.

Installation Procedure

 To install WAREHOUSE DESIGNER:

1. If you're installing from diskettes, Insert Disk 1 of the WARE-HOUSE DESIGNER Installation disks in drive A. Run setup.exe from drive A. This file launches an installation wizard that will guide you through the steps of installing WAREHOUSE DE-SIGNER.
2. If you're installing from a CD-ROM, go to the WAREHOUSE DE-SIGNER subdirectory. run setup.exe.

Successful Installation

You will know that WAREHOUSE DESIGNER has been successfully installed by checking the following:

- **Installed files.** A new directory is created. If you used the default directory name and path during the installation process, the new directory will be called **Warehouse Designer** and can be found in the **Program Files** subdirectory.
- **New program group in the Start menu.** A new program group in the Start menu is created. If you used the default directory name and path during the installation process, the new group will be called **Warehouse Designer**.

Uninstalling Warehouse Designer

WAREHOUSE DESIGNER updates the Windows Registry on your PC when it is first installed. We therefore strongly recommend against directly deleting the contents of the WAREHOUSE DESIGNER subdirectory.

WAREHOUSE DESIGNER comes with it own uninstaller, which you should use if you wish to uninstall the product.

 To uninstall WAREHOUSE DESIGNER:

1. Click on the Start menu of Windows 95. Choose Settings, then Control Panel.
2. From the Control Panel Window, double-click on Add/Remove Programs.
3. In the dialog box that appears, select WAREHOUSE DESIGNER.
4. Click on the Add/Remove button. The WAREHOUSE DESIGNER uninstaller executes and guides you through the steps for uninstalling the software.

The WAREHOUSE DESIGNER uninstaller removes all WAREHOUSE DESIGNER files that were copied into your machine. It also tries to remove any subdirectories that were created during the installation of WAREHOUSE DESIGNER.

If you have placed files of your own in any of the WAREHOUSE DESIGNER subdirectories, the uninstaller does not delete the subdirectory (and its parent directories) where your files can be found. In this scenario, although WAREHOUSE DESIGNER was successfully uninstalled, you will receive messages similar to the following: "Unable to remove the directory C:\Program files\Warehouse Designer" and "Some components cannot be removed from your computer."

▶ Basic Concepts

WAREHOUSE DESIGNER users should be familiar with dimensional modeling concepts as well as the underlying business concepts of their organization.

Dimensional Modeling Concepts

WAREHOUSE DESIGNER allows you to create dimensional data warehouses and data marts. An understanding of dimensional modeling concepts is helpful to the proper usage of this software, although it is not necessary.

Please refer to Chapter 12 for more information about Dimensional Modeling.

Business Concepts

Almost more important than an understanding of dimensional modeling concepts is an understanding of the business requirements. You must be able to map each of the data items required by your business users into actual warehouse attributes in Fact or Dimension tables.

WAREHOUSE DESIGNER merely automates the creation of data warehouse or data mart tables based on your design. It does not guarantee a design that will actually meet the requirements of your users.

The Warehouse Explorer

Start WAREHOUSE DESIGNER by selecting the Warehouse Designer shortcut from your computer's Start menu. This will open the main application window, the [*Warehouse Explorer*]. The main application window shows in an explorer-type user interface, all data warehouse object definitions that have been saved.

▶ The Warehouse Designer Toolbars

Two toolbars increase the usability of this WAREHOUSE DESIGNER.

- The [*Warehouse Explorer*] **toolbar** appears only in the [*Warehouse Explorer*] window and contains shortcuts to increase the explorer's usability.
- The **Data Form toolbar** contains tools that assist users who are entering, modifying, or browsing through the properties of warehouse objects. These shortcuts are context sensitive; i.e., they are enabled and disabled depending on the currently active window.

The [*Warehouse Explorer*] Toolbar

The following table describes the tools on the [*Warehouse Explorer*] toolbar.

Tool	Name	Description
	Report View	Displays all warehouse objects in Report View.
	List view	Displays all warehouse objects in List View.
	Icon View	Displays all warehouse objects in Icon View.
	Small Icon View	Displays all warehouse objects in Small Icon View.
	Show Properties	Opens a data form where users can define the properties of the selected warehouse object.
	Refresh Warehouse Object	Retrieves the latest information about the selected warehouse object from the database.
	Refresh All	Retrieves the latest information about all warehouse objects from the database.
	Generate SQL	Generates SQL statements for creating warehouse tables. Disabled in demo version.
	Close Warehouse Explorer	Closes the [*Warehouse Explorer*] and its related warehouse objects database.
	Exit Warehouse Explorer	Exits the WAREHOUSE DESIGNER application.

The Generate SQL button has been disabled in this demo version. However, this installation package comes with a sample script that you can view by clicking on the appropriate shortcut in the WAREHOUSE DESIGNER icon group under the Start menu.

The Data Forms Toolbar

The following table describes the tools on the Data Forms toolbar.

Tool	Name	Description
	Find	Finds the record that contains the user-specified text string.
	Find Next	Finds the next record that contains the user-specified text string.
	Replace	Allows users to find a text string and replace it with another text string.
	First Record	Displays the first record.
	Previous Record	Displays the previous record (relative to the current record).
	Next Record	Displays the next record (relative to the current record).
	Last Record	Displays the last record.
	New Record	Inserts a new record.
	Save Record	Saves the data of the current record.
	Delete Record	Deletes the current record.

▶ Applications

In WAREHOUSE DESIGNER, an *Application* groups together multiple, related data warehouse schemas and dimensions.

 To define an Application:

1. On the [*Warehouse Explorer*], select the Applications node, or select a node corresponding to a defined application.
2. Double-click on the selected node,
   −or−
   Click on the Properties toolbar button on the [*Warehouse Explorer*]. This opens a form through which you can enter the necessary application information.
   • **Name.** The name of the Application.

- **Caption.** The caption of the Application.
- **Description.** A textual description of the Application.
- **Short Name.** A short name for the Application; this name is used in the SQL DDL generation routines.
- **RDBMS.** The target RDBMS that will be used for the warehouse schema. The demo installation is limited to the Oracle RDBMS only.

3. Use the toolbar or menu to edit, save, or delete records as needed.

4. Once the Application properties have been defined, click on the **Dimensions** or **Schemas** command buttons to define the *Dimensions* and *Schemas* that belong to this *Application*.

▶ Dimensions

A *Dimension* is a warehouse table that stores data related to one or more of the dimensions of the business. Typical dimension tables are Customer, Product, Time, and Store.

 To Define a Dimension:

1. From the [*Warehouse Explorer*], navigate to the desired Application node, and select the *Dimensions* node of the application. Once the *Dimensions* node has been selected, click on the Properties button on the [*Warehouse Explorer*] toolbar.
   –or–
   If the *Application* definition form is currently open, select the desired application and click on the **Dimensions** command button.

2. In the data form that appears, enter the following information to define a *Dimension:*
   - **Name.** The physical table name to be used in the database. Follow the naming guidelines suggested by the RDBMS vendor.
   - **Caption.** The business or logical name of the *Dimension*, used by warehouse users to refer to the Dimension.
   - **Description.** The standard definition of the *Dimension*.

- **Short Name.** A short name for the *Dimension,* used in the generation of the primary key column and primary key constraint definitions for the Dimension.
- **Tablespace.** The name of the Tablespace where the physical table will reside. This is an Oracle-specific requirement.
- **Summary Of.** Specifies the *Base Table* reference of a *Summary Table.* This is a noneditable property.
- **Custom Of.** Specifies the *Core Table* reference of a *Custom Table.* This is a noneditable property.
- **Usage Type.** Indicates if a warehouse object is used as a Fact or as a Dimension. This is a noneditable property.
- **Implementation Type.** Indicates how the *Dimension* is implemented. Valid values are Table, View, or Synonym, with Table as the default value.
  The two other implementation types are used for the *Core and Custom Dimensions* or for *Multiple-Referenced Dimensions.*
- **Key Option.** Indicates how keys are to be managed for this *Dimension.* Valid values are Overwrite, Generate New, and Create Version.
- **Source.** Indicates the data source for this Dimension. This field is provided for documentation purposes only.
- **Aggregate?.** Indicates whether or not the physical table is a summary. Used only by the **R/**OLAP**XL** front-end product.
- **Online?.** Indicates whether the physical table is actually populated correctly and is available for use by the users of the data warehouse. Used only by the **R/**OLAP**XL** front-end product.

3. Click on the **Fields** button to enter the *Dimension Attributes.* For each attribute, specify the following information:
   - **Seq.** If you want the fields in the generated SQL DDL to follow a particular order, specify a sequence number for the fields.
   - **Field Name.** The name of the field as will be used in the physical table.
   - **Caption.** A descriptive name of the field.
   - **Data Type.** The appropriate data type for the field, as supported by the target RDBMS.
   - **Index Type.** Specify the type of index to be used on this attribute. If this attribute will not be indexed, leave it blank.
   - **Key?.** Indicate if this is a Key field in the Dimension table.

- **Add?.** Indicate if this field is an *Additive Fact*. This is not applicable to *Dimensional Attributes*.
- **Hide?.** Indicate if this field is to be hidden from warehouse users. This property is used for common audit columns (e.g., last update date and last update user).
- **UnGrp?.** Used only by R/OLAPXL, this indicates if the field is to excluded from the normal grouping of rows in the query results. In SQL terms, it has the effect of removing the field from the Group-By clause; instead, the MIN function is applied to the field.
- **Format.** The format of this field.
- **Description.** A description of this field.

Due to the number of properties required to fully define a field, you will have to scroll to the right of the Field table to see all properties.

To scroll down the list of fields, use the Page Up and Page Down keys on your keyboard. You can also click on the left-most column of the field list and use the Up and Down Arrows to navigate up and down the list.

4. Click on the Hierarchies button to define the drill hierarchies for the Dimension. If the fields within a dimension have a hierarchy, define the hierarchy level for each field, where Level 1 is the most detailed level. This definition is not necessary for generating the SQL DDL but is required to create the meta-data used by the **R/OLAPXL** front-end product.

For example, the Time dimension may have the hierarchy of Day–Month–Quarter–Year. This hierarchy is defined by setting the Day field at Level 1, the Month field at Level 2, the Quarter field at Level 3, and the Year field at Level 4.

▶ Schemas

A *Schema* refers to a warehouse Fact table and its related Dimension tables.

 To Define a Schema

1. From the [*Warehouse Explorer*], navigate to the desired Application node, and select the *Schemas* node of the application. Once the *Schemas* node has been selected, click on the **Properties** button on the [*Warehouse Explorer*] toolbar.
   –or–
   If the *Application* definition form is currently open, select the desired application and click on the **Schemas** command button.

2. In the data form that appears, enter the following information to define a *Schema:*
   • **Name.** The physical fact table name to be used in the database. Follow the naming guidelines suggested by the RDBMS vendor.
   • **Caption.** The business or logical name of the *Schema* as the data warehouse users know it.
   • **Description.** The standard definition for the *Schema.*
   • **Short Name.** Used in the generation of the primary key column and primary key constraint definitions for the *Schema* Fact table.

3. In the table provided, specify the Dimension tables that will be used with this *Schema.*
   • Use the Table drop-down list box to select a table.
   • Use the Seq column to specify the sequence in which these tables will appear in the generated SQL DDL.

Foreign key constraints in the Fact tables will be implemented based on the specified *Schema* Dimensions.

Similarly, primary key constraints will be based on the Dimensions that are specified to be part of the granularity of the *Schema.*

- Enable the Grain? checkbox if the Dimension table influences the grain of the Fact table.

4. A default Fact table definition (with the same name, caption, description, and short name as the schema) is automatically created after a Schema is successfully defined.

5. Click on the **Facts** button to enter the Schema facts and modify the Default Fact Table Definition. Fill up the field table to specify the attributes of the Fact table. Note that the process for defining a Fact field is similar to the process for defining a Dimension field.

▶ Custom Dimensions

A *Custom Dimension* is used when a dimension (such as Product) has many dimensional attributes that vary depending on the dimension record. For example, a company may have many different kinds of products, and different attributes are tracked for different products.

A Core Product Dimension is defined to track all attributes that are common to all products, and Custom Product Dimensions are defined for each type of Product to track the attributes that are of special interest to that product type.

➲ To Define a Custom Dimension:

1. From the [Warehouse Explorer], navigate to the desired Dimension node. Select the Custom Dimensions node for that Dimension, and click on the **Properties** button in the [*Warehouse Explorer*] toolbar.

2. In the data that appears, define the Custom Dimension as you would a Core Dimension.

   Note that WAREHOUSE DESIGNER will automatically enter the appropriate Core Dimension table reference in the Custom Of field.

▶ Custom Schemas

A *Custom Schema* refers to a related set of Custom Fact and Custom Dimension tables.

⮞ To Define a Custom Schema:

1. From the [*Warehouse Explorer*], navigate to the desired Schema node. Select the *Custom Schemas* node for that *Schema*, and click on the **Properties** button in the [*Warehouse Explorer*] toolbar.
2. In the data form that appears, define the Custom Schema as you would a Core Schema.

    Note that at least one Custom Dimension must be selected as part of the *Schema* definition.
3. Click on the **FACTS** command button to open the **DW Field** window. On this new window, modify the table definition as needed, then define the facts for this Custom Schema.

▶ Aggregate Dimensions

An *Aggregate Schema* is a set of Fact and Dimension tables that contain summarized or aggregated facts. For example, if a base-level (detailed) schema contains Daily Sales per Product per Store, then the following are possible Aggregate Schemas: Monthly Sales per Product per Store, Quarterly Sales per Product per Store, Monthly Sales per Product Group per Store, etc.

Aggregate Schemas provide faster response times to high-level, summary queries that would otherwise take a much longer time to derive if these were queried against base-level tables.

⮞ To Define an Aggregate Dimension:

1. From the [*Warehouse Explorer*], navigate to the desired Dimension node. Select the Aggregate Dimensions node for that

Dimension, and click on the **Properties** button in the [Warehouse Explorer] Toolbar.

2. Enter data as you would for a Base Dimension definition. The Summary Of table reference will be populated automatically by WAREHOUSE DESIGNER.

▶ Aggregate Schemas

Once you have defined the Aggregate Dimensions, you can now define an Aggregate Schema.

 To Define an Aggregate Schema:

1. From the [*Warehouse Explorer*], navigate to the desired Schemas node. Select the Aggregate Schemas node for that Schema, and click on the **Properties** button in the [*Warehouse Explorer*] Toolbar.

2. Enter data as you would for a Base Schema definition. Use either an Aggregate Dimension to define the *Schema,* or use base-level Dimension tables if applicable.

3. Click on the **FACTS** command button to open the `DW Field` window. On this new window, modify the table definition as needed, then define the facts for this Aggregate Schema.

Online Data Warehousing Resources

A number of data warehousing resources are freely available on the World Wide Web. Aside from the data warehousing material available online from various data warehousing vendors, readers might find it helpful to visit the online resources listed below.

Data Warehousing Associations

International Data Warehousing Association	(http://www.idwa.org/)
The Data Warehousing Institute	(http://www.dw-institute.com/)
The Meta Data Coalition	(http://www.he.net/~metadata/)

Online Resources

The Data Warehousing Information Center	(http://www.pwp.starnetinc.com/larryg/index.html)
Data Warehousing on the World Wide Web	(http://www.datawarehousing.com)

| The Data-Warehouse.Com Site | (http://www.data-warehouse. com/) |
| The Data Warehousing Knowledge Center | (http://www.dataware house.org/) |

Online Magazines and Periodicals

DBMS Magazine	(http://www.dbmsmag.com/)
CIO Magazine	(http://www.cio.com/cio)
Datamation Magazine	(http://www.datamation.com/)
Data Management Review	(http://www.dmreview.com/)

Data Warehousing List Server

To subscribe to the list: Send e-mail to dwdomo@datawarehousing. com. The first line of your message must be "subscribe datawarehousing." No subject line is required.

Newsgroups

Comp.databases.olap

Note that online resources constantly change and that there is no guarantee the ones listed above will continue to be available. Readers may want to visit the website of Intranet Business Systems, Inc. (URL: http://www.intranetsys.com), where links to online warehousing resources will be continuously updated.

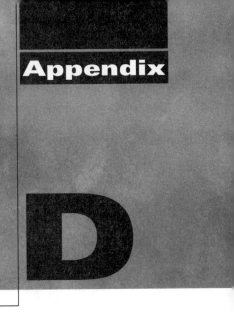

Tool and Vendor Inventory

A large number of data warehouse software vendors are distributing an even larger number of data warehousing tools. Although in this appendix we provide lists of products and vendors, we do not claim that the lists are in any way complete or comprehensive. In certain cases, the URLs were not available and are therefore left blank in the tables below.

Also, given the popularity of mergers and acquisitions among data warehouse players, some of these products may have already been sold or acquired by other companies.

Extraction, Transportation and Transformation Technologies

Vendor	Product	Contact Location
Apertus Carleton	Enterprise/Integrator	http://www.apertus.com
Apertus Carleton	Passport	http://www.apertus.com

Vendor	Product	Contact Location
DEC	messageQ	http://www.dec.com
DEC	Object Broker	http://www.dec.com
ETI	Extract Suite	http://www.evtech.com
Hewlett-Packard	OpenView	http://www.hp.com
Hewlett-Packard	ORB Plus	http://www.hp.com
IBM	MQSeries	http://www.ibm.com
IBM	NetView	http://www.ibm.com
IBM	SOM, DSOM	http://www.ibm.com
IBM	Visual Warehouse	http://www.ibm.com
Intersolv	DataDirect SmartData	http://www.intersolv.com
Momentum	Message Express	
OMG	CORBA and CORBA 2	
PeerLogic	PIPES Platform	
Prism	Data Warehouse Manager	http://www.prismsolutions.com
SunSoft	SunNet Manager	
SunSoft	ToolTalk	

Data Quality Tools

Vendor	Product	Contact Location
Belmont Research, Inc.	Table Trans	http://www.belmont.com
i.d. Centric	ACE, Merge/Purge, TrueName Library	http://idcentric.com
Mastersoft	ScrubMaster	http://www.msi.com.au/company.htm
Matchware Technologies, Inc.	AutoMatch, Auto Stan	http://www.matchware.com

Vendor	Product	Contact Location
Peoplesmith	StyleList, Personator	http://www.peoplesmith.com
Vality	Data Quality	http://www.vality.com

Data Access and Retrieval Tools

Vendor	Product	Contact Location
Acuity Management Systems	Acuity/ES	
Ambit Research	Toto	
Andyne	Andyne GQL	http://www.andyne.com
Andyne	Andyne Pablo	http://www.andyne.com
Angoss Software	Knowledge SEEKER	http://www.angoss.com
Arbor Software	Essbase	http://www.arborsoft.com
Arrival Software	Track for OLAP	
Brio Technology	DataPrism, DataPivot	http://www.brio.com
Brio Technology	BrioQuery Enterprise	http://www.brio.com
Business Objects	Business Objects	http://www.business objects.com
Cognos	Powerplay	http://www.cognos.com
Computer Associates	CA-Visual Express	http://www.cai.com
Computer Concepts Corp.	d.b.Express	
Comshare	Commander OLAP	http://www.comshare.com
Crystal/Seagate Software	Crystal Info Reports	http://www.crystalinc.com
Dimensional Insight	CrossTarget	http://www.dimins.com
European Management Systems	EIS-Eureka	
HNC Software	DMW:Database Mining Workstation	http://www.hncs.com

Vendor	Product	Contact Location
Holistic Systems/Seagate Software	Holos	http://www.crystalinc.com
Hunt Systems	Consolidation Auditor	
Hyperion Software	Hyperion Enterprise	
IBM	Data Visualizer	http://www.ibm.com
Informatica	OpenBridge	http://www.informatica.com
Information Advantage	Decision Support Suite	http://www.infoadvan.com
Information Builders	FOCUS/EIS	http://www.ibi.com
Information Discovery	Data Mining Suite	http://www.datamining.com
Informix	NewEra ViewPoint	http://www.informix.com
Intranet Business Systems, Inc.	R/OLAPXL	http://www.intranetsys.com
IQ Software	Intelligent Query	http://www.iqsc.com
IQ Software	IQ/Vision	http://www.iqsc.com
Kenan Technologies	Acumate Enterprise Solution	http://www.kenan.com
Lingo Computer Design	Fiscal	
Microsoft	MS Query, Access	http://www.microsoft.com
Microstrategy	DSS Agent	http://www.strategy.com http://www.micro strategy.com
Open Environment Systems	EnteraQx	http://www.openenv.com
Oracle/IRI Software	Express	http://www.oracle.com
Pilot	Lightship Suite	http://www.pilotsw.com
Planning Sciences	Gentium	http://194.217.8.100
Platinum/Trinzic	Forest and Trees	http://www.platinum.com
Platinum	InfoBeacon	http://www.platinum.com
Powersoft	Infomaker	http://www.powersoft.com
Praxis	OmniInfo	http://www.praxis.com

Vendor	Product	Contact Location
Renaissance Information Technology	Multi-D Lite	
SAS	SAS System	http://www.sas.com
SelectStar	StarTrieve for Windows	
Show Business Software	Show Business	
Sinper Corp	Table Manager/1	
Software AG	Esperant	http://www.sagus.com
Stanford Technology Group	Metacube	
Sterling	ANSWER:Journey	http://www.sterling.com
Sterling	VISION:Data	http://www.sterling.com

Data Modeling Tools

Vendor	Product	Contact Location
Sybase	S-Designer	http://www.sybase.com
Logic Works	ERWin	
Oracle	Oracle Designer/2000	http://www.oracle.com

Database Management Tools

Vendor	Product	Contact Location
AT&T	Teradata	http://www.att.com
Computer Associates	CA-Ingres	http://www.cai.com
ETI	EXTRACT Suite	http://www.evtech.com
IBM	DPROPNR	http://www.ibm.com

Vendor	Product	Contact Location
IBM	DPROPR	http://www.ibm.com
IBM	IBM DB2	http://www.ibm.com
Information Builders	EDA Copy Manager	http://www.ibi.com
Informix	Informix	http://www.informix.com
Microsoft	Microsoft SQL Server	http://www.microsoft.com
Oracle	Oracle 7, Oracle 8	http://www.oracle.com
Oracle	Oracle Symmetric Replication	http://www.oracle.com
Platinum/Trinzic	InfoPump	http://www.platinum.com
Praxis	OmniReplicator	http://www.praxis.com
Prism	Warehouse Manager	http://www.prism-solutions.com
Red Brick	Red Brick Warehouse	http://www.redbrick.com
Sybase	Sybase Replication Server	http://www.sybase.com
Sybase	Sybase SQL Server	http://www.sybase.com

Metadata Management Tools

Vendor	Product	Contact Location
Apertus Carleton	Warehouse Control Center	http://www.apertus.com
Informatica	PowerMart Repository	http://www.informatica.com
Intellidex Systems	Warehouse Control Center	
Prism	Prism Warehouse Directory	http://www.prism-solutions.com

External Data Sources

- Bloomberg News
- Dow Jones News Service
- Lexis
- New York Times Services
- Nexis

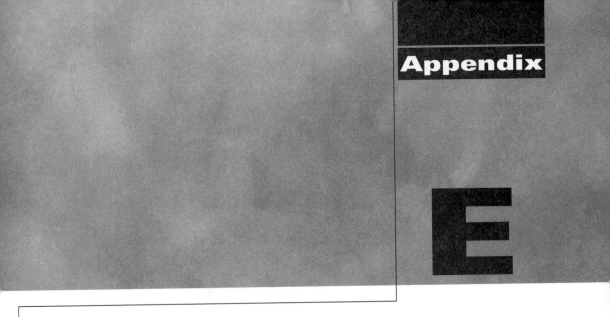

Software License Agreement

By using the software that accompanies this book, you agree to abide by the terms of the License Agreements of these products. The term "product" refers to software and any associated media, printed materials, and "online" or electronic documentation that accompanies this book.

Copyright laws and international copyright treaties, as well as other intellectual property laws and treaties protect both the R/ᴏʟᴀᴘXL® and Wᴀʀᴇʜᴏᴜsᴇ Dᴇsɪɢɴᴇʀ® software products that accompany this book. The software products are licensed for use, not sold.

Use of Software. Intranet Business systems, Inc., grants you unlimited, nonexclusive license to make and use copies of the R/ᴏʟᴀᴘXL Client and Wᴀʀᴇʜᴏᴜsᴇ Dᴇsɪɢɴᴇʀ Demo Installation software products for the sole purpose of evaluating their features.

Without corresponding server software licenses, use of the R/ᴏʟᴀᴘXL Client product is restricted to accessing the sample database schema provided in the accompanying Microsoft® Access database.

Use of Electronic Documentation. All electronic documents included with the software product may be distributed on an unlimited basis provided that such copies shall be used only for purposes of aiding your use of the software product. These documents are not to be re-published or distributed to any third party.

Intellectual Property Rights. This license does not grant you rights to any patents, pending patent applications, trademarks, copyrights or other intellectual property rights that are exclusively reserved by Intranet Business Systems, Inc.

Full Distribution. Both R/OLAPXL and WAREHOUSE DESIGNER software products must be distributed complete and intact without any modifications whatsoever. No modifications are allowed to the distribution files.

Reverse Engineering, Decompilation, and Disassembly. You agree you will not attempt to reverse compile, modify, translate, or disassemble either R/OLAPXL or WAREHOUSE DESIGNER in whole or in part and that you will make reasonable efforts to prevent anyone from doing the same.

Rental. You may not rent, lease, or lend the software product.

Termination. Without prejudice to any other rights, Intranet Business Systems, Inc., may terminate this License Agreement if you fail to comply with the terms and conditions of this License Agreement. In such event, you must destroy all copies of the software product and all of its component parts.

Copyright. This package makes reference to a number of copyrighted and trademarked products. These are copyrighted and trademarked by their respective holders.

All other titles and copyrights in and to the R/OLAPXL and WAREHOUSE DESIGNER software products, the accompanying printed materials and any copies of the software product are owned by Intranet Business Systems, Inc. The products are protected by copyright laws and international treaty provisions. You must treat the software product like any other copyrighted material. You may not copy the printed materials accompanying the software products.

No Warranty. Intranet Business Systems, Inc., its suppliers, distributors, and resellers do not warrant that R/OLAPXL and WAREHOUSE DESIGNER software products are error-free. The above parties disclaim all warranties with respect to the software products, either express or implied, including but not limited to implied warranties of merchantability, fitness for a particular purpose, title and noninfringement, with regard to the software product, and the provision of or failure to provide support services.

No Liability. Intranet Business Systems, Inc., its suppliers, distributors and resellers shall in no event be liable for any special, incidental, indirect, or consequential damages whatsoever (including, without limitation, damages for loss of business profits, business interruption, loss of business information, or any other pecuniary loss) arising out of the use of or inability to use the software product, or the provision of or failure to provide support services, even if Intranet Business Systems, Inc. has been advised of the possibility of such damages. In any case, Intranet's entire liability under this license agreement shall be limited to the amount actually paid by you for the software product.

This license is governed by the laws of the Republic of the Philippines.

References and Further Reading

Index

D

LICENSE AGREEMENT AND LIMITED WARRANTY

READ THE FOLLOWING TERMS AND CONDITIONS CAREFULLY BEFORE OPENING THIS DISK PACKAGE. THIS LEGAL DOCUMENT IS AN AGREEMENT BETWEEN YOU AND PRENTICE-HALL, INC. (THE "COMPANY"). BY OPENING THIS SEALED DISK PACKAGE, YOU ARE AGREEING TO BE BOUND BY THESE TERMS AND CONDITIONS. IF YOU DO NOT AGREE WITH THESE TERMS AND CONDITIONS, DO NOT OPEN THE DISK PACKAGE. PROMPTLY RETURN THE UNOPENED DISK PACKAGE AND ALL ACCOMPANYING ITEMS TO THE PLACE YOU OBTAINED THEM FOR A FULL REFUND OF ANY SUMS YOU HAVE PAID.

1. **GRANT OF LICENSE:** In consideration of your payment of the license fee, which is part of the price you paid for this product, and your agreement to abide by the terms and conditions of this Agreement, the Company grants to you a nonexclusive right to use and display the copy of the enclosed software program (hereinafter the "SOFTWARE") on a single computer (i.e., with a single CPU) at a single location so long as you comply with the terms of this Agreement. The Company reserves all rights not expressly granted to you under this Agreement.

2. **OWNERSHIP OF SOFTWARE:** You own only the magnetic or physical media (the enclosed disks) on which the SOFTWARE is recorded or fixed, but the Company retains all the rights, title, and ownership to the SOFTWARE recorded on the original disk copy(ies) and all subsequent copies of the SOFTWARE, regardless of the form or media on which the original or other copies may exist. This license is not a sale of the original SOFTWARE or any copy to you.

3. **COPY RESTRICTIONS:** This SOFTWARE and the accompanying printed materials and user manual (the "Documentation") are the subject of copyright. You may not copy the Documentation or the SOFTWARE, except that you may make a single copy of the SOFTWARE for backup or archival purposes only. You may be held legally responsible for any copying or copyright infringement which is caused or encouraged by your failure to abide by the terms of this restriction.

4. **USE RESTRICTIONS:** You may not network the SOFTWARE or otherwise use it on more than one computer or computer terminal at the same time. You may physically transfer the SOFTWARE from one computer to another provided that the SOFTWARE is used on only one computer at a time. You may not distribute copies of the SOFTWARE or Documentation to others. You may not reverse engineer, disassemble, decompile, modify, adapt, translate, or create derivative works based on the SOFTWARE or the Documentation without the prior written consent of the Company.

5. **TRANSFER RESTRICTIONS:** The enclosed SOFTWARE is licensed only to you and may not be transferred to any one else without the prior written consent of the Company. Any unauthorized transfer of the SOFTWARE shall result in the immediate termination of this Agreement.

6. **TERMINATION:** This license is effective until terminated. This license will terminate automatically without notice from the Company and become null and void if you fail to comply with any provisions or limitations of this license. Upon termination, you shall destroy the Documentation and all copies of the SOFTWARE. All provisions of this Agreement as to warranties, limitation of liability, remedies or damages, and our ownership rights shall survive termination.

7. **MISCELLANEOUS:** This Agreement shall be construed in accordance with the laws of the United States of America and the State of New York and shall benefit the Company, its affiliates, and assignees.

8. **LIMITED WARRANTY AND DISCLAIMER OF WARRANTY:** The Company warrants

that the SOFTWARE, when properly used in accordance with the Documentation, will operate in substantial conformity with the description of the SOFTWARE set forth in the Documentation. The Company does not warrant that the SOFTWARE will meet your requirements or that the operation of the SOFTWARE will be uninterrupted or error-free. The Company warrants that the media on which the SOFTWARE is delivered shall be free from defects in materials and workmanship under normal use for a period of thirty (30) days from the date of your purchase. Your only remedy and the Company's only obligation under these limited warranties is, at the Company's option, return of the warranted item for a refund of any amounts paid by you or replacement of the item. Any replacement of SOFTWARE or media under the warranties shall not extend the original warranty period. The limited warranty set forth above shall not apply to any SOFTWARE which the Company determines in good faith has been subject to misuse, neglect, improper installation, repair, alteration, or damage by you. EXCEPT FOR THE EXPRESSED WARRANTIES SET FORTH ABOVE, THE COMPANY DISCLAIMS ALL WARRANTIES, EXPRESS OR IMPLIED, INCLUDING WITHOUT LIMITATION, THE IMPLIED WARRANTIES OF MERCHANTABILITY AND FITNESS FOR A PARTICULAR PURPOSE. EXCEPT FOR THE EXPRESS WARRANTY SET FORTH ABOVE, THE COMPANY DOES NOT WARRANT, GUARANTEE, OR MAKE ANY REPRESENTATION REGARDING THE USE OR THE RESULTS OF THE USE OF THE SOFTWARE IN TERMS OF ITS CORRECTNESS, ACCURACY, RELIABILITY, CURRENTNESS, OR OTHERWISE.

IN NO EVENT, SHALL THE COMPANY OR ITS EMPLOYEES, AGENTS, SUPPLIERS, OR CONTRACTORS BE LIABLE FOR ANY INCIDENTAL, INDIRECT, SPECIAL, OR CONSEQUENTIAL DAMAGES ARISING OUT OF OR IN CONNECTION WITH THE LICENSE GRANTED UNDER THIS AGREEMENT, OR FOR LOSS OF USE, LOSS OF DATA, LOSS OF INCOME OR PROFIT, OR OTHER LOSSES, SUSTAINED AS A RESULT OF INJURY TO ANY PERSON, OR LOSS OF OR DAMAGE TO PROPERTY, OR CLAIMS OF THIRD PARTIES, EVEN IF THE COMPANY OR AN AUTHORIZED REPRESENTATIVE OF THE COMPANY HAS BEEN ADVISED OF THE POSSIBILITY OF SUCH DAMAGES. IN NO EVENT SHALL LIABILITY OF THE COMPANY FOR DAMAGES WITH RESPECT TO THE SOFTWARE EXCEED THE AMOUNTS ACTUALLY PAID BY YOU, IF ANY, FOR THE SOFTWARE.
SOME JURISDICTIONS DO NOT ALLOW THE LIMITATION OF IMPLIED WARRANTIES OR LIABILITY FOR INCIDENTAL, INDIRECT, SPECIAL, OR CONSEQUENTIAL DAMAGES, SO THE ABOVE LIMITATIONS MAY NOT ALWAYS APPLY. THE WARRANTIES IN THIS AGREEMENT GIVE YOU SPECIFIC LEGAL RIGHTS AND YOU MAY ALSO HAVE OTHER RIGHTS WHICH VARY IN ACCORDANCE WITH LOCAL LAW.

ACKNOWLEDGMENT

YOU ACKNOWLEDGE THAT YOU HAVE READ THIS AGREEMENT, UNDERSTAND IT, AND AGREE TO BE BOUND BY ITS TERMS AND CONDITIONS. YOU ALSO AGREE THAT THIS AGREEMENT IS THE COMPLETE AND EXCLUSIVE STATEMENT OF THE AGREEMENT BETWEEN YOU AND THE COMPANY AND SUPERSEDES ALL PROPOSALS OR PRIOR AGREEMENTS, ORAL, OR WRITTEN, AND ANY OTHER COMMUNICATIONS BETWEEN YOU AND THE COMPANY OR ANY REPRESENTATIVE OF THE COMPANY RELATING TO THE SUBJECT MATTER OF THIS AGREEMENT.

Should you have any questions concerning this Agreement or if you wish to contact the Company for any reason, please contact in writing at the address below or call the at the telephone number provided.

PTR Customer Service
Prentice Hall PTR
One Lake Street
Upper Saddle River, New Jersey 07458

Telephone: 201-236-7105

About the CD

The files on the CD are organized as follows:

Clementine Data Mining Solutions'	This directory contains a Powerpoint presentation of Integral Clementine Data Mining System in action.
RolapXL	This directory contains a trial version of R/OLAPXL, an analysis and report writing tool for dimensional data warehouses that allows users to draw data directly into Microsoft Excel spreadsheets.
warehouse designer	This directory contains a trial version of Warehouse Designer, a modeling tool used in conjunction with Microsoft Access that allows users to define data warehouse objects through a friendly graphical user interface.

System Requirements

R/OLAPXL requires:

- PC compatible system with an Intel 486/100 or faster processor
- Windows 95
- MS Excel 7.0 or or MS Excel 97
- MS Access ODBC Driver (Level 2 compliant)
- 7.7 MB of hard-disk space

Warehouse Designer requires:

- PC compatible system with an Intel 486/100 or faster processor
- Windows 95
- MS Access Runtime and ODBC Driver (Level 2 compliant)
- 1.0 MB of hard-disk space

Installation

See Appendix A for detailed instructions on how to install and use the R/OLAPXL report writing tool. To launch the installation program, double click on the `Setup.exe` file in the `RolapXL` directory on the CD.

See Appendix B for detailed instructions on how to install and use the Warehouse Designer modeling tool. To launch the installation program, double click on the `setup.exe` file, which is in the `Disk1` subdirectory of the `warehouse designer` directory on the CD.

Technical Support

Prentice Hall does not offer technical support for this software. If there is a problem with the media, however, you may obtain a replacement CD by emailing a description of the problem. Send your email to:

disc_exchange@prenhall.com